# GOD HATES

# GOD HATES

WESTBORO BAPTIST CHURCH,
AMERICAN NATIONALISM,
AND THE RELIGIOUS RIGHT

REBECCA BARRETT-FOX

UNIVERSITY PRESS OF KANSAS

Published by the University Press of Kansas (Lawrence, Kansas 66045), which was organized by the Kansas Board of Regents and is operated and funded by Emporia State University, Fort Hays State University, Kansas State University, Pittsburg State University, the University of Kansas, and Wichita State University

Library of Congress Cataloging-in-Publication Data

Names: Barrett-Fox, Rebecca, author.

Title: God hates : Westboro Baptist Church, American nationalism, and the religious right / Rebecca Barrett-Fox.

Description: Lawrence : University Press of Kansas, 2016. | Includes bibliographical references and index.

Identifiers: LCCN 2016004956| ISBN 9780700622658 (cloth : alk. paper) | ISBN 9780700622665 (ebook)

Subjects: LCSH: Westboro Baptist Church (Topeka, Kan.)—History. | Topeka (Kan.)—Church history. | Toleration—Religious aspects—Christianity. | Religious tolerance—Christianity.

Classification: LCC BX6480.T67 B37 2016 | DDC 286/.5—dc23

LC record available at http://lccn.loc.gov/2016004956.

British Library Cataloguing-in-Publication Data is available.

Printed in the United States of America

10 9 8 7 6 5 4 3 2 1

The paper used in this publication is recycled and contains 30 percent postconsumer waste. It is acid free and meets the minimum requirements of the American National Standard for Permanence of Paper for Printed Library Materials Z39.48-1992.

To my friends at Peace Mennonite Church,

for being with me during the many Sunday mornings

when I couldn't be there with you.

# CONTENTS

## ACKNOWLEDGMENTS

I am fortunate to owe debts to many colleagues and friends for their support of this project. Chief among them are Norman Yetman, American studies and sociology; Tim Miller, religious studies; Randal Jelks, American studies and African and African American studies; Ben Chappell, American studies; and Brian Donovan, sociology, who provided me with the confidence to see this project as a book. A developing scholar could not have had a more generous dissertation committee, making the University of Kansas a place where, indeed, seldom was heard a discouraging word, and I have continued to benefit from their insight and mentoring. In particular, Norm Yetman's careful and patient lessons in writing significantly improved the text found here, and his genuine enthusiasm for theology inspired me to prioritize that part of this study. Tim Miller's feedback allowed me to place Westboro Baptist Church within a framework of religious tradition and innovation. Randal Jelks has been the biggest booster for the publication of this manuscript; I am grateful for his knack for calling or e-mailing me exactly when I need to hear a friendly voice. I thank Ben Chappell for the Rogerian therapy sessions; he can accomplish a lot with a few clarifying questions. Brian Donovan has encouraged me to take the scholarly risks that make this career a joy. I hope they are pleased with the results of their hard work.

Jason Barrett-Fox, my husband as well as my scholarly colleague; Karen Lombardi, who supported this project from our first visit to Westboro Baptist Church in 2004; the always encouraging Stephanie Krehbiel; my coworkers in the graduate writing program; my indispensable writing partner, Megan Williams; and Susan Kraus, who saw my need for time and place to write and provided it, were instrumental in keeping this project moving forward. Ailecia Ruscin's talent as a photographer is equaled by her generosity as a friend and bravery as an activist and community leader. Friends at Peace Mennonite Church served as belaying partners, ready to pull me back if I ever felt the need to tug on the rope, and friends at New Creation Mennonite Fellowship rejuvenated me. Many, many others cheered me on throughout. The University of Kansas Graduate School's

Dissertation Fellowship and Summer Grant, the Norm and Anne Yetman Dissertation Fellowship, and the University Women's Fellowship provided not just financial support for this research but also an affirmation of its value. I am pleased to participate in this project with Kim Hogeland at the University Press of Kansas; everyone should get to work with such a talented editor. I appreciate the hard work of reviewers, including Cynthia Burack, whose feedback helped this manuscript find its final form.

Westboro Baptist Church produces enough public material that a scholarly content analysis of its digital culture would have been enough to fill a book. However, the generosity of church members and ex–church members allowed me to tell a different kind of story, one that, I hope, respects the lived experience of religion within the church and sees value in the members' human relationships. I am grateful for their vulnerability and generosity of spirit and time, particularly from Shirley Phelps-Roper, Steve Drain, and Sam Phelps-Roper, who were patient with me as I grew in my understanding of Westboro Baptist Church theology, and those former members who kindly shared their stories with me. I never left an interview without feeling genuinely cared for, and I hope that church members see an equal care in the analysis I share here.

Each of my three children were infants at one point or another during this research project, and I was able to travel with them to field research because of the willingness of my extended family, both Barretts and Foxes, to care for them when asked. Jason Barrett-Fox has prioritized this work, ensuring that I had the time and intellectual space to do it. Thank you, Jason, for that, without which this manuscript could not have come to fruition.

# INTRODUCTION

At the September 22, 2011, Republican presidential primary debate in Orlando, Florida, Stephen Hill, a soldier serving in Iraq, submitted a question for the Republican hopefuls via video. In it, he identified himself as gay and asked former Pennsylvania senator Rick Santorum if he would support the reinstatement of Don't Ask, Don't Tell (DADT), the defunct policy that had long prevented openly gay servicemen and -women from serving in the military. Not only did Santorum restate the right wing's unsubstantiated position that allowing openly gay men and women to serve would undermine the effectiveness of the military, but neither he nor any of the other contenders thanked Hill for his service, a convention at such events—nor did any of the debate participants rebuke the audience members who booed Hill.[1] Many who witnessed the debate agreed with the judgment of GOProud, the politically conservative progay organization, which noted, "It is telling that Rick Santorum is so blinded by his anti-gay bigotry that he couldn't even bring himself to thank that gay soldier for his service."[2] The moment revealed that "gay-bashing is a forever issue for the religious right."[3] It trumps its arguments about government staying out of people's personal lives, about the social value of marriages and stable families, and even about the dignity and respect due to soldiers and veterans.

In making their claim that America's military readiness would be undermined by the presence of openly gay soldiers (or even closeted gay soldiers), the Republican contenders linked homosexuality and homeland insecurity. American soldiers, they said, would be fighting an external threat as well as an internal threat as previously closeted gay servicemen and -women fought against the American military from the inside, traitors not only to the natural plan that God intended for human sexuality but to their comrades and their nation. The Family Research Council (FRC), a conservative Christian political advocacy group, warned, "The victims will be America's parents, her sons and daughters, absent husbands and wives."[4] But beyond that, national security would be endangered, not just by the presence of openly gay soldiers but by an increasing national commitment to the rights of gay people. Or, as Oklahoma state representative Sally Kern has said repeatedly about gay rights, including on the tenth anniversary of the attacks of September 11, "It's the biggest threat our nation has, even more so than terrorism or Islam—which I think is a big threat. . . . It will destroy this nation."[5]

Though Religious Right leaders invoked arguments that, on the surface, are about military stability, troop cohesion, and the religious rights of conservative Christian military chaplains, the language on the inside is all religious. In a "prayer alert" sent to FRC supporters on the day of the repeal of DADT, Pierre Bynun, FRC national prayer director, exhorted subscribers to pray that "this godless policy be reversed in the not-too-distant future!" Bynum cited seven Bible passages to support his claim that Christians have a duty to lead their nation away from the sin of toleration for homosexuality, for, as he quotes from Jude 7, the residents of Sodom and Gomorrah—cities, in conservative theological interpretation, destroyed because of their practice and toleration of homosexuality—"serve as an example of those who suffer the punishment of eternal fire."[6] According to this prayer alert, the duty of good Christians and God-fearing Americans is to foster social policies, including military recruitment policies, that align with God's view of sexuality as understood by the Religious Right—which is that gay people will "suffer the punishment of eternal fire." Or, in other words, gay people go to hell, and if straight Americans are not careful, the whole nation will end up there with them. Or, as another Bible verse often quoted by Christian conservatives says, "Righteousness exalteth a nation, but sin is a cancer to all people."[7]

In short, the Religious Right's argument is based not only on faulty social science that predicts that the military would be unable to function with openly gay members but also on the theological claim that God will not bless a nation that allows openly gay service members. From this perspective, God's blessing on a nation is measured in military success. This implies a grim and unspoken corollary: that military losses are a punishment from God and thus a sign of his anger. No one in the Religious Right, though, makes this claim explicitly, and all would deny it. Instead, that provocative argument is articulated by only one group on the American religious landscape: Westboro Baptist Church.

Westboro Baptist Church is the roughly seventy-person Primitive Baptist congregation that gained national attention in the 1990s for its anti-gay activism, particularly its pickets of the funerals of gay people such as journalist Randy Shilts and college student Matthew Shepard. In 2005, the church expanded its pickets to the funerals of fallen servicemen and -women, arguing, in a theological extension of the claims of other conservative Christians, not only that God would stop blessing a nation that tolerated homosexuality but that he already had—and, that, in fact, he was actively punishing America for its sins. Thus, as author of all things, God uses US military losses in Iraq and Afghanistan as a tool to punish the nation. Therefore, when anyone, straight or gay, joins the US military, he or she becomes an enemy of God. And as readers of the Old Testament know, it is God, not armies, who wins battles. Armies that fight against God's chosen army lose, and when the Israelites lost in battle, it was because God used their enemies to destroy them for his purposes, mostly to teach them obedience—and the ramifications of disobedience. In other words, God always wins—even if that means defeating his own people through the use of foreign armies. Westboro Baptists have simply updated this Old Testament model of warfare and extended the Religious Right's argument that God is going to punish America if the nation keeps on with its sinful ways. This is the message of the church founder and long-term pastor, Fred Phelps, who died in March 2014. It is a message that continues in the preaching of the small group of male elders—married men who are eligible to occupy the pulpit for Sunday sermons—in the years since his death.

On September 11, 2011, drawing from the book of Isaiah, Pastor Fred Phelps compared America to ancient Israel in a rhetorical move similar to Pierre Bynum's of the FRC:

> The ox knoweth his owner, and the ass his master's crib: but Israel (America?) doth not know, my people doth not consider. Ah sinful nation (USA?), a people laden with iniquity, a seed of evildoers, children (Americans?) that are corrupters: they have forsaken the LORD, they have provoked the Holy One of Israel unto anger, they are gone away backward. . . . Your country (America?) is desolate, your cities are burned with fire: your land (America?), strangers devour it in your presence, and it is desolate, as overthrown by strangers. And the daughter of Zion is left as a cottage in a vineyard, as a lodge in a garden of cucumbers, as a besieged city. Except the LORD of hosts had left unto us a very small remnant, we (Americans?) should have been as Sodom, and we (Americans?) should have been like unto Gomorrah. Hear the word of the LORD, ye rulers of Sodom; give ear unto the law of our God, ye people of Gomorrah (the USA?).[8]

Religious Right leaders often invoke comparisons between ancient Israel and America, both countries once blessed by God that came to reject and defy God by living in ungodly ways. This trope is as old as the earliest Puritans who came to establish a "city upon a hill"[9]—as is conservative America's linking of national survival and sexual purity. The language abounds in Religious Right materials, from political speeches to abstinence-education curriculum, but only in Westboro Baptist Church is it expressed directly to servicemen and -women. Westboro Baptist Church is writing a script and performing it at military funeral after military funeral so that the Religious Right does not have to articulate the logical end to its argument about American declension. The two can work in tandem to mount a campaign that makes gay Americans, and now openly gay soldiers, the greatest threat to national security that America has ever known.

Yet Westboro Baptist Church makes frequent headlines for its virulent antigay message whereas the broader Religious Right has ensconced its antigay rhetoric within the language of "family values" and, consequently, is less reviled. Indeed, Westboro Baptist Church first came to broad national attention when, in 1998, members picketed the funeral of gay University of Wyoming student Matthew Shepard and created a "perpetual memorial" to Shepard online that included an image of the young man in hell, screaming that people should heed the church's warning, acts that earned Fred Phelps memorialization in *The Laramie Project*, a play about Shepard's murder.[10] When Westboro Baptist church members visited the New York City site of the fallen twin towers a few days after the attacks of September 11, 2001, they gained national attention again, only this time their message was even bigger: God did not just hate gay people—he was punishing America for its tolerance of homosexuality.[11] Although Religious Right icons Jerry Falwell and Pat Robertson had suggested that God had lifted his protective covering from America on September 11, Westboro Baptist declared that, in fact, God was "America's terrorist," actively destroying the nation.[12] Protests emphasizing this theme were repeated in the months that followed at funerals for the first fallen US servicemen and -women killed in the war on terror.[13]

Suddenly, Westboro Baptist Church had found a message that brought it constant attention: God is killing US soldiers. Individual states responded by passing laws banning funeral pickets,[14] and in 2006, President George W. Bush signed into law the Respect for America's Fallen Heroes Act, outlawing such pickets in national cemeteries.[15] The Patriot Guard Riders, a motorcycle brigade, formed to counter Westboro Baptist Church's pickets.[16] Shirley Phelps-Roper, spokesperson for the church, started appearing on national television news shows and talk shows. In political speeches, news reports, and online discussion boards, disgust for the church was expressed vehemently and, frequently, with threats of violence. Then, in 2011, the Supreme Court decided against the father of a fallen marine, Albert Snyder, who had brought a multimillion-dollar lawsuit, and won at the lower level, against church members for the intentional infliction of emotional distress.[17] In preparation for the decision, the FBI prepared for increased attacks against the church and its members,[18] and, indeed, Internet attacks as well as threats increased after the decision, with many online commentators citing the failure of the juridical process to squelch Westboro Baptist Church activism as reason for their frustration. Within a few weeks of the March 2011 decision in favor of the church, Maine senator Olympia Snowe introduced the Sanctity of Eternal Rest for Veterans (SERV) Act, which was passed into law as the Honoring America's Veterans and Caring for Camp Lejeune Families Act of 2012. The act prohibits pickets of military funerals in federal military cemeteries for up to two hours before or after a funeral and sets a 500-foot buffer zone around the funeral location.[19] Individual states produced a spate of similar laws intended to stop demonstrations by Westboro Baptist Church.[20]

Though media attention to Westboro Baptist Church increased dramatically after the start of its pickets at the funerals of soldiers in 2006, the church had been running an antigay campaign since 1991 and began picketing at funerals about a year after that.[21] The church's web site reports that, to date, it has held more than 55,000 pickets, including ones in Iraq during the Saddam Hussein reign and in Canada.[22] The pickets began in 1991, when Fred Phelps complained to Topeka's city council about the use of Gage Park, a public city park, by gay men for sexual encounters. When the city failed to respond to Phelps's satisfaction, church members picketed to protest what they perceived as a cultural tolerance of homosexuality.[23] In their production of picket signs, they found that the words "God Hates Fags" fit perfectly on a poster board. Not coincidentally, the signs are highly visible, easy to read from the road or on a television screen, and inflammatory.

It was these words, according to Shirley Phelps-Roper, that really fired the church's campaign. "Fag," she says, is not the controversial word on their placards; many people participating in the events being picketed use the word themselves to refer to gay people, she argues. In other words, it is not Westboro Baptist Church's homophobia that alienates those toward whom the pickets are directed. Instead, the controversy is in the words "God hates," she says. The people of Topeka, Kansas—and Laramie, Wyoming, and even New York City—do not like homosexuality, says Phelps-Roper, and she contends that they probably agree with Westboro Baptist Church that unrepentant gay people go to hell.[24] In a 1995 interview with the *Washington Post*, Judy Miller of Topeka's Gay and Lesbian Task Force agreed, admitting, "I'm afraid there are a lot of people who secretly in their heart of hearts agree with the Phelpses, and don't really want them to be stopped,"[25] a claim bolstered by Paul Froese and Christopher D. Baden's analysis that finds that nearly one-third of Americans believe in an authoritative God who actively intervenes in human life to punish those who fail to adhere to his standards.[26] Instead, the public is most upset that its image of God as loving and merciful is challenged by the idea that God can "hate."[27] Indeed, when nine-year-old Josef Miles countered Westboro Baptist's signs with one of his own declaring, "God Hates No One" in May 2012, his act was reported in the *Huffington Post* and on National Public Radio, and he received considerable praise from the public.[28] Yet this countermessage means little to Westboro Baptist Church, which identifies the claim that "God loves everyone" as "the greatest lie ever told," listing on its web site God Hates Fags 701 Bible passages to refute this contention, which is central to the theology popularized by most evangelical Christians today.[29]

Even the words "God hates" were not enough to generate a consistent public outcry against Westboro Baptist Church on the national level, though local organizations found creative ways to protest the church's activities.[30] When the church began to picket the funerals of fallen servicemen and -women, however, public outcry against it intensified. Prior to this, some liberal churches—such as those where Westboro Baptist Church had picketed the funerals of people who had died from AIDS-related illnesses—had decried Westboro Baptist Church's activism, but the funeral pickets of soldiers prompted a wide range of Religious Right churches to publicly disavow Westboro Baptist Church. This distinction was important to other conservative antigay churches, especially Baptist churches that share the same label, because at the same time that the Afghanistan and Iraq wars escalated, the debate over same-sex marriage was becoming a major domestic issue, and Religious Right leaders were speaking out clearly against same-sex marriage and homosexuality more broadly while also supporting US-led invasions abroad. Religious Right groups, as well as conservative politicians advocating anti–gay rights laws, spoke forcefully against Westboro Baptist Church in order to avoid confusion between their own antigay rhetoric and the antigay *and* antipatriotic rhetoric of Westboro Baptist Church.[31] The result could only please

Westboro Baptist Church, for the more isolated it remains in its position, the more assured it is of its correctness. It sees itself as a lone remnant, a prophetic voice crying in the wilderness, and its isolation reinforces its special role.[32] Indeed, "many trials to our faith ensure that we follow God out of love," explains elder Steve Drain.[33] This embattled posture is expressed in church texts such as "WBC v. The World," a short, talking-head-style video about the church's lone witness against contemporary sin. Being alone in opposition to sin is not problematic for the prophets of God, though, because "that's how it has to be if we are going to find fidelity in the words of our Lord Jesus Christ."[34] As the Religious Right has maintained and even reinforced its own antigay stance, it has rhetorically distanced itself from Westboro Baptist Church, and Westboro Baptist Church has responded by claiming that the Religious Right has sacrificed its religious integrity in order to consolidate its power.[35]

This book examines the relationship between the antigay and antipatriotic theology and activism of Westboro Baptist Church and the antigay and patriotic theology and activism of the broader Religious Right. It contends that the difference in the responses of religious, civic, and political leaders to Westboro Baptist Church's pickets of gay people's funerals and to pickets of presumably straight servicemen and -women's funerals reveals that, broadly, Americans value the lives of servicemen and -women more than those of gay men and women—or, at least, that politicians find the cause of banning pickets at servicemen and -women's funerals to be more politically potent than banning pickets at the funerals of gay men and women. It considers Westboro Baptist Church's distinctive history and theology but also seeks to place these in the contexts of conservative socioreligious groups and the broader heteronormative American public. It offers a conclusion different from interpretations that marginalize Westboro Baptist Church: that the church members are speaking in a way consistent with their own history and theology, and thus their words are, for those aware of this history and theology, unsurprising. Indeed, by comprehending Westboro Baptist Church in these multiple contexts, Cynthia Burack concludes that "Phelps' importance lies in the fact that his extremism and that of other far right-wing actors [work] to center the views of Christian right leaders like Falwell, Robertson, James Dobson,

Gary Bauer, and others."[36] This book's analysis of Westboro Baptist Church also exposes the contradictions of Religious Right groups that denounce Westboro Baptist rhetoric while denying their alignment with its antigay theology and the similarity of their political visions of American nationalism. Thus, although Westboro Baptists are the central subjects of this book, they are studied in order to understand broader trends among those who collapse religion and nationalism in contemporary America.

## A NOTE ON METHODOLOGY

Although the public unanimously deplores funeral pickets, failing to engage Westboro Baptist Church beyond excoriating church members for outrageous rudeness ignores the fact that the church does more than simply act uncivilly in these contexts. Warning about researchers' temptation to use studies of unloved groups to affirm the dominant culture, sociologist Kathleen Blee notes that scholars must not use the unloved groups as "a foil against which we see ourselves as righteous and tolerant." Instead, scholars must take "a direct, hard look" at even the most unlikable research subjects, "acknowledging the commonalities between them and mainstream groups as well as the differences."[37] Similarly, Westboro Baptist Church should not be treated as a straw man in an argument against hate groups; instead, scholarship should focus on what this group reveals about broader antigay sentiment.

Research on unloved groups must be sensitive to the danger of producing results that reflect the researcher's own perspectives and desires, especially when, as with hate groups, the living research subjects and the researcher have different worldviews and different goals. "Religion," in particular, says Roger Friedland, was "used to bolster the rule of the state, to set states into conquest and war, to spark civil wars, and to establish the ethical habits conditioning the accumulation of productive wealth" but was, via the Enlightenment and modernity, "sequestered, made safe and platitudinous."[38] By articulating a public, far-reaching, and radical religion, Westboro Baptist Church sees itself as diametrically opposed to these trends. Research methods that dismiss or trivialize this self-assessment are disrespectful of the subject and, moreover, result in naive understandings of the group that may ignore or underestimate its potential power.[39]

At the same time, scholars of unsympathetic groups and people must be aware that such research projects have "the power to publicize even as they scrutinize" and "may subtly lend an academic gloss" to dangerous or hurtful behavior.[40] In *When Religion Is an Addiction*, Robert N. Minor complains that right-wing religionists in the United States today "are setting the agenda to which other political, religious, and activist groups are having to respond. And the responses have often been like those of an addict's enablers."[41] For example, counterprotests often argue that "the media" is complicit in promoting Westboro Baptist Church's message and that ignoring the church is the best way to address it. In one regard, this is true. Passersby who are confronted with offensive images on picket signs should probably ignore the church, for church members are unlikely to be persuaded by displays of anger or even respectful engagement, and the Supreme Court's increasingly narrow definition of "fighting words" has not included the words that Westboro Baptists share on the picket line, depriving would-be respondents of one legal avenue of shutting them up.[42] In short, unless addressing picketers contributes to the well-being of the passerby, he or she should simply ignore them. However, ignoring the church will not silence its members. One member explained about the church's decision not to follow through with an announced military funeral picket in April 2011: "Once the media covers the story of our coming, they do the work for us."[43] In this sense, ignoring church members might demotivate them from picketing—but if the church's announcement of a picket does *not* produce a response, members are more likely to attend. Given that Westboro Baptists have announced their intention to publicly spread their message until Jesus's second coming, ignoring it will not silence them. Therefore, scholarly research about the group is required to understand it, situate it, and learn the lessons that it has to teach about the formation and motivation of social movements. Accidentally publicizing or encouraging such a group "are dangerous outcomes," notes Kathleen Blee, "but the consequences [of not doing the scholarship] are worse."[44]

The opportunity for—or the risk of—the "possible transformative effect of the anthropological encounter"[45] occurs when researcher and

subject are culturally distant but not in conflict. "However," as Faye Ginsberg notes about researching abortion, "when the 'other' represents some
very close opposition within one's own society . . . taking on the 'native's
point of view' is problematic in different ways, especially when research is
focused on a social and political conflict."[46] In short, cultivating empathy
for Westboro Baptists is challenging, not because they have so little in
common with non–church members but because Westboro Baptists are
indeed ordinary in so many ways; the differences in theology, politics, and
civic engagement are brought into even sharper focus as a consequence.
In writing about her research with racist groups, Kathleen Blee recalls "an
eerie sense of the familiar colliding with the bizarre" as she witnessed
"disturbingly ordinary" aspects of her subjects' lives, "especially their
evocation of community, family, and social ties."[47] At Westboro Baptist
Church, though, family and community life is so intimately tied to the
church's antigay mission that such "disturbingly ordinary" moments are
frequently punctuated by reminders of the distinctive antigay activism of
the church.

At all times during this research project, church members were generous with their time and provided ample information, though they
frequently showed impatience toward those who lacked fluency in the
rhetoric of conservative Protestantism, including police officers, reporters, and ideological opponents. The church members did not interpret
such communication breakdowns as evidence of their own failure to represent themselves accurately but instead viewed them as evidence that
their audience was willfully ignorant of God. They declare on their web
site, "We are not really interested in a dialogue with you demon-posessed
[sic] perverts. We are not out to change your minds, win your soul to Jesus,
agree to disagree, find common ground upon which to build a meaningful long-term relationship, or any other of your euphemisms for compro-
mising in our stance on the Word of God."[48]

## ORGANIZATION OF THE BOOK

The first part of this book draws upon anthropological methods to provide an ethnography of Westboro Baptist Church. The first chapter, "The

History of Westboro Baptist Church," provides a historical overview from the church's founding to the present, including a biography of founding pastor Fred Phelps and an account of church membership over time and the group's political activism.

The second chapter, "The Theology of Westboro Baptist Church," analyzes the church's theology and its place in American Christianity, beginning with an explanation of its hyper-Calvinism, its focus on sin, its theology of sexuality, and its belief that individual sin and national tragedy are causally related. Though "the relationship between doctrine and life is richer and more complex than predicted by theory,"[49] doctrine plays an important role in Westboro Baptist Church members' self-understanding and activism. Because theology is "a continuous effort to relate the apostolic faith to the conditions, needs, and temptations of men,"[50] a review of the evolution of Westboro Baptist Church theology reveals the "conditions, needs, and temptations" that church members have faced over the more than sixty years of the church's existence.

The third chapter, "The Means, Ministries, and Mission of Westboro Baptist Church," describes the multiple ministries of Westboro Baptist Church, including funeral pickets and multimedia preaching. It assesses the theological motivation for the church's public activities at the local, national, and international levels, contending that the confluence of mobilized resources and a ready audience has allowed theologically justified pickets and preaching to continue.

The second half of the book considers Westboro Baptist Church in the context of the contemporary antigay Religious Right. The fourth chapter, "Cobelligerents in Antigay Activism: Westboro Baptist Church and the Religious Right," defines the contemporary Religious Right, contextualizes its antigay activism in the history of moral legislation, and articulates its theological opposition to homosexuality. It also offers explanations of Religious Right antigay activism other than those rooted in theology. In addition, it examines how, in recent years, Religious Right antigay rhetoric has generally jettisoned its use of theology in public debates about sexuality in favor of pseudoscientific arguments in order to garner more respect from a public wary of overtly religious laws. It also examines the similarities and differences expressed in the antigay rhetoric of the

Religious Right, conservative politicians who advocate antigay policies, and Westboro Baptist Church, noting the overlap in the theology of sexuality of Westboro Baptist Church and Religious Right groups. The fifth chapter, "Civility, Civil Liberties, and Religious Nationalism," considers how, given the overlap in both the theology and antigay political goals of Westboro Baptist Church and Religious Right groups, members of the Religious Right and conservative political leaders counter the church's antipatriotic, but not its antigay, message. The chapter concludes by discussing what debates about funeral pickets reveal about contemporary American culture, especially its commitment to the ideal of the straight, Christian soldier as a national hero. The concluding chapter considers changes in Westboro Baptist Church as the second generation of antigay protesters come of age in an America increasingly accepting of sexual diversity.

The goal of researchers, notes anthropologist Rosemary Wax, "is to realize what they have experienced and learned and to communicate this in terms that will illumine significant areas of the social sciences."[51] Only a more thorough examination of the theology and religious context of Westboro Baptist Church, gained through ethnographic research, rhetorical analysis, discourse analysis, visual analysis, and critical legal analysis, will yield a fuller understanding of how and why Westboro Baptist Church operates and what the public's response to it says about broader American culture. In this way, this book seeks to contribute to the meager scholarship completed on this church, which proclaims that it stands as "this world's last hope"[52] to hear God's truth.

# I

In the years after his move to Topeka, Fred Phelps told the story of how his family arrived in that community in May 1954, at the time when the Supreme Court had desegregated public schools in *Brown v. Board of Education of Topeka, Kansas*. The young pastor, who claims he left Bob Jones University (then located in Cleveland, Tennessee) over the school's racist policies,[1] had been working as an itinerant preacher among Mormons in Utah[2] and on the campus of John Muir College, where he had been a student, preaching against public expressions of sexuality. His railings there against "sins committed on campus by students and teachers," including especially "promiscuous petting" and other kinds of "pandering to the lusts of the flesh," got him removed from campus by police, but the young preacher was able to continue to preach to students from the property of a sympathizer who lived across the street from the school.[3] His confrontational style was well established by the time he and his wife, Margie, who had been a student at Arizona Bible College, were invited to Topeka by leaders of East Side Baptist Church, where Phelps would serve, planting Westboro Baptist Church in 1956 as a branch of East Side that would operate in conjunction with that church. Soon a rift between East Side and Westboro developed, and a legal battle for property ensued, resulting in a total split. At the same time, Fred Phelps grew to reject the Arminian theology of East

Side in favor of Calvinism. This significant theological shift took place over a number of years, but by 1957 the church sign identified the congregation, "having been granted the grace to slough off that hellish pretense that it was by any human power that God redeems his elect people,"[4] as Primitive Baptist. Phelps felt an additional calling, confirmed by his arrival at the time of *Brown*: to fight racism through the law.

Phelps had experienced the privilege of whiteness as a youth in Meriden, Mississippi, the midsized Southern town of his birth. His father, a railway detective, along with Fred Phelps's aunt, reared Phelps and his sister after their mother died.[5] The family was respected because of their affluence; because of their affiliation with the Methodist Church; and, according to Abigail Phelps, youngest child of Fred and Margie Phelps, because of her grandfather's likely affiliation with the Ku Klux Klan (KKK), a relationship that, she claims, inspired her father's antiracism.[6]

Despite the traumatic loss of his mother in childhood, Phelps excelled in school and as a community leader. After graduating from high school at sixteen, he was too young to attend West Point, to which he had received an appointment and which, up to that point, had been his lifelong goal. Thus, he had little to do during the summer after graduation except to attend the local junior college and wait for his next birthday. That summer Phelps attended a revival where he experienced a religious conversion. He promptly decided not to go to West Point but rather to attend Bob Jones University and switch his religious affiliation from Methodist to Baptist. At the end of the following summer, only one year after his conversion, within a year of his baptism,[7] and after having completed only one year of study at Bob Jones University, Phelps was ordained and began to pursue a full-time preaching career. While honing his style on a Western preaching circuit, he came to the attention of East Side Baptist, a Topeka-based independent church, which called him to be its associate pastor.

Though, according to his daughter Shirley Phelps-Roper, a few members of East Side were unhappy about the new preacher's admonitions against Masonry and other fraternal orders, most were pleased enough to select the pastor, described as a "commanding presence and . . . mesmerizing speaker" with a "spellbinding and chilling" speaking style,[8] to establish a new church in the Westboro area of the city.[9] Westboro Baptist

*Westboro Baptist Church is attached to the modest home of Fred Phelps, Sr., now deceased, and his wife, Margie. The front of the building is covered with a massive banner promoting the church's flagship web site. A privacy fence runs the perimeter of the block, which includes homes owned by church members. (Photograph courtesy of Ailecia Ruscin. All rights reserved.)*

Church was planted on November 27, 1955, and was formally organized in May 1956.[10]

## LAW CAREER, CIVIL RIGHTS ACTIVISM, AND DISBARMENT

The legal conflict between East Side and Westboro Baptist may have introduced Fred Phelps to the importance of legal skills. However, given his responsibilities as a new pastor, he did not graduate from Washburn University School of Law until 1964, just two years after he had completed an undergraduate degree in history from Washburn.[11] Though he had been a star law student, heading both the school of law's moot court and its law journal, Phelps struggled to gain admission to the bar because no judge would vouch for his character—a consequence, he contended, of the judges' opposition to the theology he was preaching at Westboro

Baptist Church and, at that point, on the radio.[12] He eventually did gain admittance, having demonstrated, he claimed, his character with his Eagle Scout and American Legion awards as well as by a letter from former president Harry S Truman.

Phelps soon formed Fred W. Phelps Chartered (now Phelps-Chartered), a law firm dedicated to the enforcement of civil rights legislation through litigation. Phelps pursued discrimination cases, including *Johnson v. Whittier*, a 1973 class-action case on behalf of "all Black children who were then or had during the past ten years been students of elementary and junior high schools in East Topeka and North Topeka,"[13] who, the suit contended, had been denied access to equitable facilities in the Topeka school district. The case failed to qualify as a class-action lawsuit, but it became a catalyst for the Department of Health, Education, and Welfare to examine racial discrimination in public schooling in the city, inspiring continued discussion of and litigation about Topeka's failure to live up to the promise of *Brown v. Board of Education.* Further, Phelps filed suit on behalf of African American members of the Jordan-Patterson American Legion who alleged that their post had been illegally searched in an act of racial discrimination by police in 1979;[14] he also represented racial minorities and women in employment discrimination cases.[15] Phelps's commitment to challenging racial discrimination was widely recognized. In 1986 he was the recipient of both the Omaha Mayor's Special Recognition Award for his civil rights work and an award from the Greater Kansas City Chapter of Blacks in Government. In 1987 he was recognized by the Bonner Springs, Kansas, branch of the National Association for the Advancement of Colored People (NAACP) for his legal work on behalf of African Americans.[16] Current Phelps-Chartered clients include many members of minority communities seeking assistance with immigration issues.

Some argue that Fred Phelps was and remained a racist and an opportunist who merely pursued a career in civil rights law because such cases were profitable. Nate Phelps, who left the church in the 1970s and is estranged from his family, credits his father with doing much good for African Americans in Kansas but cautions against misunderstanding his motives as altruistic. Instead, he says, his father saw an opportunity for an energetic lawyer to make money, often taking the bulk of a settlement in fees and leaving the plaintiff with very little.[17] Indeed, according to Nate Phelps, his father preached a traditional conservative Protestant racist interpretation of the story of Noah's sons, which says that Ham was punished by being made black and a servant to his brothers for laughing at his father's drunken nakedness.

Whether or not individual church members are racist, social justice does not seem to be the only motive for pursuing civil rights litigation. A common accusation against Fred Phelps was that he encouraged clients to sue for huge sums, which pressured defendants to settle for smaller amounts regardless of their liability.[18] A 1978 state investigation revealed that in many of the cases that Phelps settled outright, the settlement was one-tenth of 1 percent of the amount originally sought.[19] The accusation of abuse of the legal process followed Phelps from the start of his legal career until the end, when the *Wichita Eagle* noted that "there have been more complaints filed against Phelps, and more formal hearings into his conduct, than any other Kansas attorney since records have been kept."[20]

Phelps faced his first disciplinary case in 1969, just five years after he had passed the bar. He was suspended for two years on three of seven counts of professional misconduct alleged by the State Board of Law Examiners.[21] In 1974 Phelps landed in further trouble with the state when he filed a case against a court reporter employed by the Shawnee County District Court, claiming that she had failed to provide a court transcript promptly. Phelps cross-examined the court reporter brutally, according to the Kansas Supreme Court's assessment[22]—the kind of behavior that would, in a later case, earn him a ten-day jail sentence for contempt of court.[23] When Phelps lost the case, he sought a new trial, promising to deliver witnesses who would testify against the court reporter to establish her reputation and character, with a focus on her sex life. When she provided affidavits from those same witnesses saying that they would not testify as Phelps promised, he was accused by the state of "clearly misrepresent[ing] the truth to the court."[24] In 1977 the state of Kansas began the process of disbarring Phelps. The lawyer for the state noted the harm that Phelps's abnormally aggressive behavior and unwarranted personal attacks caused not only the defendant but also the legal system: "When attorneys engage in conduct such as Phelps has done, they do serious injury to the workings of our judicial system. Even the lay person could see how serious Phelps' infractions are. To allow this type of conduct to go essentially unpunished is being disrespectful to our entire judicial system."[25] The justices of the Kansas Supreme Court agreed,[26] concluding that Fred Phelps had "little regard for the ethics of his profession."[27] He was disbarred on July 20, 1979. Phelps was no longer able to practice law in the state courts of Kansas, and, at the same time, he was suspended from practicing law in Kansas's US District Courts for two years. According to Phelps, though, "To be wrongfully disbarred by a corrupt court is a badge of honor."[28]

Fred Phelps was able to continue practicing in federal court, and he continued to be known for his aggressive tactics, including sending "demand letters" to people whom he planned to sue.[29] Though a panel of federal judges dismissed some charges related to the demand letters, they nevertheless delivered a public censure of Fred Phelps in 1987.[30] During this time, though, Phelps and family members working for Phelps-Chartered were committing acts that would earn them more than a censure. In 1985 Fred Phelps, Sr.; Fred Phelps, Jr.; Betty Phelps, the wife of Fred Phelps, Jr.; daughter Margie Phelps; Shirley Phelps-Roper; Jonathan Phelps; and Elizabeth (Lizz) Phelps were accused of making false charges against nine US District Court judges in Kansas. The false accusations generally involved claims that the judges were racist, prejudiced against religion, and reluctant to hear civil rights cases.[31] Given that, at one time, 25 percent of all the civil lawsuits in US District Court in Shawnee County and 6 percent of the civil docket in Shawnee County District Court were handled by Phelps-Chartered,[32] both the charges and the potential consequences were serious. If Phelps's accusations were found to be false and Phelps was disbarred, it would mean that African Americans would lose a valuable ally in civil rights litigation.

In 1989 investigators concluded that the Phelpses' accusations against the judges were false and that the lawyers had violated their ethical code, echoing an earlier complaint by a local lawyer who had noted "a mean streak" in the pastor-lawyer: "Sometimes he is so filled with hate when he takes after somebody, it becomes an obsession with him."[33] Rather than fighting against the potential disbarment of all members of the family who were involved in the matter, Fred Phelps, Sr., agreed to surrender his license to practice in federal court if the other members of the family could retain their licenses. Fred Phelps, Sr., however, explained that he would retire from the practice of law "to expose judicial corruption."[34] Phelps's legal career ended ignobly but not unsurprisingly, even to him. Phelps continued to believe that it was his civil rights work, antigay activism, and defense of free speech that made him a threat to his peer lawyers and the judges of the state of Kansas who pushed for his removal from the profession.

Given his professed commitment to racial equality, how can Phelps's vitriolic antigay activity be explained? Phelps himself used theology to explain what some see as the contradiction between his commitment to civil rights for African Americans and his commitment to antigay activism. Like other anti–gay rights churches that deny a similarity between sexuality and race or homophobia and racism, Westboro Baptist Church clearly states that "the Scripture doesn't support racism," noting, "God never says 'thou shalt not be black.' However, He does say, 'Thou shalt not lie with mankind, as with womankind: it is abomination.' (Leviticus 18:22)."[35] Explained Fred Phelps in a letter to the *Topeka Capital-Journal*,

> Gays and lesbians are not legitimate minorities entitled to government's protection by force of law. . . . Legitimate minorities are characterized by immutable attributes of *being*—not by immoral, criminal *acts of conduction, voluntarily engaged in*. Skin color is an immutable attribute, not an immoral, criminal act voluntarily performed. Homosexuals are self-defined by immoral, sinful, criminal sex acts, voluntarily engaged in.[36]

Such sentiments are shared by many anti–gay rights religious believers, including many African Americans.

Potentially, their shared history of civil rights struggle and their shared antigay theology may have contributed to Topeka's black population's long-lasting support of Fred Phelps's law office. For example, in 1983 the president of the Wichita branch of the NAACP, Rev. D. D. Miller, noted, "Before Fred Phelps came on the scene, we couldn't get an attorney in Wichita to touch a civil rights case." An NAACP representative from Topeka called Phelps "a modern-day John Brown," alluding to the famed

Kansas abolitionist who led the raid on Harpers Ferry that began the Civil War.[37]

Though Fred Phelps was retired from law for more than twenty years before his death, the perception of him as a vicious litigator prepared to use the law as a weapon in personal vendettas created long-term fear among local citizens and may have discouraged early efforts to counter pickets when they began shortly after the end of his law career. Because of both his litigious tenacity and his picketing, the city of Topeka has been described as "a city held hostage."[38] In contrast to this perspective, Phelps saw himself as serving his adopted hometown through his civil rights activism, his religious leadership, and his attempts at political office.

## POLITICAL ASPIRATIONS

"If you want a law license to relieve the oppressed, you're wasting your time," Fred Phelps opined in 1994. "You can do more now by running for office and getting that platform to preach stuff and influence debate."[39] Phelps ran for public office several times in his attempt to "do more" to "relieve the oppressed," though he never won a seat. His earliest effort was in 1966, when he ran for the Democratic nomination for the 45th District of the Kansas House of Representatives,[40] and over nearly four decades and across three generations, church members have sought public office, not necessarily for the sake of winning but because, as Shirley Phelps-Roper says, "The process opens doors to speak. . . . The election is just the secondary by-product of the ability to timely say words, to draw eyes to a situation."[41] In their campaigns Westboro Baptists use in-your-face tactics and language not necessarily to win voters but to draw attention to causes important to them.

Fred Phelps ran again for office in 1990, when he won 6.7 percent of the Democratic vote in the state primary for governor, votes that, if they had been cast for incumbent governor John Carlin, would have prevented the Democratic challenger—and eventual loser in the statewide election, Joan Finney—from winning.[42] That same year Phelps received 19.1 percent of the vote to be a replacement senator representing the state of Kansas in Washington, D.C.,[43] and two years later he won an impressive 30.8

percent of the vote in the Democratic primary race for senator.[44] This election was held *after* Westboro Baptist Church had begun its antigay picketing, and Phelps's campaign included numerous examples of antigay rhetoric against his opponent.

In 1994 Fred Phelps received only 3.4 percent of the votes in the Democratic primary for governor in an election in which he barraged an opponent with questions about her sexuality, warning her that though she was "among my favorite fag-lovers and baby-killers . . . unless there's some honest-to-God confessing and repenting, I intend to clean your [clock] in 1994."[45] Had he been running for the Republican Party, which frequently has explicitly anti–gay rights planks in its platform, he might have received many more votes. In 1997 he lost badly in the race for mayor of Topeka, a town growing weary of church pickets.[46] In 1998, before Westboro Baptist Church made national news with its picket of Matthew Shepard's funeral but after it had, nonetheless, conducted many funeral protests, Fred Phelps, Sr., won 14.7 percent of the votes in the Democratic primary for governor,[47] and, though he did not win, Fred Phelps, Jr., garnered 26,054 votes in the Democratic primary for attorney general—an impressive 25.7 percent.[48] In this trajectory, Fred Phelps, Sr., increased his share of the votes in the first election during which he deployed antigay rhetoric, but he never won so many votes again, though people beyond the church did support him in future elections.

Support for Fred Phelps from Kansas Democrats might be less surprising than it first seems. First, his civil rights litigation gained him the respect of many of the state's African Americans, people more likely to be registered Democrat than Republican and also likely to support a religiously antigay stance in politics, despite their political affiliation.[49] Further, Kansans have often voted against the advancement of gay rights. For example, in 1998, after it announced its plan to study issues relating to sexual orientation, Topeka's Human Relations Commission was abolished by the city council. It was reinstated, quite weakened, after public protest.[50] The city's 2000 antihate resolution was similarly hard-fought, and the city council rejected a ban on discrimination against gay people in housing and employment in 2002, with council member Lisa Hecht, who had sponsored the bill, losing in the next election, presumably because of her support of the legislation.[51] Finally, in 2005 the council voted 5-4 to approve an ordinance that prohibits discrimination based on sexual orientation in hiring practices[52]—but the law applies only to the municipality, not to residents. Even this weak law, which passed nearly fifteen years after the start of Westboro Baptist Church's antigay picketing and won approval by only one vote, was seen by Westboro Baptists as an outrageous capitulation to gay rights advocates. The church promptly began a petition drive that aimed to repeal the ordinance as well as the 2002 hate crimes ordinance and to prevent the passage of any law that recognized gay people as a protected class for the following ten years.[53] On March 1, 2005, Topekans voted on the issue, with just 53 percent voting to keep the city's ban against discrimination based on sexual orientation in the municipality's employment practices.[54] On April 5, 2005, Kansans voted in even larger numbers to amend the state constitution to define marriage as between one man and one woman.[55] Thus, many Kansans, while they may not agree with Phelps's tactics or even his theology, supported the same antigay agenda as did Westboro Baptist Church.

When they voted to retain the city's ban on sexual orientation discrimination in citywide hiring and firing, Topeka's citizens also voted against Jael Phelps, the granddaughter of Fred Phelps, who was then a nursing student running for city council. Though Jael Phelps finished last of the four candidates in the primary, with only 5 percent of the vote, her main opponent was second-place primary finisher Tiffany Muller, the city's first openly gay council member.[56] Muller had been appointed, not elected, to the council and so faced her first election in 2005. Though Muller spent much of her campaign talking about the need for supporting economic development, she also supported the city's antidiscrimination ordinance and opposed efforts to amend the state constitution to prohibit same-sex marriage.[57] These issues, along with her sexuality, made Muller a target for Westboro Baptist Church, with Jael Phelps stating explicitly that she was running to expose Muller as a gay rights activist "so the people of District 9 would know who the incumbent is. We have someone whose goal in life is to make it so the governmental stamp of approval is put on sin, and an abomination at that."[58] Although Muller was one of the top candidates in the primary, she lost in the general election to Richard Harmon.

A protester makes the church's position on city politics and residents known at a picket in July 2010. (Photography courtesy of Ailecia Ruscin. All rights reserved.)

Though the 202 votes that Jael Phelps did win did not determine Muller's loss,[59] Westboro Baptist Church's relentless attacks on Muller may have both sparked and articulated an antigay vote in Topeka. Shirley Phelps-Roper commented regarding the contest that although Topekans do not love the Phelpses, they will not elect an openly gay council member.[60]

In other words, the climate for the advancement of gay rights in Kansas has not been ideal and remains challenging, with or without the political leadership of Westboro Baptist members.[61] That climate allowed church members as much traction as they were able to achieve in local and state elections. When Fred Phelps lost his ability to practice law, he also lost his opportunity to be a public voice in the style to which he was accustomed, to act in public in ways that garnered him praise or instilled fear in would-be opponents, and to participate in civic life as an agitator for change or a defender of what he saw as right—but, despite his faith that public office is a better place than even the courtroom to achieve his anti–gay rights goals, no one associated with the church has achieved this dream. His law career thus ended and his political aspirations unfulfilled, Fred Phelps, with the support of the many lawyers in his family, developed Westboro Baptist Church into the most provocative antigay voice on the American religious scene.

## RELIGIOUS LIFE IN WESTBORO BAPTIST CHURCH

Advanced schooling in theology is considered to be a threat to the democracy that Primitive Baptists value. Moreover, Primitive Baptists argue that theological training implies that the Holy Spirit is insufficient in preparing ministers for their work. They note that Jesus did not set accreditation standards for his gospel ministers and that, in any case, schools of theology virtually guarantee unwanted exposure to liberal doctrines. Though Fred Phelps did, in fact, have some theological training, his church adopts the goal of simplicity articulated by other Primitive Baptists, though its worship is slightly different in detail from that of most Primitive Baptist congregations. The central value in worship and organization is simplicity. Westboro Baptist Church models "the humble simplicity that attends the workings of the Lord Jesus and to his church militant on earth."[62] This means that the church service is similar each week in its organization and minimalist in its content, even now that services are led by different elders.

Services begin with a congregational hymn, accompanied by piano and organ. In its use of musical instruments, Westboro Baptist Church is different from traditional Primitive Baptist congregations, though Progressive Primitive Baptists introduced instrumental accompaniment in the early 1900s. Hymns are taken predominantly from the *Primitive Baptist Hymnal*, a text that has been unchanged for over 140 years. After the singing, an adult male offers an introductory prayer, always using King James English. After this an elder—one of the married men selected by the congregation to provide spiritual discipleship and from-the-pulpit teaching to congregants—takes the pulpit and often spends the first few minutes discussing the news of the week as it affects the church, including any appearances of church members in the media. He then launches into a sermon, provided in hard copy to those in the pews. The service varies in length depending on the preacher, from an hour to an hour and a half.

The preaching style of those in the pulpit, whether that of Fred Phelps or of one of the elders who followed in his footsteps, has frequently been described by outsiders as incoherent, repetitive, or disturbing,[63] with frequent biblical citations aimed at overwhelming the listener. Such characterizations reveal less about the individual preacher's style than about the listeners' unfamiliarity with Primitive Baptist sermon style, which has a rhetorical tradition of stitching together Bible citations as evidence for a sermon's thesis, with a focus on suffering and oppression in this world and hell in the next.[64] Primitive Baptist sermons are often extemporaneous, "frequently not even having a particular text as a basis," as John G. Crowley, historian of Primitive Baptists, notes.[65] However, sermons at Westboro Baptist Church are written in advance, and a full text is provided for congregants; later the text is posted online, as is a recording of the message.

"Allegorical 'type and shadow' preaching has always been much in favor among Primitive Baptists," notes Crowley, describing preaching that looks to biblical history, especially the books of the Old Testament, for "types" that correspond to present day or future events or people.[66] Old Testament stories are frequently central in illustrating some point. "Has

God forgotten these stories, even if we don't preach them?" Fred Phelps asked his congregation one Sunday during a service, noting his love for the often violent imagery of the historical and prophetic texts.[67]

Proof-texting, the bringing together of various scriptural passages to prove a theological point, is a common organizational strategy, with the focus of the sermon being on a theological thesis rather than on understanding a particular text in more detail. A particular sermon may include up to two dozen different scriptural references, including texts from the Old and New Testaments and at least one from the gospels, for example, in support of its thesis. Within fundamentalist preaching more broadly, "the preacher bases his address on a biblical text, and the more adept he is at cross-referencing his primary text with other scriptural passages the better his sermon is considered to be."[68] Westboro Baptist Church fits this model, but for listeners unfamiliar with this strategy of organization, sermons may appear disorganized. Some scholars of theology and preaching suggest that such a scattershot approach to scriptural study— what the church calls "connecting the dots" between passages but critics deride as stringing together passages taken out of context to support a thesis that might not be supportable through systematic study—is an abuse of scripture.[69] However, this would not be understood as a criticism by Westboro Baptists, who highly value familiarity with biblical passages but adopt, generally, a "commonsense" approach to interpretation. (It is "NOT ROCKET SCIENCE!," as Shirley Phelps-Roper explains.[70]) Mere citation of biblical passages might seem to be a dodge to those unfamiliar with the texts, but Westboro Baptists are familiar with commonly cited as well as obscure passages.

Sermons take as their focus a relatively narrow set of topics, for "Primitive preaching heavily emphasizes predestination and election," notes Crowley, adding, "Indeed, the core beliefs in the divine sovereignty cannot be expressed too starkly."[71] In the case of Westboro Baptist Church, sermons, regardless of the scripture being addressed, cover the following themes each week: the hopeless state of the world, the hoped-for election of Westboro Baptists, the need for obedience to God, and the persecution of Westboro Baptist Church as evidence of its chosen role in God's plan for humanity. "The content of [Primitive Baptist] sermons reflects devotion to their core doctrines and their almost total disassociation with the outer world,"[72] Crowley notes. Westboro Baptist Church's sermons generally follow this model, though they address issues of national and global concern—most frequently abortion, gay rights, political leadership, international conflict, and Catholic priests' sexual abuse of children in their care—frequently citing them as evidence for God's impending destruction of the world. The repetition of themes and evidence serves to reinforce key elements of theology—the limited atonement of Jesus Christ and the perseverance of the saints, for example—while also providing believers with language they can use to share the church's message publicly.

With their attention commonly held by the preacher, congregants build a relationship with each other. The service is unusually quiet for those familiar with more interactive relationships between preacher and audience or accustomed to the distraction of noisy children, nursery workers entering or exiting the room, or ushers attending to congregants. Congregants do not encourage the speaker with "amens" or "hallelujahs," though they do laugh at his jokes, which are sometimes at the expense of outside groups, are sometimes aimed good-naturedly at members of the congregation, and are sometimes self-deprecating. Attention is focused intensely on the sermon and the preacher.

Decoration is minimal. A photograph of the church from the 1950s hangs on one wall, and two or three church placards rest on easels at the front of each aisle; these are rotated, but they all highlight the main messages of the church: God hates gay people, God hates America, and God hates the world. Sometimes images of admired figures, such as the eighteenth-century hymnist Isaac Watts, appear on placards, and a large sign spelling the acronym "TULIP"—one letter for each of the five points of the Calvinist theology that the church espouses (total depravity, unconditional election, limited atonement, irresistible grace, and the perseverance of the saints), as will be discussed in chapter 2—always hangs behind the speaker. The pulpit, along with an organ to the left and a piano to the right, is on a small raised stage, and a microphone hangs over it so that the preaching elder's voice can be heard throughout the sanctuary and recorded. Below the pulpit, offstage, is a wooden communion table inscribed with the words "Do This in Memory of Me."

Religious iconography of any kind is considered idolatrous; no crosses, pictures of Jesus, or other symbols appear in the sanctuary or, for that matter, on the clothing, cars, or jewelry of congregants. "Anyone should destroy anything that stands between them and salvation," explained Abigail Phelps at the church's September 11, 2010, Koran and US flag burning, and that includes the Koran, Catholic statuary, Orthodox icons, crosses, and crucifixes. That is also why the church includes no images of Jesus (who, as God, should never be depicted as a "graven image") in its sanctuary or literature. This is not surprising, for, according to Peter J. Thuesen, "predestinarianism presupposed the utter transcendence and hiddenness of an all-determining God. It is not coincidence that the strongest predestinarians have often been equally strong iconoclasts," forbidding any images of God, including Jesus.[73]

Attendance at Sunday services is expected of church members, as is participation in other church events, including picketing and Bible readings. The church does not sponsor Sunday school, declaring that the Bible provides no model of age-specific instruction, though members gather frequently for Bible readings. All gathered members sit in concentric circles and read the selected Bible text or, occasionally, approved commentary aloud, stopping if someone raises a question or comment about the text, for, as Shirley Phelps-Roper notes, they are instructed to "help each other," as they have "gifts that vary."[74]

In addition to Bible reading, Bible memorization is valued by the congregation, and children are quizzed on memorized material. Many days when school is not in session, children participate in two sessions of Bible reading per day, overseen by an adult. If someone finds something of interest to the group while reading, he or she shares it, sometimes via e-mail. In sum, texts are central. "Fundamentalists are bound to view correct interpretation as a matter of eternal life or death," notes Kathleen C. Boone in her analysis of fundamentalist rhetoric. "If one's eternal destiny depends on a right relationship with God, and if that God is reliably known only through the Bible, it follows that one must read, and read correctly."[75] Immersion in scriptures and frequent public discussion of them is how Westboro Baptists learn biblical passages in the church's tradition.

## CHURCH DEMOGRAPHICS

As of September 2015 Westboro Baptist Church includes approximately seventy participants, people who have been baptized as professed believers whose behavior is in accordance with church standards and have joined Westboro Baptist Church as members as well as those who are on some pathway to membership; this includes several participants who have joined since the Supreme Court's ruling protecting the church's right to picket military funerals in March 2011. Because baptism is "a privilege, not a right,"[76] not all who attend the church service are members. This includes the many young children of the church as well as some who have joined in worship but have not yet been baptized, either because of their own hesitancy or the church's. The church will "lay hands on no man suddenly"—meaning that the church community has a duty to deliberate on accepting new members, who must not only adhere to the church's rules regarding proper living but also be willing to preach its message.[77] This number represents a decrease in membership since May 2004, a time of increased exclusion among church members, but many of the recent members have come from outside the Phelps family.

When the church was founded in 1955, two key families—the Phelpses and the Hockenbargers—comprised the majority of adherents, and members of the families have married each other. Because Westboro Baptist Church discourages potential alliances with outsiders and because of the church's distinctive theology, which has developed in a setting where no outside authority has sway, membership is difficult to achieve, for even if would-be members share some of the theological tenets of Westboro Baptist Church, they do not share all of them. Says Shirley Phelps-Roper, "Of a truth, we have heard from hundreds of people over these years, I mean hundreds that claim they are [believers according to the standard of Westboro Baptist Church]. Then, upon a VERY SMALL examination, you run into some error."[78] For those who do pass, the next test is willingness to participate in the church's ministry.

Antigay sentiment is not sufficient for church participation. According to the church's web site, most of those who support Westboro Baptist Church's antigay picketing from afar do so without theological justification, instead invoking personal prejudice. If you fall into this category, says the church, you are a "pretender": "You're a rebel against God that happens to think that fags are filthy. Duh. You think? You don't care about God's standard (see Rom. 1:18–32);[79] you just personally don't like something about fags (e.g. their wallowing and/or eating feces, their men behaving like little girls, or some other specific personal distaste of their particular curse from God)."[80] In passages such as these, the church invokes a politics of disgust, which "localizes discrimination against a group of Americans by references to their *natures* and the dangers of contagion posed by *unnatural* acts, peoples, and ideologies."[81] Such tactics are common in Religious Right depictions of same-sex sexuality because, though "feelings of disgust are nonrational responses to physical phenomena," they may be successfully tapped as "underlying motivations for our rational discourses," including legal arguments against civil rights for gay people or religious arguments to eject gay people from churches.[82] Westboro Baptist Church members luridly describe sex acts involving anal penetration, urolagnia, coprophilia, and anilingus, hoping to promote feelings of disgust among online readers and those passing by pickets. The stick-figure images on their signs suggesting male-male anal intercourse prompt many parents of children to cover or avert their children's eyes as they walk past, indicating that Westboro Baptist Church is indeed successfully tapping into feelings of public disgust or shame about anal sex between men. The choice to show male-male anal intercourse, rather than, say, male-male kissing does not mean that anal intercourse is inherently wrong (the church makes no prohibitions against such acts in the context of heterosexual marriage) or that male-male kissing would be acceptable. Instead, this image is chosen because it unambiguously refers to sexual relations between men (as the stick figures lack skirts, the signal that they are women) but requires no outline of a penis—as would, say, frottage—which would likely violate ordinances against pornographic images in public places. More importantly, the church chooses images of male-male anal intercourse to rouse feelings of disgust because members believe, correctly, that the public is more likely to be upset by such images—and, indeed, the very idea of queer sexuality among men—than by images of lesbianism.[83]

To be a member of the church, one must participate in antigay activism for religious, not secular, reasons because "God's hatred is not like man's hatred. His hatred is holy, pure, unchanging, while man's hatred is a sinful, fickle emotion."[84] Indeed, in field research, individual prejudice against gay people was not visible; openly gay church visitors were treated civilly, and gay journalists traveling with the church to pickets were extended welcome in the forms of bottles of water and offers of sunscreen. Indeed, a vicious personal dislike of gay people may be seen as a sign that a potential church member is motivated by the wrong reasons.

If potential converts to the church do, in fact, share its theology and a religiously motivated desire to picket against homosexuality, they must move to Topeka and join the congregation, a move that evidences their belief, for "if they were like-minded, they would be HERE."[85] Few do because, as Shirley Phelps-Roper explains, "it is nothing for some people to agree with us, NAY, with GOD on some points. It is a whole other matter to OBEY and put away your huge idol called 'MY TIME' and submit yourself to God and to submit yourself to his people."[86] Occasionally people outside the church join. One notable case is Steve Drain, who, while studying film at the University of Kansas, produced a documentary about the group titled *Hatemongers*.[87] According to Drain, he had completed his degree and returned to his home state of Florida to edit the documentary and, during the process, had a religious experience. He moved his unwilling wife and daughters to Topeka, and eventually the entire family joined the church, though his oldest daughter, Lauren, left in 2008. Since joining the church he and his wife have had two more children. Another notable case is that of Jeff,[88] a young, single man who moved from California to join the church in 2008. Though he has purchased a home near church property, he is not yet a church member. Likewise, a sometime participant, Joe,[89] travels from Wichita to join pickets. Joe had been active in the protests of Operation Save America, a Christian antiabortion group, against Dr. George Tiller, a Wichita abortion provider who was murdered while at church in 2009. Joe turned his attention to Westboro Baptist Church in 2008 upon the election of Barack Obama, whom he identifies as a Muslim threat to America. Like Jeff, Joe is not a church member. Matthias Holroyd, a man from England, successfully joined the church, then married a woman in the church and now has two children. The past few years have seen a few more people move to Topeka to join the church, only to leave for various reasons. These include a young married couple, both US Marine Corps veterans, from California and a young single man from Illinois.

Members are expected to participate in both Sunday services and pickets, and church members who fail to do so soon find themselves threatened with exclusion from Westboro Baptist Church and, as Fred Phelps hinted in sermons, eternal exclusion from heaven. It is important to God "that each time the church assembles, with a few exceptions, each member has a solemn obligation to be there and worship, and encourage his loved ones. I tell you, it is a mighty dangerous thing to forsake the assembling and ignore the thrilling call of the Silver Trumpet of God," for what if, in turn, "God neglects to give you a Silver Trumpet call to the Rapture?"[90] As a result of this pressure, church members attend church or are excluded, and most who attend are members. This practice is in contrast to that of most Primitive Baptists, for whom "emphasis upon salvation as an unconditional covenant transaction before the foundation of the world makes church membership absolutely unnecessary for salvation in their view."[91]

Married members of the church do not use birth control, and family size, consequently, is large, with several families having ten or more children. Despite this, the church does not discourage women from seeking employment outside the home. For example, all nine of Fred and Margie Phelps's daughters obtained law degrees, and some have additional graduate degrees. Though the church values marriage, it does not promote marriage, believing, as one young woman in the church said, that members should focus on God's work because "we're living in the last days anyway."[92] Single parenthood, while not desired, is not a reason for rejection from the church, provided that the single parent repents of the sin of nonmarital sex. In all of these ways, then, the church does not neatly mimic the Religious Right's veneration of traditional gender roles.

Despite accusations that marriages within the church are prearranged, only a few couples within the church met each other through it. Most met while in high school, college, or graduate school, and the non–church member of the pair then converted. Within the congregation, the married and unmarried have equal standing.[93]

Church members are relatively affluent and almost all are well edu-
cated. Most work in professional jobs, and all of the women of the church,
except for the elderly Margie Phelps, Fred Phelps's wife, work or worked
outside the home. Church members, both men and women, work in nursing, computer science, robotics, and law, suggesting some flexibility in
gender roles outside the home. Most adult church members are home-
owners, and most live within a short distance of the church. However,
financial success is not linked to value as a church member. Like the historical Primitive Baptists with whom they identify, whose "mistrust of
institutional religion led them toward an equality within the plain walls
of their churches that defied the common understanding of honor as a
function of orderly hierarchy,"[94] Westboro Baptists do not link church responsibilities or privileges with income.

## GENDER WITHIN THE CONGREGATION

As revealed in even a casual perusal of congregants during a Sunday service, Westboro Baptist Church takes a unique stance on gender issues.
Women and men sit in the same pews. Fathers actively attend to their children, assisting older children in reading sermon notes and taking younger
ones to the restroom. If a mother is ill or for some other reason unable to
attend the service, her husband still brings their children to church and
provides for their care.

The gender equality that church members display in the care of their
children is in apparent contradiction with the appearance of the women
of the church. Women do not cut their hair, ever, and men have short hair.
During Sunday services, but not during pickets, Bible readings, or other
events, all females wear some kind of head covering, either scarves tied
under the chin or at the nape of the neck or, for infants and toddlers, bonnets to cover their hair, which may be worn up or be free-flowing. Imme-
diately after the closing hymn, before exiting the sanctuary, women and
girls remove their head coverings. Head covering was not always part of
church practice; instead, says Shirley Phelps-Roper, it is something that
members came to adopt over time, once they understood the scriptures to
mandate it.[95]

All females in the church, regardless of age, cover their heads during services, though hair may be free-flowing beneath the head covering. Women generally wear scarves, and infant girls often wear bonnets. (Photograph courtesy of Ailecia Ruscin. All rights reserved.)

However, gender is not indicated by dress in other ways. For example, women wear pants to the church service, and younger women even wear shorts. Though some congregants dress in "church best" clothes, others wear more casual clothing. Although congregants dress modestly, women may wear sleeveless tops, and, especially among young women, fashionable brands are common. Women may wear precious metals or stones as part of their jewelry or eyeglasses, though decoration is never ostentatious. Unisex clothing such as T-shirts is acceptable. This is in contrast to how most conservative churches manage gender. For example, among other head-covering churches—the Amish, Mennonite, and German Baptists, for example—head coverings are generally worn at all times, not just during Sunday services. In addition, among these groups, gendered clothing is the norm, with women wearing dresses that are designed with capes or aprons to hide the outline of breasts. All of these groups also prohibit the wearing of jewelry. Though Westboro Baptist Church shares the practices of uncut hair and head covering with these other groups, members have the freedom to wear clothing that they choose, provided it meets minimum standards of modesty.

Westboro Baptist Church's gender distinctions are rooted, members say, in the biblical mandate that husbands have authority over their wives and are "the saviors of their homes,"[96] just as Jesus Christ is the savior of the church. However, Westboro Baptists quickly qualify that this does not give all men authority over all women but only husbands over wives, that husbands are responsible for the peace of the household, and that women are not compelled to accept physical violence by their husbands. For example, Tim Phelps, son of Fred and Margie Phelps, warns that those husbands who would read the command "Wives, submit yourselves unto your own husband as unto the Lord" of Ephesians 5:22 as license to bully their wives are abusing scripture, using it to justify their own laziness to avoid fetching their own slippers or making their own supper.[97] These people, he notes, are not welcome to membership in Westboro Baptist Church. Sam Phelps-Roper, Shirley's son, repeats the point, saying that if an excluded member of the church is a physical threat to his wife, the couple should live physically apart, even though the church does not advocate for married persons, even if one is excluded from the congregation, to live separately otherwise.[98] Again, this is quite different from the beliefs of conservative churches that condone spousal physical abuse through scripture.

In their interactions with their spouses, Westboro Baptists are gentle and kind. Even good-natured spousal teasing is rare, and spouses speak of each other with respect, both for the individual and for their marriage. Jonathan Phelps notes that church members are excited about their marriages, recalling that Brent Roper, a convert to the church as a teenager in the 1970s, hurried through his undergraduate degree and law school so that he could marry Shirley Phelps. Further, Sam Phelps-Roper adds laughingly, the women of the church are too independent to be strong-armed into marriage.[99] Indeed, three of Fred and Margie Phelps's daughters who are active in the church remain unmarried, though two of them have children (one through adoption and one through a nonmarital relationship). The three sons who remain in the congregation are married.

Westboro Baptist Church marriages are marked with love and tenderness, at least at this stage of the church's history. Although women do not preach or pray in the Sunday service, they do lead Bible readings, organize church time, and plan church activities; however, men are not absent in these roles. This is because, says Shirley Phelps-Roper, women and men are to be equal partners in God's work and equally able to do the work. They should be "ambidextrous," she says, applying a description of the soon-to-be-king David's warriors taken from 1 Chronicles 12:2: "They were armed with bows, and could use both the right hand and the left in hurling stones and shooting arrows out of a bow, even of Saul's brethren of Benjamin." Like David's warriors, Westboro Baptists, both male and female, are called to fight with everything they have and are supernaturally equipped to do so.

## CHURCH DISCIPLINE

Both current and former Westboro Baptists agree that disciplining members is a central function of the church. This happens by organizing life around church activities and functions, including attendance at Sunday services and participation in pickets. Adherence to church standards is expected, and the result is a high level of compliance, with most of those reared within the church among Fred and Margie Phelps's children and grandchildren remaining within the church. This is accomplished first within the home. Says Shirley Phelps-Roper, "The children in my house will obey their parents, or they will have no peace. They will serve the Lord or they will have no peace. I find that what you expect from children is what you get. For their sakes, I teach them every day in every way what the Lord their God requires of them."[100]

However, children are also seen as distinct from their parents, and their parents' status within the church is irrelevant to their own; thus, children are not encouraged to be baptized, as that is a claim to belief, but are required to attend church, as obedience is required even if belief is absent. Within the Calvinist doctrine of Westboro Baptist Church, this is not free will but a recognition of the isolation of each person before God. Speaking of her own children, Shirley Phelps-Roper says, "My hope is that the Lord my God will bless them with saving faith and that they will serve and obey God. Mostly, I pray that the will of God will be done—if that involves their salvation or their perdition, it is all fine with me."[101] Shirley Phelps-Roper, like many of the parents of adult children within the congregation, was forced to contend with this situation when her son Josh, then in his twenties, left the congregation. His departure was evidence not of the failure of the church discipline to retain members, according to church theology, but, instead, of his nonelection. "While they live in my house, they will serve God," says Shirley Phelps-Roper about her children, and if they depart, "they do as God has ordained for them to do."[102] After a departure church members no longer worry about the excluded, they claim. "Life is too short," says Shirley Phelps-Roper. "My prospects for eternity are too important to worry about anything else," including even beloved family members' salvation, over which neither she nor they have any control.[103] Mark Phelps, son of Fred and Margie, though, claimed that his father was far more passionate about his exclusion, recalling that, after he left, Fred Sr. visited him at his workplace one day. "He came right up to me and said, 'I hope God kills you.'"[104]

Exclusion, or excommunication, thus is viewed by members as a mechanism for separating the sheep from the goats, to use a biblical metaphor, in order to remind both the goats and the sheep of their place in eternity. In the disciplinary structure of the church, it is the most drastic action it can take in reining in members. This kind of discipline is unusual in most branches of American Christianity today, though it remains a practice of the Amish.

Church members contend that they practice a model of discipline taken from Matthew 18:15–19, when Jesus instructs believers to confront an individual among them one-on-one if they see him in sin.[105] If he rejects their effort to correct him, they are to approach him in a small group, and if that engagement fails to produce change, they are to confront him as a congregation. If he still fails to adhere to standards, they are to excommunicate him according to 1 Corinthians 5:12–13, in which Paul directs the church at Corinth "not to keep company" with fornicators, the covetous, extortionists, railers, drunkards, or idolators, saying, "For what have I to do to judge them also that are without? Do not ye judge them that are within? But them that are without God judgeth. Therefore, put away from among yourselves that wicked person." By placing the offending person outside the congregation, the congregation indicates its understanding that that person is failing to live up to God's standards and is not its responsibility.

Accordingly, one of the reasons cited for the closeness of the community is that members can scout for sin in each other's lives and provide corrective advice if some sin is suspected. If that advice fails to produce change, a larger body addresses the offending individual, and if necessary, the entire church addresses the person. Frequently, though, according to church members, the problem is remedied in dyads or small groups. Even when the entire church addresses a person, the goal is to return that person to good standing within the congregation. If deemed necessary, the decision to exclude is made with the consensus of the congregation, minus the offending member.

The goal, throughout, is to maintain the group's high standards, without the stain of a willfully and repeatedly offending member; this is accomplished through either a change in the member's behavior or the exclusion of the member. Even if exclusion occurs, the community hopes that it results in a return, and so those who leave are not given up forever. Within Westboro Baptist Church, various members have been excluded for misconduct but did not leave the area and were voted back in when they demonstrated change. The congregation remains open to the return of the excluded—if they properly repent. "That is amazing," comments Shirley Phelps-Roper. "From start to finish and it is mercy and it is loving kindness."[106] Exclusion is thus a tool for maintaining group purity and group identity, both through its actual and its threatened use.

Exclusion does not have to be invoked to be an effective tool for directing congregants' behavior; merely the existence of it—and the practice of it on others and other members' participation in it—serves to remind would-be dissenters of the consequences of departing from church doctrine and behavioral standards. Because the "distinguishing feature" of fundamentalist religious belief is "the assumption that life has meaning only in relation to certain [symbolic] frameworks," obedience to the community's moral precepts is vital to community self-understanding and maintenance.[107] Exclusion represents not only a removal from the community—which itself has unpleasant consequences, as one is cut off from the emotional and financial support of one's family—but also the tearing away from the framework that holds life together. Everything is in question, and even when ex-members intellectually know that they are safe outside the community, a visceral fear remains that they are hell-bound, as Nate Phelps notes about his own experiences.[108] This is because fundamentalist churches encourage members to believe that they "possess a secret road map with regard to past and future, they know where they are located in space (operational and cosmological), and they hold firm answers on questions related to nature (human and physical)."[109] Through exclusion, ex-members, if they reject the theology of the community, lose this road map, their location, and their answers. If they keep believing the theology, they are forced to see themselves as outsiders, damned.

Mark Phelps, who left the church in 1973, recalled his fear of being an outsider on his first night away from the congregation:

> That night, I stayed at a stranger's house. . . . I specifically remember that night when I lay in that bedroom in that bed and was going to sleep. I thought I was going to wake up in hell the next morning. That's how strongly I believed. . . . My dad had told me since I was 10, "If you ever leave the church, you're going to hell." I so strongly believed that. I did not think I was going to wake up. That's what I thought was going to happen to me.[110]

In this way, exclusion reinforces the boundary between outside and inside. Emmanual Sivan, describing the enclave that religious fundamentalists create, writes, "The enclave must place the oppressive and morally defiled outside society in sharp contrast to the community of virtuous insiders. A sort of 'wall of virtue' is thereby constructed, separating the saved, free, equal (before God or before history), and morally superior enclave from the hither-to tempting central community. Who but the depraved would desire to cross such a boundary and join the defectors and the evil outsiders?"[111] Thus, exclusion is the door through which the "reprobates" within the congregation are rejected, and the experience serves to define, for remaining members, the boundaries between the elect and the nonelect.

This is true even for those who are involuntarily excluded. For example, Karl Hockenbarger, a longtime member, was excluded against his will in

2006 but continues to follow the church's rules as he understands them and listens to sermons via the Internet, saying, "Whether they accept me or not, I still consider them my brethren. . . . I'd go back in a heartbeat."[112] Further, though he disagrees with his own exclusion, he supports the process of exclusion, having apparently voted, in 2004, for the exclusion of his own parents, members since 1960, and he likewise accepted the church's choice to exclude his teenaged son for disrespect shortly after his own exclusion.[113] His adult daughter remains in the church, as does a minor son.

Members are excluded for actions that are seen as signs of a lack of God's grace; thus, disobedience to church rules is equated with nonelection, and although the clearly nonelect can attend services, they cannot be members. Church members can therefore say that people are excluded for inappropriate sexual relations, lying, and fraud and that these sins—and, in some cases, crimes—are signs of spiritual rebellion against God, but the excluded can also claim that their exclusion was due to their noncompliance with church rules.

Those who vote for the exclusion of their cocongregants are likely to point to behavior problems that undermine the credibility of the group's claim to election as cause for excommunication. For example, Shirley Phelps-Roper recalls a driver who passed the picket line and yelled out information about a young, single man in the church who was having an affair with a married woman outside the congregation. When the church confronted the man, he chose to leave the congregation rather than end the affair. The affair was not only a sexual sin but a potential weapon that those critical of the church could use to undermine the church's focus on sexual purity.[114]

The purity of the church is one of exclusion's many goals. For example, Karl Hockenbarger, who had been a member for nearly his entire life when he was excluded in his early fifties, was excluded for a "lack of grace," as evidenced in his occasionally violent behavior on the picket line—behavior he admits and recognizes as wrong but excuses as the response of a man who sees his family and loved ones threatened. He recognizes, however, the value of a nonviolent religious presence. If a member cannot meet that standard, he, like Karl, cannot be "a member in good standing of the church of the Lord Jesus Christ."[115] But theological reasons for nonviolence are not the only concern; the church also needs to maintain its credibility and eliminate its liability. "This generation, this nation," says Shirley Phelps-Roper, "would love nothing more than to say we're standing on these streets brawling. We are not going to stand on these streets and brawl. We do not do that."[116] Given the tension at church pickets, violence is likely, and church members need to avoid violence that could invoke lawsuits or criminal charges.

Exclusion remains a powerful disciplinary mechanism for Westboro Baptist Church to shape the behavior of members within the group, cut off those who dare leave, and define the boundary between elect and damned. Its severity is what makes it so functional as a guard against defection. Says Shirley Phelps-Roper on a possible reunification with her son Josh, a reunification that Josh would welcome and that would allow his mother to see her grandchildren: "Before I could have him over and sit and chat . . . I would first have to line up these young people who are come to years [her younger children] and are interested in serving God and know the standards set by God and kick 'em, each one, in the shin . . . or maybe punch 'em in the stomach, if I was the punching kind of person."[117] Indeed, those other young people are reminded of Josh's absence—and what will happen to them if they dare leave—each time they glance at the refrigerator, where photos of Shirley Phelps-Roper and Brent Roper's children are lined up in order of age, with a gap where Josh's photograph was; or when they see a wall hanging of little wooden figures representing their family, the figure with Josh's name painted on it removed from the scene but the space where it hung unclosed, a visible reminder of his absence.

In Leo Booth's framework for abusive religion, exclusion as practiced by Westboro Baptist Church is a form of abuse. Says Booth, when religious groups "restrict their families' lives, continually trying to force them into a belief system under threat of rejection, punishment, or abandonment, it becomes abuse."[118] Westboro Baptist Church members strongly reject such a characterization, embracing exclusion is a loving way of holding each other accountable to their shared purpose as a church.

WESTBORO BAPTIST CHURCH AS
THE REMNANT CHURCH

Westboro Baptist Church identifies its purpose as the glorification of God, specifically through a ministry of Internet and street preaching. As a congregation, it seeks to create cohesion among members in order to more readily mobilize its ministry, and it builds that cohesion by repeating its doctrines each time the group gathers and through the practice of exclusion. In these ways, the church reinforces the boundary between itself and the outside world. Westboro Baptist Church provides members with a clear picture of who they—and their enemies—are. It depicts the church as an ark, like Noah's, that the members are building despite the derision of critics. That ark will carry the elect church members to salvation while the damned, too late, attempt to swamp the boat as stoic church members watch their demise. However, this does not mean that all members of the church are elect, for Noah took aboard his son Ham, who later proved himself to be wicked.[119] The image of Noah's ark is both metaphoric, symbolizing the spiritual safety of the church in contrast to the tempting but ultimately damned outside world, and literal, as Westboro Baptists, like many fundamentalist Christians, envision an imminent apocalypse that will result in the physical salvation of the elect and eternal bodily suffering of the damned.

The isolationist rhetoric of Westboro Baptist Church as a remnant, an authentic community directly descended from the New Testament period, has a long history among fundamentalists. Westboro Baptists' self-definition as the remnant of the New Testament church provides them with confidence that they are protected from tragedy while alive, that they are the only contemporary group that accurately understands and lives out God's commands, and that they are thus the only people who have a reason to hope that they will enter heaven. Westboro Baptist Church's place in the lineage of true churches that have been divinely preserved proves to them that God will continue to protect them. Warned Fred Phelps in one sermon, speaking to an imaginary audience of detractors, "Don't mess with Westboro Baptist Church! We've got a garrison of angels watching over us."[120] Though, as spiritual beings living in corruptible bodies, their health will decline with age, Westboro Baptists believe that they are physically protected by God because of their obedience. For example, Shirley Phelps-Roper explains that believing women who follow the church's teaching against family planning of any kind find that they have no reproductive difficulties,[121] and church members reiterate that, despite the many physical attacks they have faced on the picket line, no one has been seriously injured because God protects them and will reward them for their faithful risk-taking. Explains Steve Drain, "The fact of the matter is the Lord protects us" while on the picket line.[122] In a document detailing an August 20, 1995, pipe-bomb explosion at the church, the church explains, "In spite of and through it all, these faithful souls hit the streets every day 'going forth and weeping, bearing precious seed,' (Ps. 126:6), knowing the promises of God to sustain us and keep us were good and faithful promises."[123]

According to Westboro Baptist Church theology, because its members alone today obey the church's detailed interpretation of scripture, they alone will enjoy heaven, though the faithful of the past will also be present. "Beloved," Fred Phelps frequently encouraged his congregation, "we are the harvest."[124] If other churches adopted the theology of Westboro Baptist Church—and, consequently, engaged in the same activities—then they, too, would be in obedience to God and would have some hope for the salvation of their members. Westboro Baptists have concluded that they are likely to be elect: "Discerning the signs of the times in the light of rightly dividing and portioning out relevant Scripture passages, all as considered in the context of 20 action-packed years of 50,000+ open air street-preaching services on a daily basis on the mean streets of America—all this has led us to believe that the Gospel torch has been passed to the saints of God of the Westboro Baptist Church."[125] This pronouncement, delivered in a sermon, reminds Westboro Baptists of their remnant status, their role as defenders of a divinely preserved truth, a role manifested by (albeit not deserved because of) their pickets. Although it also recognizes that in previous times, other people and groups had this role, it declares that Westboro Baptists alone have it today. Says Shirley Phelps-Roper, just as biblical heroes and the Reformation leaders and Puritans admired by Westboro Baptists were chosen by God to preach obedience, "this is our day, we are the people on the ground that fulfill our part of the prophecies."[126]

Although current members of Westboro Baptist Church deny the authoritarian qualities that former members attribute to them, the church does conform to Gabriel A. Almond, Emmanual Sivan, and R. Scott Appleby's characterization of fundamentalist religious groups: (1) elect, chosen membership; (2) sharp boundaries; (3) authoritarian organization; and (4) behavioral requirements.[127] Westboro Baptists consider themselves literally chosen by God, who likewise winnows the nonelect from the church over time. Though Westboro Baptists, unlike many fundamentalist believers, do actively engage the outside world, sharp boundaries are a de facto consequence of the demands of church life; for example, even though Westboro Baptist children attend public school and adults work in the secular world, they spend so much time doing the work of the church that little time is left for nonchurch relationships. Indeed, Megan Phelps-Roper, with insight gained from having left the church, says, "The stronger your group identity, the more you are able to suppress empathy for the outgroup."[128]

❖ Westboro Baptist Church has, over time, evolved in its theology and practices to reshape both its internal and external practices. "To this day, we continue to learn," Shirley Phelps-Roper explains, and, indeed, Westboro Baptist Church, founded as a missionary effort of an independent Baptist church, quickly adopted a Calvinism that increased in severity over time.[129] This evolution is a group effort, Shirley Phelps-Roper says. "We are a work in progress—we have come a long way from where we began. We read and figure things about how our conduct should be and we strive to live that way."[130] Now that members' mission is clear to them, they see how the talents of individuals fit into the role God designed for them.

"The stones fit the frame," notes Steve Drain. "Some of our people will spend more time in the workplace because more money is needed either for their family or to take on needs of the church," and, in contrast, "some have jobs that aren't as lucrative but they'll have more free time to do chores and errands or go on picket trips."[131] The organization

of the church—physically around the Westboro neighborhood, spiritually around a commonly held set of unusual tenets, and chronologically
geared toward the second coming of Christ—reinforces the boundary
between elect church members and the damned rest of the world while
simultaneously allowing for quick mobilization. Church members are so
concretely situated within the church—because they live near it; because
their family members belong to it; because it organizes their time and
their friendships and love lives; because, for many of them, their liveli-
hoods are associated with it or with other church members—that they
are quick to respond to the demands that the church makes on them, demands couched in their unusual theology.

# THE THEOLOGY OF
# WESTBORO BAPTIST CHURCH

## 2

Theology plays a significant role in understanding Westboro Baptists' beliefs, actions, and self-understanding; as
for many people of other faiths, the life events of church
members and the church itself are "framed by systemati-
cally explicated doctrine."[1] For some, including Westboro
Baptists, theology addresses the most momentous of life's
questions—"questions of life and death, goodness and
truth, time and eternity"[2]—in the context of a meaningful,
purposive trajectory. To understand how Westboro Baptists
see themselves and their actions in the world, then, researchers must understand their theology, for, in their framework,
"only doctrine is competent to govern experience" for these
believers.[3] Thankfully, this task is made easier by Westboro
Baptist themselves, who are, generally, theologically informed and articulate. "Debates about the implications of
the doctrine of predestination"—the premier theological
point of every sermon and many conversations—"continue
to preoccupy . . . and permeate [the] lives and conflicts" of
Primitive Baptists more broadly, and Westboro Baptists are
no exception.[4] Indeed, all members of the congregation are
expected to be able to "give an account" of their faith, to answer questions clearly and with an overwhelming number
of biblical citations. Among Westboro Baptists, even children are encouraged to speak to the public about their faith.[5]
"Contrary to what one might expect of a denomination that

disapproved of higher learning, . . . Primitive Baptists have had to this day a strong sense of historical continuity and knowledge of their doctrinal past,"[6] notes Bertram Wyatt-Brown. Westboro Baptist Church, though rejected by Primitive Baptists as an authentic church, maintains this tradition.

## HISTORY OF THE PRIMITIVE BAPTIST CHURCH

Westboro Baptist Church self-identifies as a Primitive, or Old School, or "Hardshell," Baptist Church, though no other Primitive Baptist Church recognizes its claim.[7] Like most Baptist churches, its organizational identification is with the Reformation[8] and, more specifically, with the Anabaptist movement that critiqued the Roman Catholic Church for its practice of infant baptism, arguing, instead, that baptism was only for confessing believers, and the Catholic and Reformed churches for their desires to collapse church and state.[9] Importantly, although Primitive Baptists recognize that, organizationally, they developed and were recognized as a historical entity only after a split within American Baptists in 1832, they claim that their church as a spiritual institution begins with Jesus. Most believe in a "literal Baptist 'apostolic succession' from the beginnings of Christianity."[10] Tellingly, nineteenth-century Primitive Baptist historians Cushing Biggs Hassell and Sylvester Hassell titled their history of the Primitive Baptist church *History of the Church of God, from the Creation to A.D. 1885; Including Especially the History of the Kehukee Primitive Baptist.* Published in 1886, the text locates the origin of the church in the first generation of Christians, noting that, within 100 years, before the first creeds were established,[11] Christians had already invented their own "man-made" additions to the simple and pure—that is, primitive—directions for organization and worship that Jesus had delivered during his lifetime. Everything, then, beyond what Jesus explicitly ordered or modeled—that is, beyond adult baptism by immersion; the breaking of unleavened bread and drinking of wine in memory of his death; foot-washing; preaching; and the appointment of male pastors, elders, and deacons—was unscriptural and suggested, arrogantly, that humans could better organize a church than God. For this reason, as articulated at the Suwannee River

Baptist Association meeting in 1838, most Primitive Baptists by the early 1800s "had adopted the idea of church successionism, that there had been a continuous, unbroken succession of Baptist churches, ordinations, and baptisms from the days of John the Baptist to the present."[12] Westboro Baptists, like all Primitive Baptists, see themselves as the authentic church of Christ, as organized by his apostles and settled in the United States by God's providence.

As a small group of believers whose church was not supported by the state as an "established" church and who, in fact, disapproved of such church-state relationships, early American Baptists were political outsiders. Moreover, they were critical of attempts to impose religious law upon state activity, a position that caused them significant problems in Puritan Massachusetts and more broadly after the American Revolution.[13] After the creation of the nation, for example, they did not support temperance or sabbath laws such as those that prohibited mail delivery on Sundays.[14]

Early American Baptists permitted a certain amount of flexibility within their ranks. Some were organized into associations, whereas others shunned large-scale organization. Some were Arminians, believing that God's call for salvation was something that could be freely chosen by an individual, whereas others were strict Calvinists, believing that only those who were predestined by God for salvation would enter heaven and that they could not, in fact, resist God's grace, a position that aligned with Puritanism. Indeed, early Calvinist Baptists and Puritans shared much theology; disagreement arose around issues of establishment and the baptism of infants. Over time these differences led some Puritans to separate from the Puritan church and join Baptist congregations, but the effect of Puritan theology on Calvinist Baptists was—and is—still deeply felt. Westboro Baptists, like the churches that separated from the separatist Puritans, thus "withdrawing from the withdrawers,"[15] continue to draw heavily from Puritan texts in their doctrine and preaching.

By the late 1700s and early 1800s, the diversity of beliefs was creating problems for Baptist congregations, and congregations became divided, at first only in doctrine but soon also physically. The tension had been brewing since the Synod of Dort in 1618–1619, when Reformers met to address Jacobus Arminius's challenge to strict predestination theology.[16]

In response to these divisions, latitudinarians, who "valued moderation over zeal and morality over dogma,"[17] tried to find common ground for the increasingly theologically divided colonial Christians. For Calvinists, however, "unconditional predestination was far from nonessential"[18] and could not be compromised. Since at least the late eighteenth century, the Calvinist message of total depravity, unconditional election, limited atonement, irresistible grace, and the perseverance of saints has come into increasing conflict with the buoyancy and optimism that have come to be so central to American culture. Attacks on the "unrelieved negativism, introspectiveness, and baneful formality"[19] of Calvinism, especially the "hyper-Calvinism"[20] of British theologian John Gill that has so extensively informed Westboro Baptist theology,[21] increased during the Enlightenment as science began to be seen as an explanation for previously inexplicable phenomena, from illnesses to earthquakes. As people gained increased control over the natural world through technologies as varied as vaccines and lightning rods,[22] supernatural explanations began to appear superstitious, and the view of God as intimately involved with all details of human life—a view rejected for some time by the minority Deists[23]—crept into Christianity more broadly. Further, a general optimism about human ability undermined the view of humanity as depraved and God as arbitrarily vindictive. Non-Calvinists began to see in predestination "a peculiar sense of doom . . . derived from antique sources"[24] that were inconsistent with modernity.

In contrast, Arminianism, perhaps best articulated in the theology of Methodist brothers John and Charles Wesley,[25] empowered believers to do something about their own salvation. Although Methodism retained a lively vision of hell, it gave people an option for escaping it: they could opt into the free grace of Christ. Though, like their Calvinistic critics, Methodists believed in total depravity and thus held that people, by their natures, did not deserve such grace and could do nothing to earn it, they also believed that grace was available to every person and that each person could accept or reject it. Thus, for Arminians, salvation was conditional upon the individual's choice to accept it, in contrast to Calvinists, who believed that salvation was available to only a few, could not be rejected by those to whom it was offered, and was not conditional upon the individual but was determined entirely by God. These theological differences caused significant change on the nineteenth-century American religious landscape, particularly the 1827 split between Arminian Baptists, who went on to form the major Baptist conferences, such as the Southern Baptists and American Baptists, and the Calvinist Baptists, including the Primitive Baptists.[26]

In the early 1800s this new brand of evangelical Christianity had widespread popular appeal, especially in the context of a rapidly changing society. James R. Mathis, a historian of Primitive Baptists, writes, "The new evangelical's language of human ability, progress, science and utility was foreign to Primitive Baptists accustomed to a language of human depravity, divine sovereignty, and adherence to primitive Scriptural models."[27] At the same time, it was enticing to new Americans' ideas of individualism and autonomy, whereas Calvinism's "monarchial God" was a reminder of British rule.[28] Not surprisingly, Arminian-inflected forms of Christianity grew while Calvinist forms lost popularity. Primitive Baptists of the early nineteenth century defended their faith as an authentic expression of the simple church of the first century, rejecting the innovations that made Arminian Christianity popular. Their strong disdain for anything "extra-Biblical" and denial of the influence of culture on their own beliefs or practices continues to mark contemporary Primitive Baptists, who use "Primitive" to mean "first, earliest, original, simple, primary."[29] Primitive Baptists link theology and practice and thus reject many changes out of concern that changing practice may result in a change in theology[30]—and they accuse more overtly innovative Baptists of making changes to their theology after the 1827 split. After the division, the General Baptists— missionary in orientation toward the world, Arminian in theology— would go on to divide into various religious groups, including the largest contemporary US Protestant group, the Southern Baptists, and, at times, disagreements about predestination and election would be raised again.[31] For Primitive Baptists, the case was, overall, closed, and strict Calvinism became the rule.[32]

Similarly, today's Primitive Baptists are extraordinarily consistent in their beliefs and do not welcome dissent. Says Timothy P. Weber, "Fundamentalists' unwillingness to expect or provide for sincere differences of opinions among themselves seems to be at least partially responsible for the movement's militancy. As a result, fundamentalists have quarreled with each other nearly as much as they have quarreled with their enemies,"[33] and, even among fundamentalists, Primitive Baptists are known for their divisiveness, resulting in small individual congregations and an overall low membership.[34] In 1832 Joshua Lawrence defended the Primitive Baptist rejection of evangelical innovation at the Black Rock (Maryland) Association's meeting, where Calvinistic Primitive Baptists split from all other Baptist groups:

> Though we may not enjoy the satisfaction of seeing multitudes flocking to Jesus under our ministry, yet instead of going in to Hagar to accomplish the promises of God,[35] or of resorting to any of the contrivances of men to make up the deficiency, we would still be content to preach the word, and would be instant in season and out of season; knowing it has pleased God, not by the wisdom of men, but by the foolishness of preaching to save them that believe. And that his word will not return unto him void, but it shall accomplish that which he please, and prosper in the thing whereunto he sends it. Faith in God, instead of leading us to contrive ways to help him accomplish his purposes, leads us to inquire what he hath required at our hands, and to be satisfied with doing that as we find it pointed out in his word; for we know that his purposes shall stand, and he will do all his pleasure.[36]

Lawrence's words encapsulate Primitive Baptists' defense of the local church against any form of ecumenism; for example, they practice only what they term "close" communion, that is, communion only with other baptized members of "orderly" (that is, acceptable to the individual congregation) Primitive Baptist churches.[37] They do not ecumenically partner with churches from other denominations, even in the pursuit of commonly held political goals. This has protected them from the influences of other, more liberal theologies and has permitted their theology to remain largely unchanged since their organization. As Mathis notes, "The leaders of their churches preach these same doctrines their predecessors preached."[38] Indeed, their isolation, which is understood as "merely a manifestation of the inscrutable will of God,"[39] solidifies their theological views. "If anything, their views of the doctrines of election and predestination grew more stringent over time," notes Mathis, and have "provide[d] a permanent and safe home for a particular strain of Calvinism."[40] Though rejected as a Primitive Baptist church by other Primitive Baptist churches, Westboro Baptist Church views itself as a preserver of this tradition.

## WESTBORO BAPTIST CHURCH THEOLOGY

By identifying themselves with the New Testament church, those receiving the letters of Paul and Timothy and the other New Testament writers, today's Primitive Baptist churches affirm their authenticity as "gospel churches"—and make demands on and promises to their members accordingly. Writes Nancy T. Ammerman, "By placing life into a mythic context, people can claim their special role in creating the future."[41] Westboro Baptists view their own role in God's plan for the world as divinely ordained, and they spend considerable time in church sermons and Bible readings discerning what that role is and how they can best fulfill it. Referring to the promise that "ye might be partakers of the divine nature, having escaped the corruption that is in the world through lust," taken from 2 Peter 1:4, pastor Fred Phelps rallied his congregation with the reminder that Peter's words "are intended directly and expressly for us, at this hour, in this humble church—or they are no longer intended for anybody, except for mildly interested ancient history professors. We are vitally interested."[42] To understand the promises in which they are "vitally interested," Westboro Baptists, like other Primitive Baptists, turn to the theology of John Calvin and those who followed him.

### Calvinism

"Primitive Baptists have been reluctant to frame and adopt new confessions of faith,"[43] notes James Leo Garrett, Jr. Similarly, Primitive Baptist Web Station, a web site that archives essays, sermons, and radio broadcasts about the faith, reminds visitors that "Primitive Baptists claim the scriptures as their sole rule of faith and practice, and therefore, are not bound to creeds of faith," though some churches and associations have summarized key beliefs in articles of faith that "differ in wording but not in substance":[44] wording drawn from the Westminster Confession of Faith (1646), the Midland Confession of Faith (1655), the London Confessions of Faith (1644 and 1689), and the Philadelphia Confession of Faith (1742).[45]

Many Primitive Baptists reject the label "Calvinist" because, as churches that see themselves as influenced only by the first-century church, they cannot accept labels that were invented after that period.[46] For example, on their web sites, many Primitive Baptist churches answer the question "Are Primitive Baptists Calvinists?" with a decisive no, arguing instead that "[Primitive Baptists] and their ancestors have maintained their identity since the days of Jesus Christ and the Apostles. John Calvin was a Protestant Reformer who seceded from the Catholic Church and started Presbyterianism. Baptists derive their existence from Jesus Christ and the Apostles and as such, predate Catholics and have maintained separate existence even through the Dark Ages, hence the name, 'Primitive.'"[47] Further, they follow Anabaptist traditions regarding believers' baptism and church-state separation, rejecting Calvin's defense of infant baptism and intimate church-state ties. Their religion, though, is like Calvin's in that it is "radically theocentric,"[48] which points to "God as the first Cause and last End of all things."[49] Unlike a Christianity that focuses on human behavior or human attainment of salvation, explains historian William A. Scott,

> man fits into Calvin's concept of religion in terms of his relation to God. What is important is that man learn of God's plan for the world and, having learned it, that he fits himself into the divine scheme of things. It is not for man that God exists; rather the contrary is true and the supreme act of religion for man is to accept this and submit himself humbly to the absolute sovereignty of the all-holy God.[50]

Because God is sovereign, in Calvin's scheme, all else exists for God's glory (soli Deo gloria). From these doctrines comes "the inevitable corollary" of predestination, a doctrine nearly synonymous with Calvin's name.[51] For Westboro Baptists today, as for other Primitive Baptists as well as Calvinists within other denominations, predestination—the idea

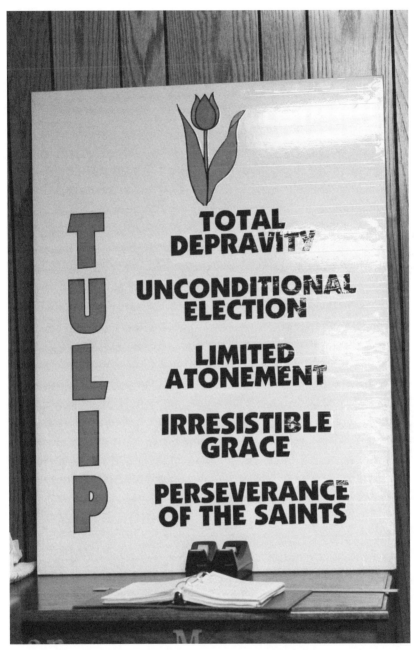

TULIP

TOTAL DEPRAVITY

UNCONDITIONAL ELECTION

LIMITED ATONEMENT

IRRESISTIBLE GRACE

PERSEVERANCE OF THE SAINTS

A sign explaining the five tenets of Calvinist theology stands at the front of the church sanctuary, directly behind the pulpit. (Photograph courtesy of Ailecia Ruscin. All rights reserved.)

that people are chosen for salvation by God at the start of time and independent of their behavior—is grounded in the five principles of Calvinism, as outlined in the following sections. These tenets are so central to
worship at Westboro Baptist Church that they are displayed prominently
in the sanctuary.

## Total Depravity

At the core of Calvinism, as for other Christian theologies, is the doctrine
of original sin, the claim that humans "inherit" the sinful nature of Adam.
Thus, before individuals ever transgress the moral codes espoused by
their faith, thus committing a sin, they are distanced from God because
of their very natures, which are sinful. Among Calvinists, this belief pre-
cludes any individual ability to seek God; that is, human nature is totally
depraved, with no ability to turn toward the holy. Jonathan Edwards notes,
"We are not only without any true excellency, but are full of, and wholly
defiled with, that which is infinitely odious. All our good is more apparently from God, because we are first naked and wholly without any good,
and afterwards enriched with all good."[52] The focus on the depravity of
humanity, though, does not necessarily create hopelessness or paralyz-
ing feelings of worthlessness. Instead, it is liberating, for it places all responsibility on the divine.[53] What seems like a brutal system is, indeed, a
comfort. "Only within contexts where this notion of original sin is taken
for granted does predestination become for its most ardent believers a
doctrine of mercy,"[54] notes Peter J. Thuesen. Indeed, the gap between absolutely depraved humanity and an absolutely holy God is a measure of
God's graciousness in saving anyone.[55]

## Limited Atonement

One of the most controversial tenets of Calvinism is its insistence that
Christ's death, understood in many forms of Christianity to be a substitute
for the blood sacrifice required for depraved humanity to be reconciled to
a holy and unapproachable God, was intended only for those uncondi-
tionally elected by God; its power does not extend to all those who live
according to Christian morality, all those who self-identify as Christians
because of their culture, all those who engage in sacraments, or all those

who claim to believe. When John 3:16, a favorite verse of evangelicals, says that "For God so loved the world that he gave his only begotten son," it means, for Calvinists, that God so loved his world of his elect, not the universe of humanity.[56] This elect has gathered in the true church of every age, and so, when the elect ascend to heaven, the group will include those from the time of Adam and Eve onward.

For many Calvinists, the doctrine of limited atonement does not undermine the duty to preach the gospel message to all people, even if it means that many nonelect will hear it. Primitive Baptists, however, understand the "free offer" of the gospel, the claim that "the benefits of the atonement should be offered indiscriminately to all hearers[,] as a denial of the doctrine of particular redemption, that Jesus Christ died for the elect only";[57] as a consequence, they do not support missionary work or efforts to seek converts. This does not prohibit them from speaking freely and publicly about their faith, however; instead, it means that, when they do so, they do not proselytize.[58]

The anxiety of Puritanism, according to Max Weber, was the consequence of the adherent's insecurity about his election. Even though to search oneself for signs of election is a sign of election, to excessively question God's logic in limited atonement is, itself, a blasphemous act. Writes Calvin:

> For [God's] will is and rightly ought to be the cause of all things that are. For if it has any cause, something must precede it, to which it is, as it were, bound. This is unlawful to imagine. For God's will is so much the highest rule of righteousness that whatever he wills, by the very fact that he wills it, must be considered righteous. When, therefore, one asks why God has done so, we must reply: because he has willed it. But if you proceed further to ask why he so willed, you are seeking something greater and higher than God's will, which cannot be found.[59]

Rather than being an unfair system, limited atonement is understood by Primitive Baptists as a gracious act, for God, in his justice, owes depraved humanity nothing. That he extends himself to anyone is cause for hope. Thus, Westboro Baptists can believe that they have a "hope" for salvation, and, if election is suspected, joy: "We are his jewel, the apple of his eye."[60] God's majesty is increased in the atoning death of Jesus Christ for the elect and is not diminished in his exclusion of other equally undeserving sinners from that gift. [61] Indeed, his majesty is just as exalted when he casts the reprobate into hell as when he saves sinners. Moreover, the limited extension of atonement makes the saints happy, not mournful, even when those cast into hell are those whom, on earth, they loved. They cannot feel pity for a sinner who receives his just punishment, only relieved that they escaped their own.

Westboro Baptists today feel the same about those they believe are among the nonelect, even those friends and family members who have left Westboro Baptist.[62] "'What can we do?' ask people," Fred Phelps said from the pulpit, imitating a bystander at one of the church's pickets. He happily replied to his imaginary bystander: "'Nothing. God is through with you. I'm through with you. Westboro Baptist Church is through with you.'"[63] For the helpless sinner, only the atonement of Jesus Christ will secure salvation, but, for those for whom it was not extended, nothing can be done to achieve it—and that delights the elect, "not as evils and miseries simply considered, nor from a private affection; but as the glory of divine justice is displayed therein."[64] Indeed, Fred Phelps rather gleefully preached the destruction of the nonelect, echoing Edwards's delight: "We're going to pray for you—that you'll go to hell, that you'll be smitten."[65] Indeed, to offer any other prayer for those whom God destined for hell would be to suggest that God is changeable and ought to change his plans according to human desire and would thus be blasphemous.[66]

### Unconditional Election

The doctrine of total depravity says that no one deserves salvation or can do anything to initiate it, but the doctrine of limited atonement says that some will be saved. The doctrine of unconditional election explains how: without consideration of human merit, for reasons known only to God. God's will thus seems arbitrary to humans,[67] who cannot be assured that God has chosen them and can do nothing to persuade God to choose them. Unlike Arminians, who argue that God foresees human willingness to believe, Calvinists do not believe that God considers future behaviors or beliefs in his selection of his elect; indeed, in the supralapsarian (also called antelapsarian) vision of unconditional election, God chooses the elect prior to the creation of humanity (and thus prior, or supra or ante, to the fall, the "lapse," of Adam and Eve), which means that sin had not yet even entered the world.[68] Writes Jonathan Edwards, "There is nothing that keeps wicked men"—which, by their nature, includes all men and women—"at any one moment out of hell, but the mere pleasure of God."[69] Church membership, moral living, one's personal experience of spirituality—these are irrelevant in God's decision to elect or damn a person, though they may be signs of one's election or damnation.

Because humans are entirely without merit, because their "righteousness is as filthy rags,"[70] they cannot engage in their own salvation. This is unlike other forms of Christianity, which, to varying degrees, suggest that humans, as beings created in the likeness of God, can participate in their own redemption, though the mechanisms for that participation vary across denominations. Although many branches of Protestantism have criticized Catholicism for its "salvation by works"—that is, the idea that particular behaviors, ranging from taking communion to confessing sins to a priest to reciting prayers, contribute to one's salvation—strict Calvinists decry even other Protestants for suggesting that any human effort, including "accepting Jesus into your heart" or "making a choice for Jesus" or "praying a sinner's prayer" is not only ineffective in generating salvation, it is blasphemous, for it suggests that salvation can be affected by human will. Or, to quote Shirley Phelps-Roper, "Rebels say, I accepted Jesus as my own personal savior, [even though] Jesus said—YOU DID NOT CHOOSE me, but I choose you!"[71] People who make this claim are not merely mistaken but are rebellious, claiming an authority and agency in salvation that totally depraved humans do not have and cannot take from God; thus, they are either denying the depravity of humanity or attempting to usurp God's sovereignty.

Among Calvinists, there is debate regarding "double predestination" or "double election"[72]—whether God *chooses* to damn people just as he chooses to save people or whether God chooses his elect and simply *allows* the nonelect to fall into hell; whether, to say it differently, God damns people or allows them to damn themselves. For Westboro Baptists, as for other "high" (or "hyper") Calvinists (those who accept a more exclusive interpretation of Calvin's views), God does, indeed, actively both damn and elect. Those hesitant to attribute an apparent mean-spiritedness to God skirt the issue by explaining that, due to their depraved nature, all people deserve damnation, so in not electing them, God does not harm them but merely does not extend an undeserved grace to them. This does not undermine the image of God as loving and gracious any more than the failure of a governor to pardon *all* death-row inmates undermines the graciousness he demonstrates by pardoning *some* of them.[73] To do so does not impute any wrong to God, for "when a man is made holy, it is from mere and arbitrary grace; God may forever deny holiness to the fallen creature if he pleases, without any disparagement to any of his perfections."[74] Westboro Baptist Church illustrates this concept in a seven-second video archived through the social-media platform Vine. In the first six seconds of the video, a teenaged boy makes a detailed figure out of clay as the lyrics "The perfect will of God Almighty cannot be frustrated" are sung. In the last second of the video, the boy smilingly smashes the clay figure. The accompanying message is "Each human is like clay in God's hand. And, yes, He makes some just to destroy. #Romans9."[75] As with the doctrine of total depravity, unconditional election is, for Calvinists, not an optional position; instead, it is central to their view of humanity at the mercy of an all-powerful and inscrutable God.

The status of one's eternity—whether a person is elect or reprobate—was a central concern for Puritans and resulted, for some, in a near-constant cycle of self-examination. As Peter K. Thuesen chronicles, the search for evidence of election in one's life was a brutal one for many Puritans, and many sermons were devoted to managing the balance between the congregants' sense of worthlessness and hope that God, in his holiness and mercy, would elect the professed believer. At the same time, many Puritans seemed relatively unbothered by the question,[76] and even Increase Mather implied that those within the church and their own children were likely among the elect.[77] Whether, as Max Weber famously argued, the Puritan's compulsion to prove to himself that he was among the elect fueled early capitalism in the colonies,[78] it certainly drove many Puritans and latter-day Primitive Baptists to serious introspection.[79] That anxiety continues to haunt contemporary hyper-Calvinists. Former Westboro Baptist Church member Zach Phelps-Roper, who left the church in 2014 at the age of twenty-three, articulates the tension of this theology:

> I felt great joy at the thought that I would be counted so dear to a God that I believed he would save me from what I thought were my sins simply because of his merciful kindness. However, on the flip side, when I would feel like my salvation was not a sure thing because I saw myself backsliding back into sin, all of the joy I had felt turned into pure terror. Nothing could comfort me, and I would have trouble falling asleep at night, or thinking straight, because I felt like I was put in the crosshairs of a raging, omnipotent, omniscient, and horrifying God.[80]

Zach Phelps-Roper's insights into his own turmoil are similar to other examples of Puritan spiritual writing and conversion narratives among Primitive Baptists, which suggest that "the elect individual's soul is . . . a battlefield between God and Satan."[81] Given that election occurred at the start of time, there is no chance that Satan will win, but the individual, unsure of his condition, may be tormented with worry that he is damned. Because the doctrine of total depravity declares that sinners can do nothing of their own volition to move toward God, strict Calvinists might lack optimism about their election, but they have more hope, they argue, than if their salvation depended upon their own depraved natures. Moreover, the elect may seek signs of their election, finding, first, that in their concern for their election is their hope of their election. Within early Calvinist churches, for example, "ordinarily a preacher urged repentance on those hearing the gospel for the first time, a strategy that seemed to suggest that repentance . . . was an initial rather than a final phase of sanctification. But actually, anguish and remorse, ingredients for what Elizabethan pietists termed 'godly sorrows,' were the first signs of election and sanctification."[82] In other words, conviction of one's depraved nature was a sign of one's election, not a step toward it, since it had been determined since the start of time. Since, still, despite one's deep desire for it and one's efforts to obey God, one is never worthy of salvation, believers can never state firmly that they are elect; instead, they refer to themselves as having "a hope" for their election.

When accused of believing that they are the only people who have hope of going to heaven, Westboro Baptists remind their accusers that they are part of an "invisible church" as well as the visible church of Westboro Baptist. That is, if they are elected, they are in a long line of other heaven-bound people. Moreover, while they cannot be certain of their own election, which would always be undeserved, they can be sure of who is not among the elect; thus, they can say with surety who is in or going to hell.[83] Though election does not depend upon moral living, immoral living, as defined by the church, is a sign that one is not elect. Thus, it can respond to charges of hypocrisy by saying that its members do not believe that they are "better" than others or "without sin"—only that, in recognizing and repenting of their depravity, they see signs of God's work in their lives. Such signs are absent, though, in the lives of people who do not recognize and repent of their depravity.[84]

*Irresistible Grace*

Just as unconditional election declares that God's elect can do nothing to persuade God to choose them, irresistible grace declares that there is nothing that God's elect can do to reject their election. When called by God, people cannot refuse that calling. "Nothing is done or undone without God's order or his permission, which are the same thing,"[85] Fred Phelps reminded his congregation one Sunday in a sermon. Not only does God foreordain every action on earth in Westboro Baptist Church's absolute predestination theology, but he also gives people no option except to obey his will. For this reason, an evangelical Christian's claim that he "asked Jesus into his heart" is subject to Westboro Baptists' scorn. "It's all right with me if you want to think you made up your mind, but I know the Lord Your God is a great mind-maker-upper!"[86] Fred Phelps chortled one day from the pulpit, reinforcing, as in every sermon, the absolute sovereignty of God, not only in human and natural events but in human thoughts.

Instead of "asking Jesus into their hearts" as the first step toward their salvation, Westboro Baptists, in line with their Puritan forerunners, experience "effectual calling"—"a work of God's Holy Spirit, whereby convincing us of our sin and misery, and enlightening our minds in the knowledge of Christ, and renewing our wills . . . he doth persuade and enable us to embrace Jesus Christ, freely offered to us in the Gospel," a calling that is effectual "because it always gains the Sinner to accept of, and close in with it."[87] Just as unconditional election removes from humans the burden of salvation, irresistible grace ensures that, if that election is there, it will be received by them. Together, these two doctrines provide a defense against the apparent hopelessness of total depravity and limited atonement.

### Perseverance of the Saints

Theologies that suggest that human beings are heaven-bound because of their partaking of sacraments, their moral living, or their willingness to "accept Jesus into their hearts" always keep their believers under a grim threat, according to Calvinism: if salvation depends upon the individual, then it can be lost when the individual fails to partake of the sacraments, fails at moral living, or loses faith. For Calvinists, the belief that God alone controls salvation brings comfort in the corollary that God will not withdraw salvation. God chooses whom he chooses, and he does not change his mind. "Will the Lord Repent of His Choice? Never; never. 'Tis unalterable," encouraged Cotton Mather.[88]

God's unchanging nature does not mean, however, that one who is elect is permitted to continue a life of sin. When he does sin, God will rebuke and correct him, often through the church: "It may be that we are sinful; but God did not love us for our goodness, neither will he cast us off for our wickedness. Yet this is no encouragement to licentiousness, for God knows how to put us to anguishes and straits and crosses, and yet to reserve everlasting life for us."[89] Thus, the elect will still suffer the natural, earthly consequences of sin in this lifetime and can still be punished by God in this lifetime. However, as the elect continue, like Christian in John Bunyan's *Pilgrim's Progress*, they reject sin. Indeed, by their changed nature, the elect *cannot* continue a life of sin. The doctrine of saintly perseverance is not equivalent, then, to the phrase "once saved, always saved," which might suggest that salvation cannot be lost regardless of the behavior of the individual. Instead, one who is elect will necessarily be a changed person, as evidenced in his or her actions.[90] If upright living does not result, then the sense of election is false,[91] for "if he hath appointed thee to life, it is certain he also has ordained thee to fruits, and chosen thee to be holy."[92] Thus, the church can exclude a member who continues to sin on the grounds that, despite his baptism, membership, and confidence in his election, he is a reprobate. This outcome is terrifying for the excluded member—akin to the terror of the virgins who, because they failed to secure the oil for their lamps before the bridegroom's arrival, were locked out in darkness and to whom Jesus said, "Verily I say unto you, I know you not."[93] For those excluded, the shame of being forced out of the community may be less psychologically difficult to bear than the assurance that they are among the reprobates. For example, Karl Hockenbarger, who was excommunicated from Westboro Baptist Church in June 2005 for "lack of grace," said of his experience, "I was terrified. . . . My expectation was not to live long enough to get home. And this is not an indication of suicidal thoughts or desires, but I'd rather be dead than in this situation."[94] It would be cold comfort for Karl Hockenbarger to remember that, as long as he is alive, he may be hell-bound but is not yet in hell. According to the theology that he has adhered to since his baptism at age nine, as a reprobate, that is his eternal home.

In contrast to Karl Hockenbarger, for those who remain secure in their election, the doctrine of the perseverance of the saints is a beautiful if undeserved gift. Writes Scott,

> His conviction of salvation is rooted in the divine will and that is unchangeable. Even though life in its passage may bring frequent doubt, sin, failure, or temptation, these can always be countered and overcome by the recollection of the divine changelessness, God's fidelity to his decree of election. He does not choose on the basis of what a man does; so too He will not change His choice because of what a man does. One may rest secure in the divine fidelity to His own will.[95]

In the end, then, Westboro Baptists will reach heaven not because of their own merit but because of the inscrutable, irresistible, and unchangeable will of God.

❖ The five points of Calvin's belief coalesce into the doctrine of predestination, which is viewed, among those Christians who remain familiar with it, as "either . . . the rock of Christian certainty, without which no true hope is possible, or . . . the most dangerous of doctrines, one that risks negating the 'come unto me' of Jesus' gospel promise."[96] The unpopularity of predestination, as measured in the outrage of Westboro Baptist Church counterprotesters who argue both that church members' pickets are uncivil and that the theology that drives church members to declare who is in heaven and hell is blasphemous, prompts Westboro Baptists to defend it in sermon after sermon. Among all Primitive Baptists, "these theological tenets are starkly explicit"[97] in preaching, and they are explained as matters of fact, not debate, that are derived from infallible readings of the Bible. "Fundamentalist discourse," generally, argues Kathleen C. Boone, "is in fact marked by an unrelenting rationalism."[98] Among Primitive Baptists, "deep mysteries are ordered by a severe theological rationalism,"[99] and even the most sensitive matters are organized by the "ruthless logic of doctrine."[100] In the end, admits Bertram Wyatt-Brown, "it might be said that the Primitive Baptists placed justice before love in their understandings of Christianity."[101] In assessing God's mercy and his justice, they do not hesitate to remind listeners that God's mercy can only be desired, never deserved. The Primitive Baptist theological argument, like the Westboro Baptist Church argument more specifically, has not yielded great returns.

The gap—both in church membership size and in theology—between strict Calvinists and non- or quasi-Calvinists grew over the first decades of the nineteenth century, with a resulting decline in Primitive Baptist congregations since then. However, their small size does not undermine belief among Primitive Baptists, nor among Westboro Baptists in particular. Indeed, it is viewed as a sign of their correctness, "for many are called, but few are chosen" (Matthew 22:14). Though they cannot be sure that God has chosen them, they have a hope that he has, and they are confident that, whether or not God has selected all the individuals in the congregation for eternal salvation, they all, like all humans, elect and reprobate, have a duty to live obediently.

In their adherence to the hyper-Calvinism of John Gill; their denominational independence; their church organization and discipline; their focus on moral living as a sign of election; and many, though not all, of their practices regarding worship, Westboro Baptists are Primitive Baptists, drawn from the separatist, antiestablishment branch of Puritans. In this way, they are not so much an anomaly on the American religious landscape as an anachronism—or, as Westboro Baptists say, "Although these doctrines are almost universally hated today, they were once loved and believed."[102] They still believe them.

## WESTBORO BAPTIST CHURCH AS AN AMERICAN RELIGIOUS ANACHRONISM

Although other religious groups are quick to denounce Westboro Baptist Church as not truly Christian and the group is popularly labeled a "cult," with frequent comparisons to groups such as the KKK[103] and the Branch Davidians of Waco, Texas,[104] Westboro Baptist Church sees itself, as do many other Christian groups, as constituting the true apostolic church. The claim to be in a line of direct descent from Jesus Christ is a bold one, but Westboro Baptist Church's claim that it teaches a theology that was once taught by major American religious figures is valid.

Pictures of religious figures such as Baptist hymnist Isaac Watts appear near the pulpit at Westboro Baptist Church, though any images of God, including images of Jesus, are forbidden in accordance with the commandment against creating images of God. Every sermon includes references to the lives of heroes in the faith, mostly seventeenth- and eighteenth-century English separatists and early Baptists, who are depicted as faithful despite persecution. For example, in his June 27, 2010, sermon, pastor Fred Phelps told the story of William Shirreff (1762–1832), a Presbyterian minister who refused to perform infant baptisms. Shirreff became part of "a handful of small and poor Baptist churches and poorer still Baptist pastors [who] could not be bought off." Reading from the memoirs of such leaders, Phelps reminded his congregants that they are part of a long and long-suffering religious line and suggested that, if the Primitive Baptist forerunners were still alive, they would support Westboro Baptist Church's activities.

Sermons also include direct quotations from the theological writings of Puritans and other early Calvinists as well as lyrics from hymns and poems—again, almost exclusively from the late 1600s to the early 1800s, when Protestant predestination theology was still popular. Jonathan Edwards and earlier Puritan leaders are quoted, their books—some of which sit in a row on the communion table beneath the pulpit—recommended, and their spirits invoked.[105] During Bible readings—churchwide study sessions in which all ages gather in concentric circles and take turns reading from the Bible, listening to commentary, and discussing what they are learning—commentary is drawn from Bible scholars from the same period, just as it is when commentary is incorporated into the sermons.

Through these means, Westboro Baptist Church not only keeps alive once widely read but now neglected authors; it also maintains in congregants a sense of belonging to a select, well-respected American tradition, for although Puritanism is, generally, no longer preached, its power in America's imaginative history is strong. By stressing its ties to an antiestablishment branch of Puritanism, Westboro Baptist Church also reminds itself that it is in tension with the state and the culture, that it is a separatist group like the Puritans, who rejected state funds.

Puritan theology was falling out of favor by the early 1800s, and, consequently, predestination theology is difficult for many modern audiences to grasp, appreciate, or believe. This difficulty, though, does not bother Westboro Baptist Church, which interprets the disdain that most Americans feel for predestination theology—especially the absolute and double predestination theology of Westboro Baptist Church—as evidence of the election of church members and the nonelection of outsiders. God has not permitted "heretic Arminians" to understand the beauty of predestination theology or its application to sexuality.

## WESTBORO BAPTIST CHURCH'S THEOLOGY
## OF SEXUALITY

Same-sex attraction and sexual contact and toleration and acceptance of gay people are key issues for all Religious Right groups. However, Westboro Baptist Church's views on homosexuality are markedly different from the views of many other groups, which claim to judge feminism, homosexuality, abortion, and "deviant" heterosexual sex (including nonmarital and extramarital relationships and anal and oral intercourse) to be similar sins, even though antigay rhetoric is usually more virulent than rhetoric attacking feminism and, for example, divorce. Moreover, Westboro Baptist Church's theology bans only homosexual sex and nonmarital heterosexual sex; the church does not dictate the details of married heterosexual sex, as do many other conservative religious groups.[106] According to Sam Phelps-Roper, all sexual acts that occur within the context of marriage are acceptable. "Once you're married," Shirley Phelps-Roper's oldest child notes with merriment, "you can swing from the lights!"[107]

Sexual intercourse, according to the church, is reserved for men and women in their first marriages—an ideal held by all major denominations. Romantic physical contact of any sort prior to marriage is discouraged. For example, when Shirley Phelps-Roper hinted that her son Sam might have kissed his wife before they married, Sam clearly and discreetly let his mother know that the two had never touched, which relieved her. Asks Shirley Phelps-Roper, "What possible value is there to such conduct except to get you into trouble—taking fire into your bosom and getting into some kind of fornication or otherwise?"[108] Within marriage, though, sexuality is private, respected, and enjoyed.

Remarriage after divorce is equated with adultery. Church belief in this principle is so strong that it was the topic of the marriage sermon at the wedding of Brent Roper and Shirley Phelps-Roper, when Fred Phelps reminded the couple that marriage "is the only legitimate place for sex. That bed is undefiled. Marriage is honourable in all, and the marriage bed undefiled. All the others are whoremongers and adulterers that God will judge."[109] Moreover, the law firm of Phelps-Chartered, staffed only by members of the church, will not serve as counsel in divorce proceedings in their first marriages, though the firm will do so for those who have previously been divorced, interpreting their second marriages as invalid in God's eyes anyway.[110] Sexual intercourse prior to marriage is a form of fornication, just as sex with someone other than one's spouse during marriage is adultery.[111] Sexual fidelity in marriage is the overarching mandate. "Remember," noted Fred Phelps at the start of the church's antigay picketing, "I've preached more and harder against adulterers than I have fags."[112]

Above, Jael Phelps (now Holroyd) pickets in Topeka, calling attention to the sin of divorce. (Photograph courtesy of Ailecia Ruscin. All rights reserved.)

This outline of ideal sexual expression is shared among many religious denominations in the United States, including Catholics, conservative Protestants, and mainline Protestants. Indeed, Westboro Baptist Church makes no prohibitions against particular sex acts between opposite-sex married couples who have not been divorced and remarried, as do many denominations. What makes Westboro Baptists different from other religious groups is that the sexual sins of members are a reason for church discipline. Only rarely do other denominations formally discipline members for sexual transgressions through means such as excommunication,[113] despite the higher-than-typical rates of some of those sins, such as divorce, among some conservative Christians.[114] Of course, they may shame people, especially women who have undergone abortions[115] or women who have had children while unmarried,[116] and pastors may be (but certainly are not always) disciplined for sexual infractions.[117] However, tolerance for heterosexual sin seems to be more readily available than it is for the sexual sin of gay people. For example. nearly one-third of evangelical pastors said they would conduct a marriage ceremony for a straight person divorced "for any reason," according to a 2011 poll by LifeWay, the Southern Baptist Convention (SBC) research and publishing resource.[118] This seems like hypocrisy to some gay-affirming Christians, such as pastor Danny Cortez of New Heart Community Church, which was dismissed in 2015 from the Southern Baptist Convention for affirming same-sex relationships. Cortez argued that the SBC had long allowed pastors to follow their consciences regarding their affirmation of marriages of divorced individuals, despite the fact that this directly contradicts the Baptist Faith and Message's prohibition of sanctioning adultery, and that this model should be used during pastoral care of gay people, too.[119] This is in direct conflict with the position of Southern Baptist Ethics and Religious Liberty Commission President Russell Moore, who has repeatedly said that the convention's failure to stem the tide of divorce (and remarriage) among its members is not an opening for same-sex marriage. According to Moore, a straight marriage may be entered into sinfully, but repentance for the sin of remarriage allows congregants to be members in good standing and sanctifies their marriage, whereas a same-sex marriage is always a sin.[120] This is the same logic that Kim

Davis, county clerk of Rowan County, Kentucky, invoked in her refusal to issue marriage licenses to same-sex couples after the US Supreme Court decision in *Obergefull v. Hodges* that the right to marriage is guaranteed to same-sex couples by the Fourteenth Amendment to the US Constitution. Davis's own marital history—a divorce from her first husband and marriage to her second husband while pregnant with twins fathered by her third husband, whom she later divorced before marrying her fourth husband—came under scrutiny by critics who wondered how Davis could credibly claim to object to same-sex marriage on religious grounds. Davis, who attends an Apostolic church known for its conservative views on gender and sexuality, sees God as forgiving her divorces and her remarriages and blessing her current marriage since, as Moore noted, opposite-sex marriage of religious believers can be redeemed from its sinful origins, whereas same-sex marriages are always inherently sinful because they do not fit the model of God's plan for human sexuality.[121]

At Westboro Baptist, however, heterosexual sexual transgressions are reason for church members to address a congregant individually and, if necessary, exclude him or her from the church. Westboro Baptist Church is concerned not only with the sexual transgressions of its own members but also with what it sees as a cultural tolerance, acceptance, and celebration of sexual sin, especially homosexuality. Same-sex sexual contact is a sin, according to the church, drawing from the same religious scriptures that are understood to prohibit same-sex acts in other denominations, particularly Leviticus 12:30 ("If a man also lie with mankind, as he lieth with a woman, both of them have committed an abomination; they shall surely be put to death; their blood shall be upon them") and Romans 1:26–27 ("For this cause God gave them up unto vile affections: for even their women did change the natural use into that which is against nature: And likewise also the men, leaving the natural use of the woman, burned in their lust one toward another; men with men working that which is unseemly, and receiving in themselves that recompense of their error which was meet"). Given its opposition to theological schooling and rejection of Higher Criticism, which places the Bible in its original context, Westboro Baptist Church will not consider any translations of the Bible except the King James version or consider alternative understandings of these texts.[122] Such language, posits Robert N. Minor, is another form of rebuffing doubts or even intellectual engagement among members: "The archaic language of the King James Bible with its 'thou' and 'ye' contributes to the thought-numbing nature of the experience. It gives the language an authority that the current everyday speech of plain human beings just doesn't have."[123] Shirley Phelps-Roper agrees with part of Minor's judgment: the King James version's English *does* take the language out of the ordinary, allowing it to be one form of expressing respect for God. However, Minor's argument that the language is "mind-numbing" dismisses the aesthetic pleasure that some listeners—and speakers—derive from the experience. Further, Westboro Baptist Church members are quite comfortable with the language, with even the children demonstrating an understanding of its grammar and rhetoric.[124] Moreover, as with fears that changes in practice will lead to errors in theology, Westboro Baptist Church has concerns that a change in language may soften its theology, especially regarding "God's righteous hatred which is his determination to send the unrepentant to hell" and in regard to God's standards for human sexuality.[125] This hatred, which is intrinsic to God and not conditioned on human behavior, allows for a God who can cast anyone into hell at any time and smite any person—no matter whether or not their behavior is moral—with an "earth judgment." In this model, God does not need to be angry in order to do malignant things to people, even as he is "angry with the wicked every day," as the frequently invoked Psalm 7:11 notes.

Though Westboro Baptist Church shares with other denominations a belief that homosexuality is a sin, the church's understanding of the nature of sin is quite different from what many others espouse. In contemporary America, predestination theology, with its denial of free will, is unfamiliar to many people. Today, even those who do not attend religious services hear predominantly Arminian theology mixed with what Peter J. Thuesen calls "providence-without-predestination,"[126] a general sense of having a "purpose driven life," to quote the religious best seller,[127] in which God assigns the purpose but people do the driving. The conservative Protestantism preached today on radio airwaves and television asks sinners to repent of their own volition, whereas Westboro Baptist Church theology denies that any sinner—which is to say, anyone—can repent without previously being regenerated, that is, having God elect this person and create an internal change in him or her. Other religious groups say that God loves gay people but hates homosexuality (the "love the sinner, hate the sin" paradox). Russell Moore, for example, explained the difference between Westboro Baptist Church and "real" Baptists this way: "God does not hate anybody and God would never countenance the use of a demeaning and derogatory word like 'fag' to describe a human being for whom His Son died. God loathes and detests homosexuality, but God loves the homosexual."[128] This theological framework gives permission and incentive to preach to gay people, pray for their conversion, and even work with them in therapeutic settings to help "strugglers" (those fighting against unwanted same-sex attraction) reorient their desires to members of the opposite sex.[129] They believe that those who do not repent of their same-sex intercourse will be damned to hell in the afterlife; that is, God, who loves them, is forced to send them to hell because they have not repented of their sins.

In contrast, Westboro Baptist Church does not preach that God hates people because they are gay but rather, in a move that confounds Arminian believers, that they are gay *because* God hates them. That is, God chose at the beginning of time who was among elect and who was not in total disregard for the worth or obedience of the individual. Hugh Binning contrasts the Arminian and Calvinist theses on the matter: "Hath he chosen us because he did foreknow that we would be holy, and without blame, as men think? Or hath he not rather chosen us to be holy and without blame? He cannot behold any good or evil in the creatures, till his will pass a sentence upon it; for from whence should it come?"[130] Because of total depravity, humans cannot be good enough to be chosen for salvation; only by being chosen for salvation can they be holy.

In choosing his elect, God also chooses the reprobates—those who will be eternally damned and will thus likely live unholy lives on earth. This double predestination, "the grand doctrine that razes free will to the ground,"[131] means that God abandons some people before they are even born, and, in their abandonment, some people pursue homosexuality. Again, Westboro Baptist Church cites Romans 1:25, which describes people "who changed the truth of God into a lie, and worshipped and served the creature more than the Creator, who is blessed for ever." Verse 26 of the King James translation continues: "For this cause God gave them up unto vile affections: for even their women did change the natural use into that which is against nature."

In this text, God's "giving up" of individuals occurred prior to, not after, their "unnatural" acts of homosexuality. Homosexuality becomes evidence, not the cause, of God's damnation; God gives gay people up to be gay, not because they are gay. Indeed, those who engage in same-sex activity do not even recognize it as sin, for "the wicked have no practical, prevalent knowledge of the malignity of sin, because they have no such knowledge of God."[132] Furthermore, there is nothing any gay person can do about it, for "the sinner doesn't see [God's word] and doesn't hear it, and he never will."[133]

However, even within Westboro Baptist Church's theology of sexuality, those who engage in same-sex intercourse can repent—or, rather, they will repent, if they are drawn through God's irresistible grace to do so. This is in accordance, not in conflict, with the doctrine of unconditional election "because if Christ died for them, the Holy Spirit will surely call them, God will in fact draw them, they will leave off that uncleanness, vile affections, and reprobate mind, and the inevitable result will be that they will inherit heaven and not hell."[134] As with all sinners, according to Westboro Baptist Church logic, the only hope for gay people is in their election. Their nonelection causes them to pursue same-sex sexuality, and God's election will invariably lead them away from it.

Given Westboro Baptist Church's belief that gay people were hell-bound before they engaged in same-sex intercourse, the impetus for its activism is not clear to those who understand Christianity only in terms of Arminian theology. Christians who believe that God judges people based upon their actions, rather than the Westboro Baptist belief that people's actions reflect God's prejudgment of them, try to reorient gay people in order to align them with God's plan for them: heterosexuality or, if that fails, celibacy.[135] Westboro Baptists argue that gay people are already engaging in God's plan for them—a plan for their eternal damnation. According to this theology, any activism seems unwarranted, and, indeed, church members have no goal of gaining new converts or stopping people from engaging in same-sex acts. In response to the question "Have any homosexuals repented as a result of your picketing?," the church provides a decisive answer: "Yes, but this doesn't matter. Christianity is not a game, consisting of who can get the most people to repent. Our job is simply to preach, and by the foolishness of our preaching, we hope that people will be saved. However, Jesus is the Savior, not us. No man can come unto Him unless the Father in heaven draws him, and He will call His sheep."[136]

This answer is precisely in line with the "no free offers" hyper-Calvinism of Westboro Baptist Church hero John Gill and much of Primitive Baptist belief today. As double predestinarians, Westboro Baptists go further than refusing to offer the gospel message to the nonelect, recognizing, as Steve Drain noted, that "if the Lord has it that these people won't believe in him, there's nothing I can do for them";[137] they refuse to pray for the nonelect, including gay people, because "you simply cannot read the accounts given throughout the scriptures without recognizing that those who are clearly condemned of God are beyond any hope of intervention by prayer."[138] To pray for them would not only waste church members' time, it would also suggest that God's design to send those people to hell was erroneous and thus would be an affront to God's sovereignty. Thus, concludes the church, "we would not dare to do so." Especially for those who are gay, the church asks, "What arrogance would we display to pretend we could pray them back into the good grace of Him who has given them up?"[139]

Despite the belief that their preaching is not aimed at converting people to their church or changing people's sexual orientation, members still picket seven days a week. This is one of the central puzzles of Westboro Baptist Church, setting the church apart from both evangelical (that is, Arminian) conservative Christians who also oppose gay rights as well as other predestinarian groups who do not engage in social activism. This puzzle is explained in three ways. First and most broadly, social activism such as picketing or publishing on web sites—both of which the church considers a form of preaching—may be the way that God chooses to reveal someone's election to him or her. Says Ben Phelps, an elder in the church, "Preaching has a two-fold purpose: it saves believers and damns the wicked."[140] Here, though, Ben Phelps does not mean that the preaching itself changes a person's eternal destination, which was decided before time began. Instead, he means that it reveals whether the listener is righteous or wicked. Individuals cannot be persuaded by Westboro Baptist Church (since only God saves us, our own "persuasion" is irrelevant—that is, in Westboro Baptist Church, you cannot "make a decision for Christ," as a figure like evangelical Billy Graham would argue), but it could be that God has selected Westboro Baptist Church to be the mouthpiece through which individuals will hear his message.

Second, this message to obey God (according to Westboro Baptist Church standards) is for everyone, not merely the elect; everyone is to obey God, even if they are damned. Indeed, since election is limited and is doled out by God without regard to individual merit, even some members of Westboro Baptist Church may not be elect—yet they still must be obedient. To those who find this unfair, Westboro Baptist Church members point to Paul, who is asked in Romans 9:19, "Why doth he yet find fault? For who hath resisted his will?" How, wonder early Christians, can God both hold them accountable for sin and deny them free will? Paul responds in Romans 9:20: "Nay but, O man, who art thou that repliest against God? Shall the thing formed say to him that formed it, Why hast thou made me thus?" Paul points to the impossibility of humans understanding God's righteous judgments—in short, "the ways of the Lord are passed finding out" but there is "beauty" as well as security in knowing that salvation is "not a human meritocracy."[141]

Finally, Westboro Baptist Church must preach out of that obedience to God, not because of any expectation that God will use the church. Picketing may serve all of these purposes, for God "can do more than one thing"—that is, achieve more than one purpose "at a time."[142] As Steve Drain smilingly confessed one Sunday morning as he stood outside Topeka's St. David's Episcopal Church, which has had a temporary restraining order in effect against Westboro Baptist Church since 1993,[143] "I just have to be here!"[144]

3

The Religious Right's organized antigay activism emerged
in the 1970s and developed in the 1980s, but the 1990s provided challenges to antigay activism that required the antigay
movement to shape itself differently if it hoped to maintain
its successes and include Americans who were uncomfortable with same-sex sexuality and opposed to gay rights but
generally resistant to seeing themselves as intolerant. Even
as gay Americans continued to live (and die) with the consequences of institutional homophobia that had long denied them basic rights such as health care in addition to
tolerating interpersonal violence in the form of hate crimes,
anti–gay rights groups adopted what David Ehrenstein calls
"kinder, gentler homophobia,"[1] at least in the tone they took
in public discourse.[2]

This included a shift from an antigay rhetoric that was
outright hostile to one that was pitying and a shift from the
use of theology to the use of science and social science to
argue against same-sex sexual contact. At the same time,
national, state, and municipal legislation and policy were
increasingly sought to prevent the extension of gay rights
to areas where gay people had traditionally been denied access, such as the US military, which enacted President Bill
Clinton's Don't Ask, Don't Tell executive order in 1993, and
legally recognized marriage, which was regulated by the Defense of Marriage Act (DOMA), signed into law by Clinton

in 1996 to legally define marriage as between one man and one woman in federal law while allowing states to deny marriage rights to same-sex couples married in other states.[3] Although such laws represented a "win" for anti–gay rights activists because they extended anti–gay rights laws, they were also a recognition that long-held assumptions about the fitness of gay soldiers for service or the desire for gay people to marry were questionable.

This was the setting in which Westboro Baptist Church launched its first antigay campaign. According to *Hatemongers*, a church-approved documentary film about Westboro Baptist Church, church members were walking in Gage Park in Topeka one day in 1991 when Fred Phelps's school-aged grandson was propositioned by a gay man; such encounters, in this public park, according to church members, were frequent.[4] In response, the church sent a letter to the city requesting that laws against public sex be applied more forcefully, especially since the park had been named as a "cruisy" area in a gay-sex tour guide.[5] "I can't imagine anyone wanting their picnics interrupted by fags making out," Fred Phelps recalled in a 1994 interview, appealing to a politics of disgust quite separate from the church's theology. "I thought it wouldn't take but a time or two," he suggested.[6]

When the city failed to respond in what the church saw as an adequate way, Phelps concluded that the city was controlled by gay rights interests, and he began researching the topic of the gay rights movement in America. He recalled in a *Washington Post* story, "It was breathtaking how far down that road this country's gone. . . . And the more I found out the more resolute I got and began to look upon myself gradually as the last, best hope of this miserable, godforsaken country."[7] Soon the church began what it termed "The Great Gage Park Decency Drive"—a campaign, starting in the spring of 1991, to draw attention to illegal homosexual encounters happening in the park and what church members saw as the failure of local government to address the issue.[8] In those days before widespread Internet use, the church used faxes, media outlets, and public forums[9] to decry public toleration of homosexual acts, which were, until the US Supreme Court's 2003 *Lawrence v. Texas* decision, illegal in the state of Kansas.[10]

Since then the church has expanded its media output to include a variety of web sites and Twitter, Vine, and YouTube. It also began military and police funeral pickets—demonstrations involving singing hymns and parodies of patriotic songs; carrying signs; dragging the American flag on the ground; and, depending on the state, preaching anywhere from 50 to 1,000 feet from a funeral. It broadened its targets to include all "fags and fag enablers"—including high-profile gay men and women such as celebrities and politicians and those supportive of gay rights—and soldiers, victims of crimes and natural disaster, Catholics, Muslims, and Jews. In his documentary film *The Most Hated Family in America*, British documentary filmmaker Louis Theroux browses through a collection of Westboro Baptist Church picket signs, noting that the church calls Princess Diana a "Royal Whore in Hell" and Archbishop Desmond Tutu "Fag Tutu." "There's no logic here," he complains to Steve Drain, to which Drain replies, "Actually, there's plenty of logic. Anybody who's in the news who supports the filthy fag agenda, we're going to make a sign about."[11] Theroux, like many in the audience of such pickets, understands Westboro Baptist Church pickets only as antigay, failing to understand that the strict sexual code that the church preaches is concerned with more than same-sex sexuality. Moreover, he fails to comprehend members' claims that the church's Calvinistic theology justifies their participation in pickets not only of gay people but of all who do not support their means of communicating their message, ministries, and mission.

Westboro Baptist Church critics accuse the church of exploiting protest scenes for profit, claiming that the church deliberately provokes an illegal or even violent response from local governments or members of the public in order to then sue for damages, thus funding future pickets. A scouring of Westboro Baptist Church legal history provides no evidence for this claim. Though Phelps-Chartered, under the leadership of Fred Phelps, did file several wasteful lawsuits, church members have endured many physical attacks, often without police intervention, without legal retaliation. Westboro Baptist Church has not been aggressive in torte action, though it is concerned with protecting what it sees as its First Amendment right to picket. When the church does file a lawsuit, it is to recover the cost of legal fees associated with action taken against church members, such as the case, settled in 2010, in which the town of Bellevue, Nebraska, was forced to pay Shirley Phelps-Roper nearly $17,000 in damages related to her wrongful arrest or the fees that Albert Snyder is required to pay since the Supreme Court decided in the church's favor in *Snyder v. Phelps*.[12] In such cases the church is entitled to recover costs it expended in defending its position, but this money does not provide sufficient income to fund church activities, which include approximately $250,000 a year in travel.

## WESTBORO BAPTIST CHURCH MEANS

What the *Santa Fe Reporter* characterized as "the most offensive and ingenious theological campaign in modern memory"[13] began in the early 1990s with local picketing and faxing and soon expanded into a national campaign involving a variety of new technologies of protest, particularly digital and social media. Indeed, like many conservative Christians, Westboro Baptists are innovators in their adoption and adaptation of media technologies. "While fundamentalists claim to be upholding orthodoxy (right belief) or orthopraxis (right behavior), and to be defending and conserving religious traditions and traditional ways of life from erosion," note Gabriel A. Almond, Emmanuel Sivan, and R. Scott Appleby, "they do so by crafting new methods, formulating new ideologies, and adopting the latest processes and organizational structures."[14] In controlling their own media—through their maintenance of web sites and Twitter, Vine, and YouTube accounts; video production; and old-fashioned press releases— Westboro Baptists have greater control over their message, and they are able to quickly respond to current events, including misrepresentations of them in other media. However, Westboro Baptists frequently leave such media misrepresentations of their church uncorrected, for such presentations isolate them further from the public while ensuring that they retain some media attention.[15] As Shirley Phelps-Roper says, "Any news story about us is going to say, 'God Hates Fags.' If that's the only thing they [the reporters] get right, we've done our job."[16] Church members thus make outside media into an accomplice in spreading their message.

However, the church has its own robust multimedia ministry, including a number of high-quality web sites that provide podcasts of sermons, sermon texts, church-produced news videos, music videos, and blogs as well as a stable of social media. Indeed, the church provides a user guide for accessing its content in a video titled "Our Commission: Saturation."[17] Each of the church's means for communicating its message has a distinct history, but all have the same aim: to disseminate the message of Westboro Baptist Church and engage an unbelieving public. Explains Steve Drain, "Our job is to preach the whole counsel of God to you out of our love and obedience to God and out of a Christ-commanded love for our neighbors, which is you. And whether you'll hear or whether you'll forbear hearing, be sure of this one thing: We will preach the God of the Bible to you until our testimony be finished at the hand of God Almighty."[18]

## Fax Campaign

Westboro Baptist Church's fax campaign began in the early 1990s, before Internet access was widely available, with daily or near-daily faxes distributed to businesses, organizations, and individuals. The faxes, like church-produced, Internet-distributed press releases today, included offensive graphics, reputation-damaging accusations, and challenges to local authorities. In particular, the faxes focused on the immorality of gay sex and the way in which allegedly closeted gay men and women—in short, nearly everyone who crossed the church—lied, church members claimed, about their sexuality. In this way the church "outed" gay men and women or forced heterosexual people to publicly affirm their sexuality while they sidestepped the issue of their support for gay rights. The accusations were often cruel but effective, and they were also manipulated by outsiders. For example, the faxes included medical information drawn from anonymous sources.[19] Inspiration for claims about local politicians or public figures was sent "in the mail or sometimes . . . left in the mailbox outside the church. Some information [came] from longtime city, county, or state politicos," according to the church, though the church did require two corroborating sources for any anonymously supplied information.[20] For example, blood-bank records of a city council candidate who was once supported by Fred Phelps were left in the church's mailbox, and the church published faxes that suggested that she was HIV-positive.

The records indicated that the candidate had been rejected as a blood do-
nor because she tested positive for hepatitis B. "Well that's something
like AIDS!" defended Fred Phelps in a 1995 interview. "So I put out a flyer
saying, 'Does she have AIDS?' I used a question mark." Such grammati-
cal nuance escaped recipients of the fax, says the candidate, as coworkers
and family members found themselves confronted with doctored images
of their friend with Kaposi's sarcoma lesions.[21] In these early faxes, the
church established its reputation for offensive graphics, personal attacks,
and specious accusations.

## Picketing

Fred Phelps defended picketing as preaching, saying, "Picketing is just
preaching, what I've been doing for 40-some years."[22] The act is justified
by church members with a Bible verse from the prophet Habakkuk: "And
the LORD answered me, and said, 'Write the vision, and make it plain
upon tablets, that he may run that readeth it.'"[23] In writing their words
on posters that they display at busy intersections, Westboro Baptists can
spread their message quickly to a variety of passersby.

Pickets involve teams of various sizes—often as many people as can
fit into a church member's van—holding church-produced poster-sized
signs with graphics and words articulating the church's main beliefs;
these signs are produced on church property. Picketers include church
members of all ages, and because so many of the members are minors,
children are often on the picket line.

While on the picket line, picketers may stand still or walk, and they
remain on public areas such as sidewalks. They are careful to obey state
laws regarding public space and "time and distance" rules that limit the
picketing of church services and funerals to certain hours and distances
from the scene of the event. Picketers are careful to stay connected with
each other via cell phone so that they can report potential dangers to each
other. The threat of danger is real, and church members are directed to
"retreat until they can retreat no more" if attacked and, if necessary, to defend themselves by covering their bodies with their signs.[24] Though picketers are always met with hostility—expressed through revved engines

and squealing tires, glares, vulgar hand gestures, profanity screamed by drivers, or more overt violence—the mood on the picket line is generally upbeat, with picketers chitchatting about movies they recently watched or their plans for the day. "I go on the theory that outdoor exercise is good, preaching the Gospel is good, helping the country is good," explained Fred Phelps about the pickets in an interview with Topeka's *Capital-Journal*. "There's just so much good stuff attending those things that I can't hardly wait for the next one to come."[25] Since the church claims that it has performed more than 55,000 pickets to date, members do not have to wait long for the next one; pickets occur daily.

## Church Web Sites

In 1996 the church launched its flagship web site under the direction of then–college student Ben Phelps. The Matthew Shepard funeral picket had drawn national attention to the church, and the neon signs proclaiming "God Hates Fags" that picketers held at the funeral drove traffic to the web site, where the group's outrageous rhetoric appalled visitors.[26] Visitors who returned to the site found "epics" explaining why each person the church had picketed—from local folks to national figures—was in hell. These included Diane Whipple, a California woman who had been savagely mauled by two dogs in the stairwell of her apartment. Lurid, detailed descriptions of her death and her sins—including lesbianism—were provided. These documents provided the template for future epics about each of the funeral pickets in which church members would participate.

The church's web presence has expanded greatly since then, and web sites now include blogs, video footage of pickets, press releases, schedules of upcoming pickets, photographs, frequently asked questions, sermons, documentary videos, talking-head-style commentary on news events, songs, music-video parodies, audio recordings of sermons, and more. Further, different web sites promote different aspects of the church's theology. For example, Beast Obama details the church's argument that the current president is the Antichrist and outlines the church's ideas about the end of the world. God Hates the World includes an interactive map that visitors can use to select different nations of the world; when users click on an area, they are provided with information about why God hates that particular nation. Sign Movies allows users to click on various signs that church members hold during pickets to learn the theological justification for the claims made on them. More web sites are in development. After years of struggling to find a server that could securely host its web site, the church now maintains its own server. The web sites are of professional quality, which is especially impressive given the small size of the church. The sites are constructed and maintained by church members with skills in information technology and media design.

## Social Media

Westboro Baptist Church and its members maintain active social media accounts across a variety of platforms, including YouTube, Facebook, Twitter, and Vine, inspiring them to craft their message in innovative ways that make use of emerging technologies and genres.[27] The process of developing so many outlets for preaching was organic, according to church members. Says Shirley Phelps-Roper, "We didn't go out with a game plan or a strategy, we just had some words on some signs and we stood in the public places and were obedient to the laws of God and man!" Out of their obedience to God, they were blessed, not with new converts or monetary donations but with assurance, say church members. "Our God taught our hands to engage in this warfare and our fingers to fight—that is to say—in the details and the minutiae,"[28] Shirley Phelps-Roper notes. They learned what they were doing as they went along, adding new places to preach and new media and developing and articulating their message more fully.

❖ Regardless of their method for preaching, Westboro Baptists share a highly disciplined message, articulating the same theology in press releases and faxes, at pickets, and in their Internet and social-media activities. The language and images are consistent across media and speakers. Church members stress that Jude 1:23 provides instructions for two ways of reaching an audience: on some, church members should "have compassion, making a difference," but they should approach others as unpleasant and potentially contaminating influences. These people, too, need to hear the message of Westboro Baptist Church, so church members continue to address them "with fear, pulling them out of the fire, hating even the garment spotted by the flesh." Envisioning themselves in the lineage of other prophets with outrageous messages and innovative media, Westboro Baptists preach to these people with a message that is consistently bold, graphic, and offensive because such words are the only kind that some people will pay attention to. As Fred Phelps noted repeatedly, everyone thought Noah was crazy when he was building the ark, but where the rest of the world sees craziness, Westboro Baptists see obedience—which did not persuade God to save Noah and his family but may have revealed that Noah and his family were going to be saved. In other words, we cannot know that Noah or his family members were elect and thus heaven-bound, but we can know that such obedience to God in the face of ridicule may be a sign of election. Just as God demanded bizarre behavior of his Old Testament prophets, ways of acting that made little sense to their contemporaries, Westboro Baptists are prepared to be mocked for their faithfulness. "If they think our signs are outrageous," Fred Phelps encouraged his congregation, "they should see what God said for Ezekiel to do": bake bread over human dung. Ezekiel's message to God's people was the same as Westboro Baptist Church's is to the world today: "You are filthy."[29] The message from the pulpit, along with the images on picket signs and graphics in videos and on web sites, is explicit. This provocativeness is deliberate, not to harm people but to help them, according to the church, which contends that "the truth is harsh. We use great plainness of speech, and will not beat around the bush when it comes to someone's eternal soul. Watch out for those people who tell you that it's okay to be gay—they'll take you to hell with them."[30] Indeed, upsetting people is precisely the goal, a kind of theatrical, theological shock to their system that forces them to confront Westboro Baptist Church's message and reveal, either by agreeing or disagreeing with the church, their status as elect or nonelect. The process is unpleasant for listeners, who are virtually guaranteed that they will be challenged. Indeed, that is the point. "I'm here to fray them,"[31] declared Jonathan Phelps at a picket in front of the Metropolitan Community Church in Topeka, referring to

Zechariah 1:21[32] and describing the experience of the congregants who see members from Westboro Baptist Church outside their church regularly: irritated, unraveled, worked over until they fall apart.

The message that those being picketed are hell-bound is so important that Westboro Baptist Church members believe it justifies tactics that even they recognize as otherwise cruel. For example, church members have defended sending letters to the parents of young adults who have died of AIDS-related illnesses, picketing the funerals of murder victims, or yelling cruel words to a father about his preteen daughter's attempted suicide.[33] Westboro Baptists describe their apparent cruelty as the only act of true love. Explains member Brent Roper, "'Love thy neighbor' means rebuking him."[34] This love must extend to everyone and explains the zeal of church members. Asks Steve Drain, "Who shouldn't I care about? If I believe [in church doctrines] in the core of my being, why are you going to fault me for preaching?"[35]

## SOCIOLOGICAL EXPLANATIONS OF WESTBORO BAPTIST CHURCH'S PUBLIC MINISTRIES

The judges of the Fourth Circuit Court of Appeals in 2009 noted when reversing the original decision against the church in *Snyder v. Phelps*, regarding the signs that picketers hold at funerals, that "as distasteful as these signs are, they involve matters of public concern, including the issue of homosexuals in the military, the sex-abuse scandal within the Catholic Church, and the political and moral conduct of the United States and its citizens. Such issues are not subjects of 'purely private concern,' but rather are issues of social, political, or other interest to the community."[36] When framed as one way of addressing commonly held concerns about issues of national importance, the actions of Westboro Baptist Church may be defined as unusual and uncommon without being defined as irrational, even if the methods members use are uncivil.

Like many believers who adopt a fundamentalist or conservative theology, Westboro Baptist Church members appear to be struggling to make sense of a broader American culture that seems to them to reject foundational truth, dismiss supernatural authority, and advocate cultural relativism.[37] Conservative Christianity's former status as the (or even an) authority on life's biggest questions may have eroded. More specifically, a contemporary understanding of sexuality as something other than God-given (whether that is socially constructed or genetic or something else) is unacceptable to a church that adopts the concept of absolute predestination. In the context of postmodernity, Westboro Baptists could adopt a different means of defining themselves, but they deliberately adopt tactics that the general public finds offensive. This does not mean, however, that their feelings about the changing nature of the world are necessarily incomprehensible, even if they are expressed in ways considered cruel by others.

Westboro Baptists share with the Religious Right more than their concern about shifting sexual mores and the declining prestige of religion. Members participate in American culture broadly, and the families involved with the church are of the sort that would make the listeners of Focus on the Family's radio show envious—hardworking, polite, respectful. Individual church members and families are often described as "for the most part, kind and sensitive people" in their interactions with the outside world.[38] Notes Louis Theroux, who spent three weeks with the church while filming his first BBC documentary on the church,

> In some ways they're a model family. All these things that you associate with the breakdown of families, like the dad's gone to the pub all the time or they just watch TV and the parents don't talk to the kids, well, you can't put that on this family. They spend all their recreational time together, and they all look out for each other. They don't really have friends outside the church because all their best friends are in the church. It's important to recognise the good qualities of the family, as it helps explain why so many of them have stayed in it and embraced the hateful stuff.[39]

By all measures except for their public ministries, church participants are exemplary citizens and employees.[40] Also, notably, Westboro Baptist Church members have not retreated from secular culture. The children attend public schools and work in enterprises unrelated to the church. In fact, many church members are employed by the state of Kansas,[41] and they participate in politics at all levels.[42] They all use modern technology and enjoy contemporary entertainment and popular culture, from video games to trendy fashions. Church members' tension with the secular world rests upon what they perceive as its tolerance of homosexuality, not any general disdain for popular culture (except in its supposed tolerance for homosexuality and other sins). For Westboro Baptists, the emergence of secular modernism and postmodernism represents a threat to fundamentalist Christianity, a trend that Fred Phelps was preaching against at the start of his career,[43] and the success of the gay rights movement in winning increased broader public acceptance of gay people has given Westboro Baptist Church the evidence it needs to say that fundamentalist Christianity has lost its place in America.[44]

Although Westboro Baptist Church has not been effective in harnessing the resentment of those who share its hostility toward gay rights, the broader Religious Right has gained political power through the use of "status politics."[45] For church members, Westboro Baptist Church's identity as the lone prophet of God's word has prevented them from allying with other groups that hold similarly antigay beliefs;[46] moreover, other proponents of similarly antigay theology refuse to align with Westboro Baptist Church's tactics.[47] Thus, according to William R. Hutchison, the Religious Right, on the one hand, has generally avoided the isolation that comes from extremism;[48] Westboro Baptist Church, on the other hand, has embraced that isolation. In order to manage their anxiety about a decline in their prestige, members of the Religious Right have sought political power, hoping to legislate a permanent place for themselves in the American hierarchy of prestige. In contrast, because of its demand for doctrinal purity, Westboro Baptist Church has refused to build the alliances that would make a politics of resentment successful and, like other Primitive Baptist churches that "view the numerical decline of their church as part of the mysterious outworking of divine providence,"[49] is unbothered by the lack of alliances.

Westboro Baptist Church represents itself as so at odds with society that the respect of the broader culture matters little to it; in fact, social rejection affirms its unique role in God's plan.[50] A politics of resentment, then, cannot be built by a group that sees the society that despises it as hopelessly in conflict with the group's goals. For this reason, rather than seeking political reform that would advance the church's own teachings on sexuality with any hope that it would be met with voter approval, Westboro Baptist Church flies the American flag upside down—a sign of a sinking ship, a nation in decline.[51] The church's mission is not to transform the culture or to increase the size and influence of the church but to purify its own ranks and warn the broader culture of the consequences of its sins. Says the church:

> First, our goal is to preach the Word of God to this crooked and perverse generation. By our words, some will repent. By our words, some will be condemned. Whether they hear, or whether they forbear, they will know a prophet has been among them. It is the solemn job of a believing Christian to preach the Gospel to every creature, and warn them to flee from the wrath to come. . . . Second, our goal is to glorify God by declaring His whole counsel to everyone. Third, we hope that by our preaching some will be saved. As Jude said, on some have compassion, making a difference, but others save with fear.[52]

Westboro Baptists view themselves as a kind of sorting mechanism, forcing listeners to recognize whether they are sheep or goats, wheat or chaff. In their response to the church, listeners reveal whether they are people who repent or people who are condemned, whether God has elected them or damned them. Regardless, the church notes, every listener is confronted and forced to admit his or her position, for or against Westboro Baptist Church and thus for or against God, reinforcing the boundary between the church and people outside it. It does not seek, then, to conquer, transform, or re-create the world, which it has labeled as hopeless and beyond redemption, but to renounce it. World renouncers, in the categorization of Gabriel A. Almond, Emmanuel Sivan, and R. Scott Appleby, are "a relatively rare mode of fundamentalism" who seek "purity and self-preservation more than hegemony over fallen outsiders."[53] Westboro Baptists both renounce the outside world and engage in it, even as they do so hopelessly, without any confidence that it will change. This paradox—the "consistent logic of purity and contamination"[54]—is an unconquerable difficulty for Westboro Baptist Church's opponents, who wonder why church members bother to picket if they have no expectation that their targets will change. The answer comes back to theology: because Westboro Baptist Church prizes obedience to the inscrutable will of God, a will that demands its public ministry to the world but has predestined that change, if it occurs at all, will not be culturewide as the world moves toward the end of time.

## SCENES OF WESTBORO BAPTIST CHURCH PUBLIC MINISTRY

Some Westboro Baptist Church members cultivate an image of church members as delighting in the destruction of their fellow Americans, but a closer analysis of interviews reveals that many of them approach their public protests as necessary and loving acts. Shirley Phelps-Roper, for example, recounts a time when a grieving mother whose son's funeral was being picketed grabbed her hand at the funeral. The woman pulled Phelps-Roper close to her and asked how she, herself a mother, could interrupt the grief of the family with a picket. Tearing up during the retelling, Phelps-Roper responded that she was there *because* she is a mother; she feels a duty to warn all mothers not to "raise their children for hell" by allowing them to align with a culture that she believes condones homosexuality and a military that supports that culture.[55] Similarly, she reports feeling "so sad" as she drove toward the funeral of fallen marine Matthew Snyder, recalling how, in media appearances, his father had called him "the love of his life," a feeling that Shirley Phelps-Roper shares about her own children.[56] Though many consider Phelps-Roper's method uncivil and her central thesis that God hates gay men and women objectionable, her story—as well as the theology espoused in sermons and in church publications—illustrates that members of the church are not, at least in their view of themselves, inspired by hatred but are driven by a religious mission to love others. Though "compassion is itself a contested dimension of Christian Right politics," remind Cynthia Burack and Jyl J. Josephson, and though it may be used strategically, researchers should nonetheless "judge these [compassion] projects in the full knowledge of the affective and theological commitments of their proponents."[57] In other words,

Shirley Phelps-Roper's claims to identify, as far as she is able, with the feelings of those mourning can be both strategic and sincere.

Moreover, when Westboro Baptists rejoice in the tragedies of others, they are expressing gratitude to God, for the just suffering of other depraved people reminds them of how deserving they are of the same punishment and of how much God loves them to withhold it. Jonathan Edwards describes the reaction of the elect to the suffering of others this way: "When they see others who were of the same nature, and born under the same circumstances, plunged in such misery, . . . O, it will make them sensible, how happy they are."[58] Or, as one member of the congregation explains in a church-produced video titled "Thank God for 9/11," "Not one innocent person died on September 11, 2001, even a woman who was carrying a child that died, even a newborn babe. . . . You thank God for September 11. You thank God for September 11 because you weren't killed that day. You were given the chance to see that God is taking his vengeance upon this evil nation and repent of your sins and serve the Lord your God."[59] Preaching the message of total depravity along with gratitude for escaping deserved destruction, though the message feels cruel to the listener, is thus actually an act of love for one's neighbor and worship of God.

Although church members do not make clear in their picket signs that they consider their public activity an act of love (and reporters and producers, untrained in theology and sometimes unconcerned about accurate depictions of attention-grabbing stories, do not grasp or report on this distinction themselves), they do make this clear in their publications and sermons. Though observers are likely to call the church hateful and quote biblical passages about the love of God to counter Westboro Baptist Church passages preaching damnation of unrepentant sinners, church members see their ministry as evidence of their obedience to God and a way of glorifying God, an act of love to their listeners. Or, as Fred Phelps wrote in an open letter requested by the *Capital-Journal*, "We are the only people who truly love you—enough to tell you the truth. The highest form of love from one human to another is to care, genuinely, for the state of a man's soul."[60] This theology is preached at a variety of scenes, to the widest audience possible, and Westboro Baptists are expected to be able to speak articulately about their faith generally—and this particular dimension of it specifically—wherever they go.

## Antigay Ministry

Westboro Baptist Church members understand biblical passages that they say condemn homosexuality in the light of what they view as their strict adherence to Calvinist doctrines: total depravity, unconditional election, limited atonement, irresistible grace, and perseverance of the saints.[61] These tenets are held by a variety of believers, of course, many of whom believe that homosexuality is an individual sin that can result in punishment from God in this lifetime as well as eternal punishment in the afterlife. Further, many believers, including non-Calvinists, make public this message of God's punishment as a response to individual and collective sin. Indeed, at the start of their antigay campaign, Westboro Baptists were not always distinguishable from antigay Religious Right protesters, many of whom argued that AIDS was God's punishment for homosexuality, either as divine punishment for the sin of gay sex[62] or as a natural consequence of gay sex;[63] that gay people threatened the security of the nation's blood supply;[64] that homosexuality should be punished with death;[65] that people with AIDS should be "humanely quarantined," as Fred Phelps suggested in his 1994 campaign for governor;[66] and that homosexual sex was unnatural and sinful.[67] Much of the same rhetoric continues to circulate among antigay religious activist groups, though few antigay activists go so far as to link specific national tragedy with gay rights, as does Westboro Baptist Church, and few others are willing to use the phrase "God hates fags," perhaps fearful of being associated with the Topeka church.

Westboro Baptist Church's antigay message was preached within the church decades before church members began their pickets. In 1993, around the time that psychologists were debating homosexuality's removal from the *Diagnostic and Statistical Manual*, Phelps advertised the church's sixteenth anniversary with a sermon that examined whether homosexuality was a "sickness or a sin."[68] Westboro Baptist Church has never been alone in its protests at gay pride parades, as conservative religious believers all over the United States protest in response to a visible gay culture, but the church is uniquely focused in its physical targeting of businesses that cater to gay consumers, including gay bars; businesses that employ openly gay or lesbian employees; churches that permit gay members or clergy; and even churches that host reparative therapy ("ex-gay") conferences. Even if other antigay protesters will not stand on the street next to Westboro Baptists at these events, they show up to lodge their own protest against what they see as the moral decline of America. For example, when Topeka was considering a repeal of the city's ordinance that prohibited discrimination based on sexual orientation in municipal hiring and firing, three protests occurred outside the city council meeting: one by supporters of the ordinance; one by Westboro Baptists, who argued for the repeal of the law; and one by other conservative Christians who also wanted to repeal the law but did not want to be associated with Westboro Baptist Church.[69] These groups are quick to point out that, unlike Westboro Baptist Church, they are active in the anti–gay rights movement because they love gay people and want them to escape from sin and the natural and supernatural consequences of it.

Not so, say members of Westboro Baptist Church. "We never said that we hate fags,"[70] Fred Phelps noted in a 2005 interview, and the point is repeated by other church members; the church thinks that God hates gay people, and because human hatred, unlike the hate of God, is not holy, they are not to hate gay people. Indeed, "we're the only ones who love the filthy little perverts," defended Fred Phelps.[71] Church members argue that the best way to "love thy neighbor" is to be honest with him, to warn him as he wanders near to danger and, if necessary, to hurt his feelings to save his soul. Reflected Fred Phelps in regard to a story about him that ran in The Advocate in the 1990s, "I didn't ask for it, but circumstances, in the Providence of God, appear to have made me chaplain to the international fag community, and I cheerfully accept the job."[72] He contrasted himself with other pastors who substitute toleration of sin for the brutal love he advocates, pastors who would allow a congregant to sin rather than correct him: "I warn you . . . these kissy-pooh fag preachers telling you it's OK to play with gerbils and worship the rectum will send you to Hell! And Fred Phelps is the best friend you fags have got in this world."[73] At every opportunity, he provided evidence for his claim to honest preaching:

Even money-grubbing hucksters like Pat Robertson and Jerry Falwell will lie to you for lucre. But not Fred Phelps. Old School Baptists never take collections at their meetings or beg for money on TV, following the patriarch Abraham who eschewed the taking of so much as a worn shoelace from the King of Sodom lest the gospel of salvation by free grace alone be compromised. (Gen. 14:23) So I happily serve as Chaplain to the Fags free of charge.[74]

Contemporary preachers, such as Joel Osteen, will "blow hot air up your keister," as one church-produced parody of The No-Spin Zone promises,[75] and, just as the Israelites preferred false prophets who promised them wealth and abundance, gay people prefer to hear a "kissy-pooh" message of tolerance. Instead, says Westboro Baptist Church, they need to hear about hell.

No time is better for preaching hell than during mourning, and no space is better than a funeral, as Fred Phelps explained, for "dying time is truth time. These poor homosexual creatures live lives predicated on a fundamental lie. It seems to me to be the cruelest thing of all to stand over their dead, filthy bodies keeping the lies going."[76] Thus, after they became interested in the issue of homosexuality, church members quickly moved to preach about the deaths of people who died of AIDS-related illnesses, preaching, if possible, at their funerals. For example, when Kevin Oldham, an Overland Park, Kansas, native who had moved to New York to pursue a career as a composer, died of an AIDS-related illness in 1993, his parents, who remained in the Kansas City area, received a letter from the church. Expecting a note of condolence, they were shocked to read a fax that Westboro Baptist Church distributed widely soon after. It included a picture of Oldham's face with the words "KEVIN OLDHAM, DEAD FAG" beneath it and declared that by "defying the laws of God, man and nature, KEVIN OLDHAM played Russian roulette with a promiscuous anal sex and lost big time when he died of AIDS March 11." The church picketed Kevin Oldham's memorial service a few weeks later.[77]

Even in the early days of funeral pickets, the church was mobile. An early event was the funeral of Randy Shilts, an openly gay reporter for the San Francisco Chronicle and author of The Band Played On: Politics, People, and *the AIDS Epidemic*, who died in 1994. The church's picket was met with a nearly 2,000-person counterprotest that included egg throwing, and the ten-person picket group left within minutes of beginning.[78] Still, church members recall it as a time when they gained national attention to their cause, testifying to the many "amazing events of that day."[79]

Even though Westboro Baptist Church is not alone in its vision of a literal hell, it is alone in its perceived calling to publicly preach this message at funerals. Moreover, the church's dogged focus on double and absolute predestination, unfamiliar and incomprehensible to many Americans and offensive to the evangelicals who often otherwise share with Westboro Baptist Church condemnation of homosexuality, inspires it to preach its message of impending apocalypse with a twist. Whereas other churches preach that sinners must repent, thereby "stamping out large-scale sinfulness, the kind of sin that prevailed in Sodom and Gomorrah and that persuaded God to destroy mankind while saving Noah and his family,"[80] Westboro Baptist Church preaches that it is too late to repent, that God will destroy the United States, as is his prerogative as the creator and sovereign ruler of all creation, regardless of how individuals hearing the church's words respond. Repentance is possible but improbable—yet, admits Steve Drain, the improbable has happened before. When Jonah preached in the city of Nineveh, his message was not "repent or perish." It was, instead, "Forty more days and Nineveh will be overthrown" (Jonah 3:4). There was no "unless" in Jonah's messages, points out Drains. With no promise of rescue, the Ninevites stopped their evil ways and repented. God spared Nineveh, and though God could spare the United States— "You can't discount that completely from consideration," admits Drain— it seems unlikely.[81]

The only hope for the individual listener is that God has elected him and will allow him to hear the truth of Westboro Baptist Church's words, turn his wayward heart and mind to the church, and enable him to live by its doctrines; even then, salvation is not guaranteed. For the rest—just like the huge number of people the church believes were killed in the flood while Noah and his seven family members floated to safety—destruction is imminent. These include not only gay people but all those who support gay people or merely fail to preach the message of Westboro Baptist Church.

Westboro Baptist Church's theological objections to homosexuality frame same-sex acts, approval or toleration of them, or failure to speak out against them not as mere personal affronts to God but as national sins that threaten to bring the punishments of God on the entire nation. It is that threat to the entire nation, as well as their belief that God has ordered them to picket, that motivates them, church members say. They find support for their position that America has come to tolerate homosexuality in the celebration of the lives of gay people and gay rights supporters at their funerals and, more broadly, in American popular culture. For this reason, and because such events provide church members with large audiences, they also have a ministry that focuses on cultural events.

### Ministry around Cultural Events

Many Kansans first hear the Westboro Baptist Church message as they attend a play at the Topeka Performing Arts Center, a rock concert at Kansas City's Sprint Center, a talk at the University of Kansas's Lied Center, or a high school graduation. All these events are sites where Westboro Baptists picket and events that they deride in faxes and on their web sites. At the same time, church members also participate as audience members in some of these events. For example, church members both picket and attend sporting events, saying, "We know the difference between using a recreational event and abusing it"[82]—and when children from the church graduate from high school (as they do every year), parents start the evening by picketing the event, then enter the graduation venue to watch the ceremony and cheer for their children.

Westboro Baptist Church extends its criticism of popular culture beyond Topeka, often adding pickets at local cultural events to their schedule when they are in an area to picket a funeral. Cultural events are chosen for three reasons: (1) they draw large crowds, sometimes tens of thousands, and receive media coverage; (2) they are often celebrations of behavior that the church considers sinful; and (3) even if the performers are not celebrating sin, they are failing to use their influence to preach against it.

Nationally known entertainers are frequently cited by the church for their promotion of sexual practices of which the church disapproves. For example, the pop singer Lady Gaga has received much Westboro Baptist Church scorn for teaching young listeners to be "proud whores,"[83] and the church has produced parodies of some of her songs and music videos, calling attention to her vague and gay-affirming theology and her hyper-sexualized lyrics and performances. Parodies, tweets, and pickets of several of her concerts have prompted the singer to address the issue. In a tweet, she cautioned her fans that, in coming to her concert, they might face "lude [sic] and violent language and imagery,"[84] and on her Facebook page, she warned, "This group in particular to me is violent and dangerous. I wanted to make my fans aware of my views on how to approach, or rather not approach, these kinds of hate activists."[85] As she noted in her post, though, Lady Gaga's recognition of Westboro Baptist Church's ministry against her draws attention to it.

Although some cultural events—such as Lady Gaga concerts, which include many gay fans; productions of The Laramie Project; or the nomination of a gay homecoming king or same-sex prom king and queen—clearly violate the church's theology of sexuality, other events that are not explicitly about sexuality also catch Westboro Baptist Church's attention. For example, singer Justin Bieber is a target for the church's ministry, not, like Lady Gaga, because of his hypersexualized lyrics or performances but because he fails to preach the church's message. Bieber, says the church, "has a platform given to him by God to speak to this world; he has a duty to teach obedience by his actions and words." Like all people, Bieber has a duty to obey and to preach God's word as the church understands it, but instead, Bieber, a "whoremonger in training," "teaches millions of impressionable brats that God is a liar when he solemnly proclaims his standard."[86]

## Ministry Aimed at Other Religious Groups

Westboro Baptist Church wages campaigns both against churches that are gay-friendly and against those that are simply not sufficiently, in its assessment, antigay. Because hyper-Calvinism "emphasizes irresistible grace to such an extent that there appears to be no real need to evangelize [because] Christ may be offered only to the elect"[87] and because of

Westboro Baptist Church's belief in supralapsarianism—the belief that God's decisions about election were made before the introduction of sin into creation—members do not pray for anyone outside the church, rhetorically asking, "What arrogance would we display to pretend we could pray them back into the good grace of Him who has given them up?"[88] Moreover, the church says, "We certainly know that we have absolutely no power or ability to show anyone where he or she went wrong. Everything begins and ends at the commandment of God and we are altogether content to leave all matters of the heart to Him."[89] This "no offers" form of Calvinism, in which nonbelievers are not "offered" the salvific message of Christ's death and resurrection, does not prevent Westboro Baptist Church from relaying the message that all nonbelievers are hell-bound. This includes all non-Christians, Catholics, Mormons, and even other Protestants who reject the church's teachings.

### Jews

Non-Christians are dismissed as hell-bound because they reject Jesus as the savior of those humans who receive salvation. Jews, in particular, are targeted because, according to the church, Jews literally rejected Jesus and demanded his execution, promising Pilate, in Matthew 27:25, that "his blood be on us, and on our children," a responsibility that first-century Jews accepted when they approved Jesus's execution. The church highlights this claim repeatedly in pickets and on the web site Jews Killed Jesus.

Since the death of Jesus, says Westboro Baptist Church, Jews "have never repented, and they try to bully into silence anyone who states that fact."[90] Further defying God, they have continued to deny the necessity and effectiveness of Jesus's death by constructing a complicated and legalistic form of religion, working "'orthodox' false religion like a cripple's cane, for which God hates [them],"[91] and have become "famous worldwide for being fag-enablers, babykillers, pornographers, adulterers, fornicators, and greedy idolaters."[92]

These are claims that the church supports with images of Jewish entertainers famous for their outrageous or offensive performances, such as Gene Simmons of the band KISS, comedian Sarah Silverman, and actor

At a 2010 picket in Virginia, Jonathan Phelps wears an Israeli flag splattered with paint to look like blood to remind Jews that their ancestors placed responsibility for Jesus Christ's death upon them and, consequently, upon Israel. (Photograph by Rebecca Barrett-Fox. All rights reserved.)

Adam Sandler. Church depictions of Jews rely heavily on stereotypes of Jews as greedy and dirty, and the church pronounces them "the basest of men,"[93] recalling racial hierarchies of the early twentieth century (though the church in fact uses this term to describe various groups, including gay people). In addition, some Westboro Baptist Church depictions of Jews (for example, describing them as "filthy") resonate with racial stereotypes of Jews as subhuman[94]—but, since these words are also used by church members to describe nonracialized groups such as Swedes,[95] politicians, and rock stars, members likely do not think of themselves as using racially coded language.

For Westboro Baptists, as for many other conservative Christians, Jews' most egregious sin is their failure to fulfill their duty to obey, which means repenting of their sin of murdering Jesus and becoming Christians, according to Westboro Baptist Church. The standard of God should be clear to Jews, argues Westboro Baptist Church, for the Old Testament includes important biblical texts that outline God's laws about sexuality, as found in Leviticus 18:22, which commands, "Thou shalt not lie with mankind, as with womankind: it is abomination." Because Jews are familiar with these scriptures and claim to obey them, those Jews who are offended only expose the fact that they are not one of the "good figs"—the Jews who will convert to Christianity—whom God has elected. All Jews who reject Westboro Baptist thinking about sexuality show that they are hell-bound. Indeed, whenever they depict a star of David, a traditional symbol of Judaism, Westboro Baptists insert a pink triangle—a symbol of gay pride, though in gay pride depictions the triangle is inverted—inside the star. Both symbols, of course, were used to label victims of the Holocaust. This is appropriate, argue Westboro Baptists, for when God punishes today's Jews for their continued rejection of Jesus and their toleration of homosexuality, they "will pine for the days of a good-old-fashioned Holocaust when God is through!"[96]

Since June 2009 Westboro Baptists have been actively searching for the "good figs." This targeted attention is due to church members' sense that, as evidenced by the election to the presidency of Barack Obama, whom they identify as the Antichrist, the end of the world is nearing and the Jews who will convert to Christianity are thus ready to be found. To find them,

Noah Phelps-Roper shares the church's criticisms of Catholic priests as pedophiles. Noah was a child when this photograph was taken but has remained in the church since entering adulthood. (Photograph by Rebecca Barrett-Fox. All rights reserved.)

church members picket synagogues, Jewish schools, and Jewish cultural centers, but as far as the church knows, reports Shirley Phelps-Roper, no Jews have yet repented because of their preaching.[97] The church has also sent a DVD of materials explaining its theology about Jews to Jewish religious leaders. In addition, the church directs its message through its web site Jews Killed Jesus, which includes news videos called "Jew News" about issues of concern to Jews worldwide but especially those in the United States and Israel.

*Catholics*

Catholic churches have been targets of Westboro Baptist Church pickets for decades, but recent sexual-abuse scandals in the Roman Catholic Church worldwide have given Westboro Baptist Church new ammunition in tirades against Catholics and allowed it to declare that the phrase "priests rape boys" is "an air-tight, three word case against the Catholic church."[98] Although Catholic theology has always placed Catholics outside of the realm of the elect for Westboro Baptists—after all, many conservative Christians do not believe that Catholics are Christians—cover-ups of sexual abuse by priests are understood by Westboro Baptist Church as confirmation that the Catholic Church's secretive, hierarchical organization is unholy. According to Westboro Baptist Church, popes have special responsibility for this problem, and Westboro Baptist Church has preached about papal responsibility for ignoring it. Priests, too, are responsible for the problem, and they are consistently mocked as pedophiles and supporters of "the largest, most well-funded and organized pedophile group in the history of man!"[99] Asks Westboro Baptist Church rhetorically, "Are there any priests preaching against this horrendous sin from the pulpit, denouncing the 'church' and demanding that his parishioners have nothing to do with it? Every member of the Catholic clergy, without exception, is a minister of Satan."[100] From the Westboro Baptist Church perspective, Catholic clergy are guilty not only of their false religion but also of sexual abuse, covering up sexual abuse, or failing to reform their church from within.

Further, even parishioners are responsible for the problem of sexual abuse of children within the church, for

> Every time any person gives any amount of money to the Catholic Church, that person is paying the salary of pedophile rapists. Not merely looking the other way, mind you, but actually paying the salaries of thousands of criminal, sexual deviants, who try to pass themselves off as men who have moral authority, but who are, in fact, the basest of men (Dan. 4:17). Who would rationally conceive of actually paying the salaries of pedophile rapists? And yet, that is exactly what all the parishioners of the Catholic Church are doing today.[101]

All Catholics, then, from parishioners on up to the pope, are guilty of perpetuating or ignoring the crimes and sins of their leaders. Westboro Baptist Church carries this message to Catholic churches and schools as well as scenes of papal visits and promotes this message on its web sites, especially Priests Rape Boys.

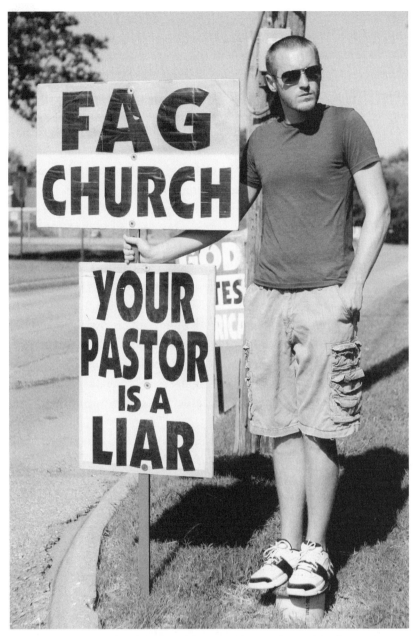

Jacob Phelps stands outside a church in Topeka one Sunday morning, waiting for congregants to arrive to see his sign. Westboro Baptists picket area churches in teams each Sunday morning before convening for their own service. (Photograph courtesy of Ailecia Ruscin. All rights reserved.)

*Other Protestant Churches*

Despite differences in theology, Westboro Baptist Church anticipated that its early antigay campaigns would meet with support from other churches. Quickly, though, the church found that even churches that did not support gay rights or welcome gay congregants distanced themselves from it. Indeed, says Lizz Phelps, members of other churches were some of the most vigorous counterprotesters at the church's earliest pickets in Topeka's Gage Park.[102] Though Westboro Baptist Church briefly had a relationship with a like-minded church in Indiana, it currently has contentious relationships with all other Christian churches.

All churches that participate in ecumenical councils with Catholics are "more guilty of the sins of the Catholics priests than the priests *themselves!*"[103] because they do not have the excuse of lust to justify their failure to reprimand Catholics, according to Westboro Baptist Church. All denominations that knowingly include gay clergy—such as the Episcopal Church—are targeted, as is Topeka's Metropolitan Community Church, which was organized as a church welcoming to gay people. Westboro Baptist Church messages repeat that denominations that allow gay leaders or do not exclude gay leaders are "fag churches," even if the particular church that members are picketing has no gay members or leaders. Mainstream churches that fail to loudly denounce homosexuality are also considered "fag-enabling churches."

When faced with the rising tolerance of homosexuality, Steve Drain says to churches that do not speak against homosexuality, "you whores get lockjaw."[104] When these pastors do speak, they convolute the clear meaning of the scripture, making it "impossible for a single soul to hear and obey."[105] Instead, participants in mainstream churches remain confused about the biblical standard of sexuality, argue church members. Instead of serving a prophetic purpose, churches spend time "cultivating a phony motivational speaking and 12 step Moose Lodge program," criticizes Drain, warning, "It's a social club, people!"[106]

Westboro Baptist Church is critical of megachurches, wealthy pastors, and those preaching the prosperity gospel, warning against those "snake oil hawkers"[107] who are "preaching for a salary, preaching for a pension" because they refuse to state that God's blessings are dependent

Paulette Phelps pickets outside Topeka's Metropolitan Community Church, a denomination founded as a welcoming and affirming church. (Photograph courtesy of Ailecia Ruscin. All rights reserved.)

upon obedience since this message would offend their audience. "If these pastors told you what the Bible really said about your sin and your manner of life and the eternal prospects for your soul, you wouldn't be in the pews when the plate gets passed," remarks Steve Drain, declaring that "the churches in American today work like a whorehouse. You pay them some money and they make you feel good."[108] Even other Primitive Baptist Churches have been rebuked by Westboro Baptist Church for producing a message that is "irrelevant, inconsequential, out of touch, and completely lukewarm" on the issue of the destruction of the sinful world.[109]

Most other Christian churches fail to properly address sin because "the pastors lie and the people want them to lie."[110] The biggest "big lie," says Steve Drain, is that "God loves you."[111] This lie is profitable for pastors because congregants prefer to believe a "very attractive lie . . . that God loves them no matter what kind of a filthy sinner they are"[112] since this "lie" allows them to continue comfortably in their sins. These pastors are guilty for the sins of their congregants because these preachers "taught people they could fornicate and that God would still love them."[113] In the end, though, argues Westboro Baptist Church, this message is not at all loving. Says Drain, "This is deadly serious stuff. Every one of these lying whore false prophets is way more than just a bungling Bible mangler. Each one of them is a minister of Satan himself."[114] So-called false churches do have a place in God's plan for humanity, though, argues Westboro Baptist Church: God creates deceptive churches to lead people astray because God, in Westboro Baptist Church's hyper-Calvinist view that espouses a strict limited atonement, does not want all people to believe.[115] Further, God is destroying these churches through their own disobedience to God's commandments on homosexuality. In a news video produced by the church, Steve Drain says mainstream churches that have failed to aggressively meet the gay rights movement "are getting their asses handed to them by militant fags on every front."[116] According to this logic, because they tolerate gay people, these churches will be brought down by gay people. This includes gay people within their own congregations, especially closeted antigay gay preachers. When journalist Joshua Kors asked Fred Phelps his opinion about antigay activists Ted Haggard and George Rekers, both of whom were caught having sexual relationships with men, Phelps replied, "I know more about these preachers than anybody else does. I've been paying close attention for 64 years, and my question is, what's taken them so long to come out? I believe that about half of these preachers and priests are closet homosexuals—I mean practicing homosexuals."[117] The sexual sins of his fellow pastors, then, did not surprise Fred Phelps. Such behavior is a consequence of teachings that stress God's unconditional love for everyone and do not preach stridently against sexual sin.

Westboro Baptists refer to pastors in other denominations as "liars" and "whores" in their pickets of church services and on their web sites. For example, while traveling to funeral picket sites, Westboro Baptists frequently stop at other churches nearby in order to picket, and they participate in dozens of pickets at other Christian churches in Topeka each week. Members maintain a rotating schedule of Sunday-morning pickets that includes Topeka churches from a variety of denominations, both those that are welcoming and affirming to lesbian, gay, bisexual, and transgender (LGBT) participants and those that are not.

## Ministry around Scenes of National Tragedy

Besides their pickets of military funerals and, more recently, of police officers, no other scene of Westboro Baptist Church public ministry has prompted such public outrage as that around what the church has come to term "GodSmacks"—acts of God that contribute to human suffering and so reveal God's hatred toward the world, illustrating the absolute predestination of all things for the purpose of sorting the elect from the damned, as believed by hyper-Calvinists. The church calls these acts "God's Wrath Revealed," saying,

> You know there's no "Mother Nature" just randomly running around with her magic wand and floaty crowny thing magically making earthquakes, tsunamis, tornadoes, hurricanes, blights, floods, blizzards, hail storms, droughts, mall shootings, postal shootings, multi-car pileups, kidnappings, apartment fire[s] and every other ass-kicking you get dealt to you by the LORD your God happen. You know God is in control. He's doing it. Just admit it. Just because you won't admit it and fear Him, and PRAISE Him, doesn't mean we aren't going to put every one of these events right in front of your nose. Read the words. Fear Him.[118]

Here, "Fear Him" strikes a double meaning: to be awed by God and to be afraid of God, for he uses violence, suffering, and death to exercise "his right to do whatsoever he will amongst the inhabitants of the earth."[119]

Westboro Baptists picket scenes of national disasters and produce commentary in the form of press releases and web videos about such events, including terrorist attacks in New York, Virginia, and Pennsylvania on September 11, 2001; the *Columbia* space-shuttle explosion in February 2003; the Sago Mine disaster in West Virginia in January 2006; the shooting of Amish schoolgirls in Pennsylvania in October 2006; shootings at Virginia Tech in April 2007; the I-35 bridge collapse in Minnesota in August 2007; the mining explosion at Upper Big Branch Mine in West Virginia in April 2010; the mass shooting of elementary schoolchildren in Newton, Connecticut, in 2012; the 2013 US government shutdown; the deaths of nineteen elite firefighters in 2013; the bombing of the Boston

Marathon in 2013; the disappearance of a Malaysian airplane in 2014; deadly tornadoes in Moore, Oklahoma, in 2014; an Amtrak train derailment in Pennsylvania in 2015; and public shootings in 2015 in Charleston, South Carolina, Chattanooga, Tennessee, and Lafayette, Louisiana.[120] Sites are chosen based on the media attention likely to be given to them and accessibility, but all tragedies, whether they are picketed or not, are understood to be expressions of God's hate toward the individual, the community, the nation, and the world.

In response to these events, Westboro Baptists are to express gratitude for God for five reasons: (1) because people should be thankful for all of God's judgments, including his punishment of the damned in both the current moment and the hell eternal; (2) because God promises to curse the wicked and bless the obedient, and disasters reveal that God keeps this promise; (3) because all humans, including Westboro Baptists, deserve death due to their absolute depravity, and any who escape death should be grateful; (4) because God has promised to avenge his prophets, and by generating disaster for America, God avenges Westboro Baptist Church; and (5) because people can find physical proof of God's hate in disasters.[121]

Despite its unpopularity today, the interpretation of disaster as God's punishment for sin was common throughout much of Christian history and certainly in the United States. Writes Peter J. Thuesen about seventeenth-, eighteenth-, and nineteenth-century American believers:

> Nothing fell outside of God's control, which he exerted either directly (through miracles such as the biblical manna from heaven) or indirectly (through kings and kingdoms and other early instruments). Whether working directly or indirectly, however, God engineered all historical developments toward the preservation and ultimate glorification of his church. Even the oppression and other calamities periodically endured by the church were all part of God's plan for his elect people, to whom he gave the power, through the Holy Spirit, to interpret the providential significance of events.[122]

Like these earlier Christians, Westboro Baptists interpret the "signs of the times" and "connect the dots" to explain how God's hate is manifested in disasters. In the process of identifying how God punishes others, they see how God preserves and glorifies Westboro Baptist Church.

Individual disaster, then, is viewed as a means of God communicating with the person suffering or with his or her loved ones. In seeing themselves as prophets—not in the sense that they are delivering a new revelation or predicting future events but in the sense that they interpret current events in light of their understanding of God—Westboro Baptists insert themselves into a cosmic story. James L. Peacock and Ruel W. Tyson, Jr., note this inclination among Primitive Baptists more broadly, as Primitive Baptists view their individual lives "within a richly perceived historical stream, one which is interlaced with doctrinal issues seen as significant not merely in a single time but for the eternal fate of humankind as willed by God."[123] Thus, Westboro Baptists are confident in the connections they make between individual deaths, public morality, and God's punishment as physically expressed against people. Tragedies in the public realm are manifestations of God's corrective anger at the society's failure in its corporate task.

Indeed, in this framework, God can even bring disaster to a single person in order to illustrate his hate toward an entire community. For example, in 1995, when Topeka police officer Tony Patterson was killed in a drug raid, a church-produced fax identified the officer as "a friend to Westboro Baptist Church" and declared its intention to "send flowers to his funeral and gifts of money to his little family in honor and respect to his memory" but also explained that Officer Patterson "died for Topeka's sins against Westboro Baptist Church" and that he "was part of a corrupt system that has wrought systemic, and sustained, state-sponsored, bloody persecution against the sheep and lambs of God's flock."[124] From Westboro Baptist Church's perspective, Officer Patterson received God's punishment for the behavior of the entire police department. Indeed, in 2015, the church began to include police officers' funerals among their regular picketing targets.

God also punishes the entire nation through disaster. Westboro Baptist Church is not alone in understanding disaster to be God's way of disciplining or punishing the world. Disaster is used by God to draw attention to the absolute dependency of humans on God and to illustrate his absolute sovereignty in order to inspire the elect or to punish the damned. These points are made by other conservative preachers during times of natural disaster. For example, after Hurricane Katrina destroyed much of New Orleans in 2005, Rev. Franklin Graham, son of the evangelist Billy Graham, argued that the hurricane was a means for God to correct a sinful city and inspire repentance, saying that, possibly, "God is going to use that storm to bring revival."[125] Michael Marcavage of Repent America, a Religious Right group, said explicitly that "this act of God destroyed a wicked city," citing, in particular, the gay-culture event Southern Decadence as evidence of New Orleans's wickedness.[126] Antiabortion activist Steve Lefemine, who circulated a weather map of the hurricane that he suggested included the image of a fetus, considered the hurricane a punishment for abortion, and on the answering machine message of his prolife organization, he simply declared, "Providence punishes national sins by national calamities."[127] These contemporary speakers seem to be in agreement with Puritans and earlier Calvinists such as Puritan pastor Thomas Foxcroft, who argued in 1756, "It would be Atheism to ascribe these Events to meer Casualty or Chance."[128]

Foxcroft's claim emerged from his belief—shared by Westboro Baptists—in the predestination of all things, not just election, and the engagement of God in human affairs. As a result of this belief, individuals can be judged to be elect or damned depending on the presence or absence of blessings or curses in their lives, and, likewise, nations can be assessed as blessed or cursed by God, according to the "GodSmacks" afflicting them. "Only one theory explained the grave disparities in national and individual fortunes," argues Thuesen of earlier American Christians' beliefs: predestination.[129] For Westboro Baptists, individual sins are punished with individual pain from God, and national sins likewise result in national punishment. Says Steve Drain, "GodSmacks are ringing throughout this land, from sea to shining sea"[130] as evidence of God's displeasure with America broadly: its people, who are gay, support gay rights, or fail to act against gay rights; its government; and its religious believers and leaders. Particular blame is reserved for religious leaders. "You," accuses Drain, "open your blasphemous sludgeholes and lie on God over and over again."[131] In contrast, say church members, Westboro

Baptist Church, in its faxes and pickets, on its web sites and in outside media, tells the truth.

## THE MISSION AND THE MESSAGE

Though it is notorious for its picketing ministry and its flagship web site, Westboro Baptist Church remains incomprehensible to many who encounter it. This is in part because the church lacks a mission that is clearly linked to individual or political change, which the public might expect of such an active group. "We're not here to persuade people but to let them know that God has a standard for them," explained Sara Phelps at a Sunday-morning picket at a neighboring church.[132] The goal is not to change people's minds, for only God can do that. Writes John Gill, an eighteenth-century theologian and the best articulator of the hyper-Calvinism embraced by Westboro Baptist Church:

> [The gospel] is not a call to them to regenerate and convert themselves
> . . . which is the pure work of the Spirit of God . . . nor to any spiritual
> vital acts, which they are incapable of, being natural men and dead in
> trespasses and sins. Nor is the gospel-ministry an offer of Christ, and
> of his grace and salvation by him, which are not in the power of the
> ministers of it to give, nor of carnal men to receive; the gospel is not
> an offer, but a preaching of Christ crucified, a proclamation of the un-
> searchable riches of his grace. . . . Yet there is something which the
> ministry of the world, and the call by it, have to do with unregenerate
> sinners: . . . the fullness, freeness, and suitableness of this salvation,
> are to be preached before them; and the whole of it to be left, to the
> Spirit of God, to make application of it as he shall see fit.[133]

Westboro Baptist Church preaches that salvation is unconditional, de-
sirable, and impossible for humans to achieve through their own efforts.
It leaves humans with a mandate to obey but without the guarantee that
obedience will bring salvation. Listeners understandably struggle with the
paradox of no-offers hyper-Calvinists both preaching to them and saying
that they are hopeless to act on the message they hear. Church members
do not concern themselves with the conversion of others, believing, like

their early-nineteenth-century predecessors, that God alone, not Bible tracts or Sunday schools or missionaries, inspires conversion. Says Shirley Phelps-Roper, "We don't want to reform the devil. What we want to do is deliver a faithful message of the Scriptures. After that, we've done our job. We don't care how you receive it."[134] In this sense, Westboro Baptists' public ministry is more about them than it is about the listener. As church members explain to those who criticize their efforts: "Listen to God. If you are one of His elect, you'll hear."[135]

4

Though the rhetoric of Westboro Baptist Church is offensive, antigay rhetoric circulated by the Religious Right and its sympathizers similarly focuses on the threat of homosexuality to gay people and the nation, the punishment of God as a response to gay sex, and the "unnaturalness" of same-sex attraction. For example, readers might find it difficult to distinguish among the famous speakers of the following quotations.

- "If God does not then punish America [if same-sex marriage is legalized], He will have to apologize to Sodom and Gomorrah."[1]
- "Like Adolf Hitler, who overran his European neighbors, those who favor homosexual marriage are determined to make it legal, regardless of the democratic processes that stands in their way."[2]
- "Homosexuals are now more than non-productive 'sexual bums.' They are recruiting others, forming communities, beginning to mock and undermine the old pieties of loyalty to family, country, and God. They have redefined 'good' and 'evil' and view with contempt the idea that honest work and sex within marriage are communal acts necessary for human survival."[3]
- "I don't think I'd be waving those [gay pride] flags in God's face if I were you. This is not a message of

hate—this is a message of redemption. But a condition like [gay-friendly events] will bring about the destruction of your nation. It'll bring about terrorist bombs; it'll bring earthquakes, tornadoes, and possibly a meteor."[4]

· "I've never seen a man in my life I wanted to marry. And I'm gonna be blunt and plain, if one ever looks at me like that I'm gonna kill him and tell God he died. In case anybody doesn't know, God calls it an abomination. It's an abomination! It's an abomination!"[5]

· "I figured a way out, a way to get rid of all the lesbians and queers but I couldn't get it pass [sic] the Congress—build a great big large fence, 50 or a hundred mile long. Put all the lesbians in there, fly over and drop some food. Do the same thing with the queers and the homosexuals. And have that fence electrified so they can't get out. And you know what? In a few years they will die out. You know why? They can't reproduce."[6]

· "Turn to Leviticus 20:12, because I actually discovered the cure for AIDs. . . . Everybody's talking about having an AIDS-free world by 2020. . . . Look, we can have an AIDS-free world by Christmas. . . . Because if you executed the homos like God recommends, you wouldn't have all this AIDS running rampant."[7]

Surprisingly, none of these quotations come from a member of Westboro Baptist Church. Instead, all are from leaders in the Religious Right, leaders who share an antigay theology but have power far beyond Fred Phelps's. The first speaker, John Hagee, pastor of the San Antonio megachurch Cornerstone Church and author of several books about the end of the world, was an outspoken supporter of Republican political candidates. The second speaker is Dr. James Dobson, Christian psychologist and former head of Focus on the Family, whose media empire produces radio shows, religious curricula, and volumes of "profamily" literature. The third is Paul Cameron, antigay psychologist and founder of the Family Research Institute. The fourth is Pat Robertson. The fifth statement was spoken by Jimmy Swaggart during a 2004 telecast of a sermon; a week later he offered a halfhearted apology "if anyone was offended."[8]

The sixth statement was made by Charles Worley, a North Carolina pastor of an independent Baptist church, shortly after President Barack Obama announced his support of same-sex marriage and North Carolina voters passed a state constitutional amendment defining marriage as between one man and one woman. The final statement is from the pastor of Faithful Word Baptist Church of Tempe, Arizona, a relatively small congregation with an extensive online presence, including, by its accounts, more than ten million downloads of church materials, which have been translated into eighty-five languages.[9] Although none of them include the word "fags," these comments, all made in public, reveal antigay sentiment that dehumanizes gay people; posits same-sex sexuality as sinful, unnatural, and deviant; caricaturizes gay citizens as enemies of the state; and predicts the justified destruction of gay people and the societies that accept them. Nonetheless, these speakers would denounce the rhetoric and activism of Westboro Baptist Church.

Though Westboro Baptist Church is commonly dismissed as a fringe group that is not representative of American Christianity, the overlap in religious rhetoric and political goals between it and members of the Religious Right is noteworthy and places the Religious Right in the uncomfortable position of defending antigay theology and politics while repudiating its affinities with Westboro Baptist Church. The Religious Right has deployed multiple strategies to distance itself from Westboro Baptist Church. Its goal is to use Westboro Baptist Church as a foil to construct itself as compassionate to gay people but critical of gay sex. In other words, by characterizing Westboro Baptists as "haters," the Religious Right can recalibrate the scale of homophobia so that its own homophobia is seen as moderate—as, indeed, compassion rather than hate. At the same time, "the emergence of more militant actors may lead to the redefinition of existing spokespersons and organizations as *more* radical than previously thought."[10] Westboro Baptist Church's fringe behavior, then, serves Religious Right goals even as the Religious Right denounces the church. In addition, Westboro Baptist Church antigay activism serves to keep alive antigay sentiment and gives potentially "loose cannons" in the Religious Right a place to voice their antigay sentiment in abrasive ways.

ANTIGAY THEOLOGY OF WESTBORO BAPTIST CHURCH
VERSUS ANTIGAY THEOLOGY OF THE RELIGIOUS RIGHT

The theological differences between Westboro Baptist Church and the Religious Right should not be understated, especially given the importance of theology to Westboro Baptist Church's self-understanding. Westboro Baptists strongly identify with the hyper-Calvinism that distinguishes them from other Christian groups and view their theology as a reason why any alliance between their church and other churches will fail. In particular, those who preach "lying Arminian bilge," which is "buckets of warm spit"[11] to hyper-Calvinist Westboro Baptists, cannot cooperate with Westboro Baptist Church because Westboro's belief in double and absolute predestination offends their notion of self-determination. "Arminian will-worshippers will go to Hell rather than suffer reproach for the cause of God and Truth in the world," Fred Phelps noted in his March 28, 2010, sermon.[12] However, they cannot be blamed for their failure to understand the beautiful justice and mercy of Calvinism, for, "as to the non-Elect, they have no light because a sovereign God has never commanded the light to shine upon them, but has chosen to leave them in gross darkness."[13]

Because Arminians believe that people can change through their own volition and that sexually active gay people, like all people, are agents in their own salvation, they are less likely to preach about hell and are thus, ultimately, less loving toward gay people, argue Westboro Baptists. According to Westboro Baptist Church, cooperation among Arminians and hyper-Calvinists is thus unlikely because, although they may both despise homosexuality, their differing beliefs about people's ability to change drive them to seek different responses from their audiences. Compounding this theological difference is Westboro Baptist Church's fierce independence. As Fred Phelps noted, "It's supremely, supremely irrelevant to us what anybody thinks or says,"[14] and as the church's main web site, God Hates Fags, notes, church members lose "0 nanoseconds of sleep . . . over your opinions and feeeeelllllliiiiiings." Given that perspective, Westboro Baptist Church will not allow any outside group to determine its goals or strategies, so cooperation is impossible. On the rare occasion when it has partnered with an outside group—as when Westboro Baptists visited the

University of Florida to picket area churches and a Jewish student center in April 2010, and members of the Gainesville, Florida, Dove World Christian Outreach picketed alongside them[15]—Westboro Baptist Church sets the agenda.

The Religious Right addresses Westboro Baptist Church theology delicately—for the Religious Right includes Calvinists. Thus, the Religious Right cannot renounce the doctrine of predestination and other theological tenets embraced by some of its members, including Orthodox Presbyterians, those in the Dutch Reformed tradition, and many Baptists. Further, it cannot renege on its conclusion that unrepentant gay people go to hell, for to do so would mean to reject the beliefs that same-sex intercourse is a sin or that God does not allow unrepentant sinners into heaven, and these beliefs are justifications for antigay politics and prejudices and evangelism. In sum, members of the Religious Right are in the delicate position of defending their antigay politics and belief in the damnation of gay people without being confused with Westboro Baptists.

The Religious Right does this, first, by renouncing the claim that "God hates fags" and claiming instead that God does not hate anyone. In this view, God hates sin but loves sinners. This position, which is frequently repeated by Christian counterprotesters, dismisses the hyper-Calvinist claim that God both actively damns and elects people, and the corollary that God in fact loves everyone is a criticism of limited atonement, the claim that Jesus's sacrificial death was intended only for the elect. When "God doesn't hate people" and "God loves everyone" are stated by opponents of Westboro Baptist Church, both claims are an expression of a theological position and a distancing of the religious believer from Westboro Baptist Church's homophobia. "There is a reason why Christian conservative leaders now proscribe the phrase, *God hates* in public discourse regardless of its object," notes Cynthia Burack. "Such beliefs are common bases of religious discourse, but they are not—or not yet—successful bases for political arguments in liberal democracies."[16] Moreover, they offend Christians who prefer to think of themselves as believers in and representatives of a loving and kind God, even if this God does, ultimately, send people to hell. For example, conservative Christian counterprotesters interviewed for this research never expressed the idea that being gay or engaging in same-sex activity was acceptable to God. Instead, conservative Christian opponents of Westboro Baptist Church consistently claim that God loves all people, *even sinners such as gay people*—which is sufficient theological grounds for fighting against gay rights.[17] Despite theological differences, then, conservative Christians and Westboro Baptists emerge at the same political conclusion, which is not surprising considering the strong evidence that "measures of a specific religious belief (Biblical literalism) and image of God (wrathful) are both significant predictors of intolerance toward *all* groups"[18] and willingness to "deny free expression to groups which they believe are unreceptive of God's guidance."[19] In part because "engaged and judgmental images of God are significantly related to conservative religious beliefs, increased religious involvement, and attitudes supporting a closer connection between religion and the state," the Religious Right and Westboro Baptist Church might be expected to be natural allies in the fight against gay rights.[20]

However, despite areas of political agreement, conservative Protestant Arminian theology is mocked by Westboro Baptists; for example, Fred Phelps said, in his rejection of those who counter his message of God's hatred by insisting that God loves everyone, "Don't stand there on the street corner with me when you know you've never cracked a Bible in your life."[21] Conservative Christian counterprotesters respond by insisting that God distinguishes between people, whom he loves, and their sin, which he hates. By positioning itself, like God, as not anti–gay people but only anti–gay sex (which is a form of sin in this view), the Religious Right thus uses Westboro Baptist Church as a foil to deflect criticisms of its own antigay sentiments and politics. In contrast to Westboro Baptist Church's message that homosexuality is a punishment from God, the Religious Right emphasizes choice in sexuality (as in salvation) so that it can ultimately blame the unrepentant gay person for being gay.

Cynthia Burack and Jyl J. Josephson have noted that the Religious Right provides two different "origin stories" about homosexuality. By emphasizing that sexual identity and sexual behavior are separate and that, even if queer people cannot choose their orientation, they can choose their behavior, the narrative of choice "neutralizes both queer claims of discrimination and public support for legal remedies,"[22] for, as Jean Hardesty concludes, when "gay sexuality is a choice . . . it is not a candidate for civil rights protections."[23] Didi Herman detects a contradiction in the claim that gender is intrinsic, natural, and essential (though the production of so many Christian gender manuals/how-to books suggests that conservative believers think it can and should be taught—and perhaps needs to be taught![24]) but that sexuality is not.[25] The narrative of choice may generate little sympathy for gay folks because it blames them for the suffering that the Religious Right imagines they must endure due to their lack of sexual fulfillment and the peace of mind that comes from living in accordance with the will of God, and the consequent lack of compassion may serve to maintain an image of gay people as deliberately ignoring, mocking, or destroying straight culture. "Always unstable in its political effects, compassion can undermine the message that homosexuals are unregenerately evil corruptors of society and manipulators of a democratic political system," Burack and Josephson observe.[26] For this reason, the narrative of choice is deployed when gay men and women are being depicted as a threat.

In contrast, the narrative of development views gay people less as deliberate corruptors of straight culture than as victims in it. In this view, emphasis is on "the continuity and force of same-sex desire over time in certain individuals."[27] Like the narrative of choice, it aims to repudiate immutability and thus undermine civil rights claims but also to assure parents that hope for emerging queer kids is warranted and to justify antigay education efforts. According to Burack and Josephson, the narrative of development rests on three claims: (1) homosexuality is an emotional response to damaged parent-child relations, including the failure of a parent to model appropriate gender behavior, the failure of the child to mirror this behavior, and the failure of the parent to notice a child's nonconformity, all of which may implicate even parents who follow relatively traditional gender roles; (2) an absent same-sex parent, especially a father, creates an environment more likely to produce sexual and gender confusion; and (3) sexual and other trauma contributes to the likelihood of same-sex desire. In the narrative of development, "although the onset of same-sex desire does not sentence individuals to a life of homosexuality, predispositions and homosexual desires are not easily reversed once they are formed."[28] Fortunately for parents, says this model, "pre-homosexuals" can opt to avoid scenarios and habits that could cement same-sex attraction and thus "further entrench their dysfunctional sexual identities."[29] Like the narrative of choice, the narrative of development has political implications, but, also like the narrative of choice, it may also be sincerely held, and, notably, it may "disrupt other forms of Christian Right political work"[30] because it does not find fault in would-be gays but instead seeks compassion for them, calling not for stoning them or casting out their demons but for viewing their sexuality as a problem to be overcome, like other personal problems of a developmental nature.

Westboro Baptist Church's view of homosexuality, as explained in chapter 2, falls into neither category. As absolute and double predestinarians, Westboro Baptists do not believe that homosexuality is a choice, for nothing is a choice. Instead, homosexuality is a punishment, a sign of God's "giving up" of a person to his or her own sinful nature. At the same time, gay people are a threat to a society and its national future, not merely or primarily because of the "scientific" consequences of homosexuality (such as the disease and family breakdown that Religious Right groups cite) but because God will destroy a nation that protects gay people. America completed the process of becoming God's enemy with *Lawrence v. Texas*, which overturned state laws against same-sex sex acts. When the legalization of gay sex was codified into law, America became "a nation that does not forge its laws at statues upon God"[31] and so invited God's destruction. What happens to such a nation? Psalm 9:17 says, "The wicked shall be turned into hell, and all the nations that forget God." That is, God will intervene to punish "both the individuals responsible for forging a godless policy but also those who follow it."[32] In the Westboro Baptist perspective, gay people are not to be treated with compassionate condescension but with strong—and offensive—words of rebuke; even worse for the nation than queer people, though, are those who support them, the "fag pimps" and "fag enablers," in the words of the church, who have permitted the legalization of same-sex sexual contact. The result is that Westboro Baptist Church is seen (and strategically constructed as) a hateful church or even a hate group,[33] whereas the Religious Right touts itself as loving. "Compassion can work to shore up support for 'mainstream' antigay initiatives by

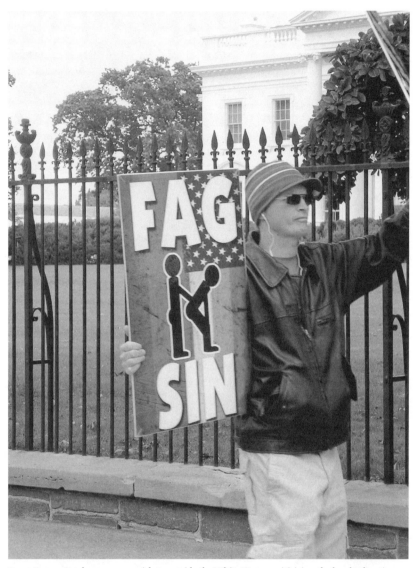

Brent Roper, October 4, 2010, pickets outside the White House, criticizing the legal toleration of same-sex sex acts by the government as sin. (Photograph by Rebecca Barrett-Fox. All rights reserved.)

Abigail Phelps seeks some relief from the heat while picketing in Topeka on a hot July day.
(Photograph courtesy of Ailecia Ruscin. All rights reserved.)

assuaging the suspicion that these programs are driven by group-related bias or defended by arguments that are pretexts for bias," note Josephson and Burack.[34] Westboro Baptist Church's hyper-Calvinism, especially the double predestination of all people and the absolute predestination of all things, seems cruel in comparison with the "compassion" of the Religious Right's depiction of gay people as victims, even if both believe that unrepentant gay people go to hell in the end. The Religious Right thus uses "compassion" to "'center' cultural and political actors"[35] and escape the criticism that faces Westboro Baptist Church.

## ANTIGAY POLITICAL GOALS: WESTBORO BAPTIST CHURCH VERSUS THE RELIGIOUS RIGHT

According to Marty E. Martin and R. Scott Appleby, religious fundamentalists show special concern for how "the intimate zones of life are ordered."[36] The Religious Right organizes across the boundaries of traditional faith categories to include Protestants, Catholics, Mormons, and Jews around concerns about the perceived threats of modern notions about sexuality, gender, and reproduction, among other issues organized under the topic of "family." Within the context of American culture, these concerns are expressed in "a secular religion which teaches that the particularities of one's nation are not the result of history, but are rooted somehow in the eternal nature of things."[37] For both the Religious Right and Westboro Baptist Church, increasing tolerance of homosexuality in American culture is linked to national decline, both sociologically and spiritually. Contemporary political issues are addressed in relation to a perceived national slide into sin. "Certainly Westboro Baptist Church is in the minority when it brandishes placards such as 'God Hates America' or 'Thank God for 9/11,'" observes Michael Cobb, "but the anger it feels toward nearly the entire world emanates from the permissiveness and sinfulness of a nation that does not hate fags enough."[38] For example, in 2010, shortly after an explosion at a British Petroleum Deepwater Horizon drilling rig began to send nearly five million gallons of oil into water off the coast of Louisiana, Tony Perkins of the Family Research Council said,

America is in deep trouble. Consider the following:

> Environmental disaster of epic proportion in the Gulf of Mexico
> Economic struggles with unemployment at nearly 10%
> Protracted bloody wars in Iraq and Afghanistan
> Political leadership bent on promoting what God forbids

Ignoring the role that the Family Research Council played in electing public officials who fight against environmental and banking regulation and oversight and who pushed for and continually supported military engagement in foreign nations, Perkins blamed national problems—including the Obama administration's alleged support for gay rights—on the failure of Americans to be properly moral. He did this, though, without explicitly saying that the tragedies he listed are a direct punishment from God. In language that neither claims nor denies that God uses environmental disaster, economic trouble, war, or political leadership to correct or punish a nation, Perkins claimed, "We are a broken nation full of broken people who have broken God's laws and God's heart. Consequently, in these difficult days, the Lord has continued to impress upon me the greatest need for us, as followers of Jesus Christ, to take responsibility for the broken state of our nation and go to God for help because He is the only one who can help us."[39] But, for Perkins, merely asking God for help is insufficient. The nation needs to demonstrate ("to take responsibility"), via political change, that it is no longer breaking God's laws and heart, for how else "can we possibly expect God to continue blessing this nation?"[40]

Westboro Baptist Church looks at the same evidence—oil spills, economic downturns, wars, and the Obama administration—and makes the claim that Perkins never explicitly states: that such troubles are the direct hand of God, rebuking a nation to seek God but questioning the nation's sincerity in doing so. For example, Louisiana Senate Resolution 145 urged residents of Louisiana to pray on June 10, 2010, for a solution to the problem of what would soon become the world's largest oil leak. In announcing that resolution, state senator Robert Adley noted, "Thus far, the efforts made by mortals to try to solve the crisis have been to no avail. It's clearly time for a miracle for us."[41] For Westboro Baptists, the belated call for prayer—unaccompanied by a call to repentance and a pursuant changing of American culture—*after* human efforts have failed is symptomatic of American arrogance toward God.[42] In Adley's call for prayer, as with Louisiana governor Bobby Jindal's call, the people do not seek God first, do not repent, and do not change. Instead, God is invoked when all else fails and is sought without any sense of remorse or desire or intent to change. God does not even *hear* a prayer like that, emphasizes Shirley Phelps-Roper.[43]

Although Westboro Baptists and members of the Religious Right both call for a return to godly living and the imposition of law allegedly derived from biblical standards, Westboro Baptists have little hope that such a change will occur. This was not always the case. In the 1990s, when Fred Phelps ran in the Democratic primary for governor of Kansas, he called for a coalition of like-minded Republicans and Democrats to advance what is basically a Religious Right agenda. In his 1990 campaign, he sought a "Coalition of Righteousness" of voters who supported "zero tolerance for abortions"; the right to keep and bear arms; the "death penalty for *all* premeditated murders"; "zero tolerance for crime," with caning as a potential punishment for offenders; lawful prayer and Bible reading in public schools and a voucher system to support students in private religious schools, "zero tolerance for tax hikes, budget hikes, and waste"; and "no same sex marriages and zero tolerance for AIDS." Of special note is his early opposition to same-sex marriage and his linking of the tolerance of homosexuality and the decline of national prosperity. For example, in a press release explaining his views, he said, "The sanctity of holy matrimony shall not lie dead on the plains of Kansas. AIDS will inevitably bankrupt this state and nation unless humane quarantining of the guilty AIDS spreaders is begun,"[44] and "So long as criminal sodomy . . . or any crime is winked at there is no moral authority to control violent crime or any other crime."[45] Here, as in the Religious Right, gay people ("guilty AIDS spreaders") are constructed as a national threat, and, as in Tony Perkins's argument, the state's tolerance of queer people undermines its ability to protect its (nonqueer) citizens.

The political goals of Westboro Baptist Church and the Religious Right are thus not that different—and, as the above planks in the "Coalition of Righteousness" indicate, not merely in the regulation of sexuality. Both want marriage to be defined as one man and one woman, though the

Religious Right is far more tolerant of divorce among its members and leaders than is Westboro Baptist Church. The Religious Right saw *Lawrence v. Texas*, which decriminalized sodomy, as the government's abdication of its role as a hegemonizing force for heterosexuality, as did Westboro Baptist Church. Both groups oppose openly gay politicians.[46] Though Westboro Baptist Church openly calls for capital punishment for sodomy and the Religious Right does not, members of the Religious Right have been implicated in the promotion of such policies in nations such as Uganda, where the citizenry will possibly tolerate them.[47] Further, the Religious Right does not univocally oppose the death penalty for same-sex contact.[48]

In sum, the Religious Right and Westboro Baptist Church both legally oppose advancing gay rights, marriage between same-sex partners, the acceptance of openly gay members of the armed forces, and the legalization of same-sex contact. Culturally, they both warn against the normalization of queerness or the acceptance of gay subcultures. Theologically, they both believe that unrepentant gay people go to hell, though one believes, generally, that a loving God who grants free will sends them (or at least allows them to self-select) and the other believes that a just God has damned them there since before the start of time. These two groups, though, cannot work together for their shared political goals, despite the fact that the Religious Right includes a number of theologically diverse believers and could likely tolerate the hyper-Calvinism of Westboro Baptist Church. Two blocks prevent cooperation: (1) Westboro Baptist Church's explicit linking of national sin to national tragedy, a link that the Religious Right makes only tentatively and only when aimed at particular kinds of sins (homosexuality but not, for example, divorce or corporate dishonesty) and particular kinds of tragedy (hurricanes that destroy majority-black cities and nations, not war deaths of American soldiers), and (2) differences in strategy.

## RELIGIOUS RIGHT AND WESTBORO BAPTIST CHURCH STRATEGIES

Westboro Baptist Church began its antigay activism in the early 1990s, a time when the Religious Right was shifting its antigay rhetoric from biblical to social-scientific arguments that claim that same-sex sexuality is dangerous for the common good. Rather than attacking gay people individually for their sexuality, the Religious Right now focuses on particular sites of potential gay rights advancement—like the end of Don't Ask, Don't Tell or the legal recognition of same-sex marriage—and explains why acceptance of gay rights in those areas is bad for the entire society, including gay citizens, who, if they do not renounce their sexuality, harm themselves just as they harm the nation.

In contrast, Westboro Baptist Church deliberately deploys explicit images and rhetoric that will be perceived by its audiences—especially individuals grieving the loss of a loved one or communities reeling from a disaster—as hateful. Though Westboro Baptist Church's theology is more complicated than "God hates fags," the church has not been effective in preaching its message that Westboro Baptists believe that they, in fact, love gay people. Members of the Religious Right and members of Westboro Baptist Church both claim to love gay people, but only the Religious Right has effectively used compassion politics to project the idea that it, like God, loves gay people but hates homosexuality. Westboro Baptist Church, on the other hand, in promulgating an image of God as hateful, does not make clear that its members do not share the emotion that they assign to God. Of course, for individual gay people, such a difference may not matter much. However, for the broader public, the Religious Right has more effectively constructed its antigay activism, from support of "gay conversion" groups such as the now-defunct Exodus International[49] to anti–gay rights legislation, as a compassionate response to a sin that God hates.

In affirming religious conservatives as compassionate, the Religious Right retains a respectability that Westboro Baptist Church lacks. The Religious Right is thus able to seek influence over politicians, frequently by mobilizing its grassroots forces to contact political representatives and leaders. Members create policy documents and legal briefs as well as primary research aimed at filling in the facts the Religious Right uses in those documents and briefs. It publishes newsletters, magazines, and Sunday school curricula, and it broadcasts television and radio programs aimed at persuading readers and listeners to adopt and enact a particular political stance, expressed in voting choices but also in the public sphere. In contrast, Westboro Baptist Church no longer expects to be politically persuasive. Its goal is to "help" people articulate their own "acceptance" of homosexuality; thus, "by their words they will be condemned."[50] For this reason, members do not engage politicians or the political process with any real hope of changing the political landscape (even when they have run in elections) but instead engage people at scenes where their message is likely to gain a wide audience and where their shocking words and images are likely to provoke a response. The meaningful difference between the Religious Right and Westboro Baptist Church, then, is not in their theologies (though this prevents Westboro Baptist Church from cooperating with other groups) or political goals but in the way in which they share their message with the greater public.

## THE RELIGIOUS RIGHT'S RESPONSE TO WESTBORO BAPTIST CHURCH'S ANTIGAY ACTIVISM

The Religious Right claims no relation with Westboro Baptist Church. Rejections of the church can be outright dismissals that Westboro Baptist Church is Christian or a church at all. For example, when asked if Fred Phelps "give[s] the Christian right a bad name,"[51] Jerry Falwell denied that Fred Phelps had the power to do so, saying:

> Fred Phelps does not give the religious right a bad name, because nobody claims kin to that guy. He's a certified nut. He's got papers to prove it—he doesn't, he should. Anybody who goes to a funeral of a little boy who's dead, and his parents are looking at a big placard Fred Phelps puts up saying "Matt is in hell," is either mean as the devil or a nutcase. Either way, he doesn't represent anybody credible.[52]

At the same time that he recognized Fred Phelps's power to hurt Judy and Dennis Shepard and other parents of deceased gay people, Falwell did not recognize or acknowledge his own role in creating an atmosphere in which gay people are devalued. Thus, Falwell is correct in saying that "nobody claims kin to that guy"—but just because Falwell does not "claim kin" does not mean that he is unrelated.

Here, Falwell is performing a common tactic of the Religious Right in regard to Westboro Baptist Church: preaching a theology that results in the damnation of gay people (for Falwell never said that Fred Phelps's claim was false, only that declaring it on a placard at a funeral is mean or crazy) and working against gay rights while denying any similarity to Westboro Baptist Church. This strategy is especially important to Baptists, such as Falwell, because they share with Westboro Baptist Church the name Baptist. "New School" Baptist churches (that is, non–Primitive Baptist churches) have overwhelmingly distanced themselves from Westboro Baptist Church without espousing support for gay rights or gay people.[53] For example, Dwayne Hastings, the Southern Baptist Convention's director of communications for the religious-liberty commission, says, "The slogans that Fred Phelps and his group are promoting are unscriptural and very inappropriate. . . . Southern Baptists stand on the word of God in believing that homosexuality is wrong and that, as the Bible says, it's an abomination to God."[54] He distinguishes his own group from Westboro simply by saying that Westboro Baptist Church is "unscriptural" while Southern Baptists "stand on the word of God"—that is, one is more authentically Christian than the other. At times, other mainstream Baptist churches such as the Southern Baptist Convention or American Baptists simply drop the word "Baptist" from reporting about Westboro Baptist Church, as if to deny Westboro Baptist Church its historical or theological ties to their denomination.

Not surprisingly, Primitive Baptist churches do not like being categorized with Westboro Baptist Church. Elder David Montgomery, writing on behalf of Primitive Baptist Online, says,

PB-Online and the Primitive Baptist Church do not recognize the ministry of "pastor" Fred Phelps, nor do we have fellowship with the Westboro Baptist Church of Topeka, Kansas, which styles itself as an Old School (or Primitive) Baptist Church. We find the actions of these people to be deplorable and against the very Scriptures they claim to believe. Let it be firmly noted that the Primitive Baptists do not and will not endorse, condone, or support the base actions of this group.[55]

Like other Christian detractors of Westboro Baptist Church, Elder Montgomery uses quotation marks to indicate that Fred Phelps is not a real pastor, and he uses the words "styles itself" to suggest that Westboro Baptist Church has usurped the name "Old School" or "Primitive" and does not properly deserve it. No scriptural evidence is provided for these claims—an oddity in a denomination that answers nearly every question with a biblical citation. Elder Montgomery's declaration seems defensive rather than informative, for it provides no explanation of the difference between Westboro theology and the theology of the Primitive Baptist churches for whom Elder Montgomery claims to speak—itself a problem since Primitive Baptist congregations are independent of each other.

Elder Ben Winslett, writing a socially and politically conservative blog from Huntsville, Alabama, similarly attempts to speak on behalf of Primitive Baptists, identifying himself as a fourth-generation Primitive Baptist with "Primitive Baptists in my genealogy in both sides since my ancestors stepped foot on 'The New World'" and as the pastor of Alabama's oldest Primitive Baptist congregation, host of a Primitive Baptist radio program, and webmaster of a Primitive Baptist web site. After he establishes his credentials to speak on behalf of Primitive Baptists, Winslett stresses, "Please take it from me, that **Primitive Baptists have no fellowship or association with Fred Phelps.** He is no Primitive Baptist Elder. He has taken it upon himself to use our name. . . . Westboro Baptist 'Church' is a **counterfeit** Primitive Baptist group."[56] Elder Winslett, like Elder Montgomery, and like other Christians who fear being painted with the same brush as Westboro Baptist Church, denies fellowship with Westboro Baptist Church, denies that Fred Phelps has a claim to a designation as a church leader, uses quotation marks to indicate that Westboro Baptist Church is not a real church, uses boldface to stress the outsider status of Westboro Baptist Church, and complains that Westboro Baptist Church is unfairly using the name "Primitive Baptist."

The frustration of Elders Montgomery and Winslett is clear and shared by many other Primitive Baptists. "Our sentiment has been universal," says Winslett, "coast to coast." "Every time this group is publicized in the media, our people cringe. . . . We do not want to be associated in the minds of Americans with Westboro or their heinous antics," he complains;

indeed, repeated requests for insight into the distinctions between Primitive Baptist churches and Westboro Baptist Church from leaders such as the webmasters, pastors, and the archivist at the Primitive Baptist Library in Carthage, Missouri, were met with either a curt refusal or silence. Like Elders Montgomery and Winslett, they did not want to explain how authentic Primitive Baptists differ from the "counterfeit" Westboro Baptist Church. Winslett notes only that "our order of faith does not condone the actions of Phelps. In fact, we DETEST his behavior."[57] Undoubtedly, Primitive Baptists do detest Westboro Baptist Church's protests at the funerals of fallen soldiers and sites of national tragedy, even if they agree in whole or in part with Westboro Baptist Church's view on sexuality. For example, in 1993, shortly after the start of Westboro's picketing, the publisher of the *Primitive Baptist Newsletter*, pastor W. H. Cayce, commented, "Lord knows there's something that needs to be done [about homosexuality], but personally I wouldn't think that adding to anyone's grief or sorrow at a funeral would be the right approach."[58] In other words, funeral protests are an ineffective approach to a real problem for other Primitive Baptists. What is most interesting about Primitive Baptists' denial of Westboro Baptist Church's claim to be Primitive Baptist is that they foreground Westboro Baptist Church's behavior at funerals rather than articulating a much simpler theological objection: Fred Phelps was not baptized by a Primitive Baptist, and so, in the Primitive Baptist vision of apostolic succession, any church he plants or people he baptized are not Primitive Baptist. The choice to focus, instead, on Westboro Baptist Church's funeral picketing suggests that the negative media attention, not the church's theology, causes the lack of fellowship.

Indeed, the claim that the Primitive Baptist faith does not "condone" the actions of Westboro Baptist Church is complex. Certainly, many Primitive Baptist churches are both absolute predestinarians and double predestinarians, so they would agree with Westboro Baptist Church's claims that all actions are foreordained by God and that those in hell are there because God selected them to be there. In their admiration of Puritan writers and theologians, many Primitive Baptists would agree that preachers can preach on the themes of the eternal damnation of the nonelect and the undeserved eternal salvation of the elect. In their own sermons, they quote from people, such as Jonathan Edwards, who preached earthly punishment for sin. What they may dislike, then, is Westboro Baptist Church's choice to make this theology public in justifying the practices that have brought it such notoriety. That is, other Primitive Baptists likely believe that Matthew Shepard is in hell, but they are unlikely to show up at his funeral. They likely believe that God punishes a nation for its sexual sins, but they are unlikely to see that punishment in the form of military deaths and even less likely to show up at a military funeral to say so.

Winslett ends his letter this way: "True Primitive Baptists love the Lord and love His people. We believe in the salvation of sinners by Sovereign Grace. We worship in a simple, New Testament pattern. We are in no way related to or like Westboro 'Church.'" Again, Winslett emphasizes the difference between "true" Primitive Baptists and the "counterfeit" Westboro Baptist Church. However, in defining Primitive Baptists as people who "love the Lord and love His people"; believe in salvation by sovereign grace; and worship in a simple, New Testament pattern, Winslett fails to distinguish his vision of Primitive Baptists from that of Westboro Baptist Church. Like Winslett, Westboro Baptists claim to love God and to love "His people"—language that reveals that both Winslett and Westboro Baptists believe that Christian love is reserved for one's fellow elect, not for the broader world. Both believe in salvation by sovereign grace—that is, the doctrine of unconditional election. Both claim to adhere to a New Testament model of worship, though, admittedly, Westboro, unlike many Primitive Baptist groups, uses musical accompaniment and prepared notes for preaching. However, Winslett's claim that the two churches are unrelated does not rest on those differences.[59] Even Winslett's declaration that "We have no fellowship or association with them" is not particularly meaningful, considering how fractured fellowship is among Primitive Baptists. Thus, Winslett's denunciation that Westboro Baptists "do not represent mainstream Primitive Baptists in any sense, *period*" rings rather untrue.[60]

The Primitive Baptist responses to Westboro Baptist Church are indicative of the broader response of the Christian community, which seldom denounces the antigay sentiments or even the predestination theology of the church. Rather, other Primitive Baptists appear uncomfortable sharing any label—"Primitive Baptist," "Baptist," or even "Church"—with West-boro congregants because of the church's funeral pickets, especially pick-ets at the funerals of soldiers and those who have died in national tragedies. Similarly, other Baptist churches are quick to note that Westboro Baptists are not "real" Baptists, and non-Baptist Christians remind their audi-ences that Westboro Baptists are not "real" Christians. The issue is not merely one of being tainted by association with Westboro Baptist Church in the eyes of the broader culture, either. Westboro Baptist Church uses offensive language and images and exploits media to draw attention to its message. The general impression to those who know Westboro Baptist Church only through its public activism is that it is loud, offensive, and self-promoting. These qualities do more than alienate the broader public. For those seeking evidence of Westboro Baptists' spirituality, it suggests that church members are cruel and self-righteous. Evidence of this atti-tude may be the cause for other Primitive Baptists' suspicions about West-boro Baptist Church, despite their theological similarities.

However, because Westboro Baptist Church self-identifies as a Primi-tive Baptist Church; because it shares with other Primitive Baptists a vision of itself embracing an antiestablishment, anti–infant baptism Puri-tanism; and because its doctrines, organization, and discipline are identi-cal to at least some Primitive Baptist churches' doctrines, organization, and discipline, the descriptor "Primitive Baptist," which is how Westboro Baptists speak about themselves, is sociologically appropriate, even if it causes other Primitive Baptists to cringe. In its public activism—and in the cruelty that other Primitive Baptists see in that activism—Westboro Baptist Church is quite different from other Primitive Baptist churches, and, in that difference, it angers them and brings them public scrutiny that they do not desire.

In an open letter addressed to all Primitive Baptist churches, dated De-cember 10, 2009, Westboro Baptist Church takes an urgent tone in asking "Are There Any Candlesticks Left among the Primitive Baptist?"—refer-ring to the church's opinion that Primitive Baptists have "hid their light under a bushel." "This letter," Westboro Baptists write, "is meant to pro-voke you unto love and to good works (Heb. 10:24) and to exhort you with longsuffering and doctrine (2 Timothy 4:2)."[61] Repeatedly in the letter, the church reminds the broader world of Primitive Baptists that they share much in common, including, for example, Calvin's five points and "the tenets of the Bible (also known as the doctrines of the Old School Baptists and Primitive Baptists)." In contrast to Elder Winslett, who denies any relationship between Westboro Baptist Church and other Primitive Baptists, Westboro Baptists identify their identical theological positions. The letter invokes shared heroes, including Primitive Baptist writer Gilbert Beebe, again highlighting a similarity. After asking Primitive Baptist churches twenty-seven questions aimed at proving whether they are acting in accordance with the special role God has given them, the letter ends "with great news!" Readers are reminded that they still have time to join in Westboro Baptist Church's efforts, for, as stated in the parable of the workers in Matthew 20, "The reward for those that only worked one hour is the exact same as them that worked 12 hours and bore the heat of the day!" Again, in this way, Westboro Baptists are identifying a common mission with Primitive Baptists and thus underscoring the legitimacy of their inclusion in the Primitive Baptist tradition.[62]

As other antigay churches, including those most theologically similar to Westboro Baptist Church, struggle to distinguish themselves from Westboro Baptist Church by denying its claims to authenticity, Christians outside the Religious Right—including mainstream and progressive Christians—face less of a struggle to be distinct since they do not adopt outright antigay theology or seek antigay policies. Indeed, the earliest counterprotesters were other Christians, recall Westboro Baptists. As early as 1993, when the church had already articulated its narrow focus on homosexuality but had not yet picketed at many cultural events or at the funerals of straight people, a group of Topeka clergy signed a declaration "in response to the Environment of Hatred and Violence." None of the dozens of signatories were representatives of theologically conservative churches in the city.[63]

The Religious Right's hesitation to denounce Westboro Baptist Church early in its antigay ministry reflects the agreement between Religious Right and Westboro Baptist Church theology and politics. Soulforce, an organization working to increase acceptance of sexual minorities among Christians, has illustrated these similarities in "Southern Baptists May

Not Say 'God Hates Fags' as Fred Phelps Does but the Effect Is the Same," a presentation that places official statements from the Southern Baptist Convention and prominent Southern Baptists next to statements by Fred Phelps.[64] Like the quotations that opened this chapter, they are difficult to distinguish, but Southern Baptists—like others in the Religious Right— seem unable or unwilling to hear how their own antigay theology, along with the social-scientific evidence they present about the danger of be- ing gay, drives their antigay politics and echoes that of Westboro Baptist Church, even if their posture is more pleasant, their graphics less graphic, and their words more tactful. This respectability, though it gives the Reli- gious Right greater access to the public than Westboro Baptist Church, is criticized by Westboro Baptist Church, which argues that other religious leaders have traded in their prophetic voice for access to power.

## CONCLUSION

The nuances of Westboro Baptist Church's theology of sexuality would matter little to the Religious Right, which adopts a "big tent" philoso- phy that accepts theological difference for the sake of political expedi- ency, if Westboro Baptist Church was willing to adopt Religious Right tactics—in other words, to come into the tent. However, Westboro Bap- tist Church refuses to wear the "mask of compassion" that characterizes the "repackage[ed]" Religious Right's antigay movement.[65] It refuses to exchange Bible-based arguments against homosexuality for the respect- ability of social science or to temper its language. Members of Westboro Baptist Church keep their focus on theology, but, note Carin Robinson and Clyde Wilcox, "doctrinal talk is bad politics,"[66] so they make little headway toward the goals they share with the broader Religious Right. Westboro Baptist Church is ostracized by the Religious Right not because of its theology, which the Religious Right could tolerate, or its antigay politics, which the two share (for there is "something about homopho- bia that arouses a deep religious fervor"[67]), but because of Westboro Baptist Church's refusal to adhere to the Religious Right's tactics. Like anti-Catholic tract writer Jack Chick, whose work has been dropped from many Christian bookstores because it is too divisive, Fred Phelps is "an old-school Christian in a focus group world."[68] However, Westboro Baptist Church's message of a hyper-Calvinist God who uses national tragedy to rebuke a nation for individual and collective sin has deep roots in American religious history, and Westboro Baptists pride themselves on their place in this tradition.

Many used to preach "as I am preaching," reminisced Fred Phelps, but "they're gone!"[69] And this is true. Just as Calvinist Puritans of the seventeenth and eighteenth centuries and Westboro Baptists of today share a belief in predestination that links individual and community tragedy to sin, the Religious Right has shared with Westboro Baptist Church a tendency to dehumanize gay people and describe same-sex contact as "loathsome" and "detestable" and gay people as a threat to themselves and the nation. Individual actors within the Religious Right continue to use this language, as the quotations at the start of this chapter reveal, even as the Religious Right as a movement has adopted social-scientific arguments against homosexuality in order to avoid appearing prejudiced. Over the last two decades, then, Westboro Baptist Church's rhetoric did not change, even as members are aware that their approach puts them at risk of "being seen as an uninformed person, Neanderthalic, and less evolved in your thinking,"[70] but the Religious Right's official rhetoric changed to *sound more* compassionate, even if the old prejudices against same-sex sexuality remain. The failure of new preachers to rise up to preach the old message of personal and national destruction as a consequence of sin only reinforces Westboro Baptist Church's perception of itself as the only remaining authentic voice of Christianity. This criticism of other churches is sharpened by the perception that many Religious Right leaders falsely claim compassion; Westboro Baptists, like many suspicious of the Religious Right's intentions, sense the hypocrisy.

Despite the Religious Right's disavowal of Westboro Baptist Church and Westboro Baptist Church's disdain for the "kissy pooh" theology[71] of the "softer, gentler gay bashing" of the Religious Right,[72] the two groups contribute to an atmosphere that is hostile to gay people and gay rights, even as both deny that they foment violence.[73] Westboro Baptist Church keeps alive so-called Bible-based arguments against homosexuality, giving the Religious Right room to agitate politically without fear of association with Westboro Baptist Church. Indeed, antigay activists can affirm their own "compassion" by opposing Westboro Baptist Church without backtracking on their support for anti–gay rights policies. Or, as Soulforce concludes in its comparison of the Religious Right and Westboro Baptist Church, "the effect is the same."[74]

5

As argued previously, the Religious Right shares antigay
sentiments with Westboro Baptist Church but expresses
these sentiments in terms that are more palatable to an
American public that is antigay but does not want to appear
intolerant of social diversity and finds the graphic and confrontational tactics of Westboro Baptist Church offensive.
Thus, the Religious Right distances itself from Westboro
Baptist Church in public statements, even as it advocates antigay policies and as both groups share the claim that God
will stop blessing (or is destroying) America for its sexual
sins. In his study of Christian Patriot groups in Idaho, *The
Politics of Righteousness*, James A. Aho writes,

> The story line is familiar. America has a covenant with the
> Lord. If she remains faithful to its edicts, as expressed in
> the Constitution and the biblical lawbooks, she shall be
> favored. Her crops shall be plentiful, her people well-fed,
> prolific, and happy, her children obedient to the voice of
> their parents. But now she has faltered in her obligations
> and her cities lie corrupt, her waters and air are befouled,
> and wantonness, crime, and dissolution follow her peo-
> ple everywhere.[1]

In religious fundamentalist belief, "outside of the biblically
revealed way, everyone is doomed to eternal damnation, and
societies are doomed to chaos."[2]

American churches have long encouraged the connection between individual and collective sin and national doom, a theological coalescence of the state of the church and the state of the state. In early America, churches "contributed to the construction of a religious nationalism that provided the new nation with a sacred canopy under which it could develop its own characteristic national style. . . . In turn, the nation itself provided the churches with a symbol of unity and wholeness that they could not generate out of their own resources."[3] America became perhaps the most religious secular state in the modern world. A hegemonic Christianity—Protestant in orientation but generic in its theological details—saw America as uniquely blessed by God. Because "God's world is pure, not pluralistic,"[4] those who threaten this vision of a sacred America worthy of God's blessings represent threats to national prosperity and security.

To many, this pessimistic narrative turns upon the sexual sins of the people. Because appropriate sexual expression is narrowly defined as monogamous, lifelong, and heterosexual and idealized as procreative—that is, heteronormative—those who express sexuality outside those parameters invite God's punishment upon a nation. Impurity, in the form of deviation from heteronormativity, threatens to undo the blessings God has already provided, stop God from further blessing the nation, or even prompt God's destruction of the nation.

A Christianity that declares that God blesses America and that this blessing is contingent upon heteronormative behavior will thus be antigay in defense of its nationalism. Its antigay theology will be an effort to protect the nation from the withdrawal of God's blessing or the provocation of God's wrathful punishment. This religious justification of heteronormativity in defense of nationalism inspires members of the Religious Right to fight, sometimes quite cruelly, any public policy that recognizes the dignity of same-sex desire, not merely or even primarily because of the social consequences of such policies but because of the supernatural consequences.[5] Sociologist Ruth Murray Brown neatly summarized the optimism that informs Religious Right activism by titling one of the chapters of her impressive study on the Religious Right "Saved People Can Save the Country."[6] Here, "save the country" means to ensure not only the country's continued functioning but its continued blessing by God: it is both materially and spiritually saved. Americans could "get the blessing of God back on it [the nation] rather than his curse" if they just stopped sinning.[7]

The Religious Right therefore views homosexuality as one of the foremost threats to the state. Indeed, religious conservatives have a duty to fight against "homosexual activism" because such activism is itself a threat to liberty. Advances in gay rights threaten the ability of believers "to practice their religious beliefs—including their religiously-based moral convictions about God's will concerning the nature of marriage and human sexuality."[8] Such fears fueled much of the Religious Right's argument against the legal recognition of same-sex marriage as opponents of same-sex marriage held up instances of caterers, florists, and photographers who faced legal trouble for refusing to serve same-sex couples as evidence of religious bias; indeed, warns the American Family Association's Bryan Fischer, "every single advance of the homosexual lobby comes at the expense of religious liberty."[9] Likewise, facing the legal recognition of same-sex marriages, signees of the Manhattan Declaration pledged not to "bend to any rule purporting to force us to bless immoral sexual partnerships, treat them as marriages or the equivalent, or refrain from proclaiming the truth, as we know it, about morality and immorality and marriage and the family."[10] Promising civil disobedience if the law requires them to recognize same-sex unions, the signees envision themselves as heroes defending religious liberty. Similarly, objections to antibullying programs in public schools have focused on Christian students' right to speak frankly about their objections to homosexuality, and supporters of such programs are depicted in the Religious Right as threatening free speech.[11]

Because religious liberty is one of the nation's founding principles, by depicting gay rights as antithetical to and undermining religious liberty, members of the Religious Right can describe homosexuality as anti-American. "People who favor gay rights face no penalty for speaking their views, but can inflict a risk of litigation, investigation, and formal and informal career penalties on others whose views they dislike," complains "traditional marriage" defender Maggie Gallagher.[12] Timothy J. Dailey encourages believers "who feel that their right of religious freedom and expression under the Constitution has been denied" to "seek redress." In this mind-set, believers must band together to fight the tyranny of gay rights. Says Dailey, "By doing so, you may also help to protect others who are facing or will face similar situations by establishing legal precedent for the protection of such rights."[13] Gay rights advocates are thus constructed as enemies not only of heterosexuality but of freedom.

Further, homosexuality is a threat to the state because it invites outside threats from both other nations and God. For example, the presence of openly gay soldiers in the US armed forces would lead to national insecurity, grimly predicted Tony Perkins of the Family Research Council in the days leading up to the repeal of Don't Ask, Don't Tell (DADT): "If open homosexuals are allowed to serve, it will break our all-volunteer force, dangerously weaken the military's war-fighting ability, and put national security and our country's future at risk."[14]

In the Religious Right's imagined post-DADT future, gay servicemen and -women are threats to their peers, who are the unwanted objects of their lusts. Discipline within the ranks will disintegrate as gays and lesbians use their sexuality to curry favor with higher-ranked officers. Lovers will prioritize each other over the straight members of their fighting units, endangering straight troops. Ten percent of current military members will not reenlist, forcing conscription. Drafted troops, pressured by gay superiors into unwanted sex and betrayed by gay peers who care only for each other, will be unable to win wars.[15] Gay soldiers will infect their straight comrades with HIV during battle. "If open homosexuals are allowed into the United States military, the Taliban won't need to plant dirty needles to infect our soldiers with HIV. Our own soldiers will take care of that for them," warned Bryan Fischer of the American Family Association, referring to claims in British newspapers that the Taliban was attempting to build bombs that contained dirty needles. Indeed, the interests of gay citizens are depicted not merely as irrelevant to American security but as in opposition to American security and tradition, which is why Fischer titled his article "Gay Sex = Domestic Terrorism."[16] Once gay people serve openly in the military, the nation will be insecure and thus open to attack. Asked Perkins, rallying his supporters to pressure legislators to defend DADT, "It comes down to this: Whose flag will fly over the US military? The flag of our Founding Fathers? Or the rainbow flag of the homosexual rights movement? Now is the time to fight for the red, white, and blue—for God, for country, for those who serve, for our families, and for our future."[17] On one side stand Washington, Jefferson, Madison, and the other (assuredly heterosexual) men who founded the nation, defending God, country, the military, families, and "our future." On the other side, in defiance of God, are gay rights activists: unpatriotic, subversive, and antifamily.

Self-centered gay people, complains Cliff Kincaid of America's Survival, a Religious Right group, do not care about the troops or national security:

> They want their "rights" and they want them now. They simply don't care if a premature policy change causes thousands of our soldiers to leave the Armed Forces in disgust and dismay and thousands more never to sign up because they don't want to room or shower with individuals sexually attracted to them. . . . Our troops have become cannon fodder in the gay rights campaign to force their views and acceptance on the rest of us. The rights of gays are now supposed to take precedence over our soldiers' lives.[18]

Homosexual sex is a national security threat, both because God has previously destroyed entire communities—à la Sodom and Gomorrah—for the sin of homosexuality and because the social consequences of homosexuality are disease, disorder, the destruction of heterosexual marriage, and a decline in military prowess. Gay Americans, then, are not merely un-American but *anti*-American, for homosexuality, "a sin that baffles those who would be true followers of Liberty and Righteousness," seeks "to destroy the freedom and liberty of all."[19] Oklahoma state representative Sally Kern spoke for many conservative Americans in 2008 when she warned that "no society that has totally embraced homosexuality has lasted . . . more than a few decades. So it's the death knell in this country."[20] For this reason, gay sexuality is not merely a private issue but a collective social concern for all patriotic Americans who want to see their nation continue to exist.

Saving the country from this threat means "transforming American culture in ways that are consistent with the [Religious Right's] conception of sexuality and sexual immorality," explains Cynthia Burack, while "in eschatological terms, turning God's wrath away from an America that is perceived to court divine judgment with every cultural and political shift."[21] Thus, Westboro Baptist Church's linking of homosexuality and military death is consistent with the tradition within the Religious Right that generally links homosexuality and national doom. Westboro Baptists believe that America, as represented by its legal system but also by its culture, has given approval to homosexuality and is thus being collectively punished by God. This is precisely the threat that the Religious Right invokes in its effort to contest gay rights. Unlike the Religious Right, Westboro Baptists do not subscribe to the notion that God cares in particular about America, but they do believe that God uses tragedy, including military deaths, to capture the attention of, rebuke, and punish an entire nation, including those who are elect. This logic actually has a long history in American religious rhetoric, even if it has not been asserted so blatantly as Westboro Baptist Church states it. "*Fundamentalist movements are organized efforts to shape the future of a people in the light of a past that is seen through the lens of . . . authorities traditionally available in the culture,*" notes Nancy T. Ammerman.[22] Westboro Baptist Church taps into a latent fear of same-sex sexual desire and thus gay people as threats to the national future, a fear "available in the culture" in large part thanks to the work of Religious Right antigay activists who keep such fear circulating.

Under close analysis, then, the Religious Right agrees with the message that Westboro Baptist Church preaches at military funerals or other scenes of national tragedy or during moments of national mourning: that, because America does not collectively condemn homosexuality, soldiers die. Westboro Baptists preach at funerals, explains the church, "to remind you that we warned you"[23] in advance that military deaths result from a nation's failure to obey God. Westboro Baptists, like all believers, they argue, have a "non-delegable duty . . . to warn your neighbors that their proud sins are bringing their destruction upon themselves (harbingers of that national and then eternal destruction are your individual dead soldiers)."[24] Westboro Baptist Church's double predestination, though, means that the church declares that God is actively destroying America, whereas many in the Religious Right think of God as merely removing "the veil of protection which has allowed no one to attack America on our soil since 1812," as Jerry Falwell noted about the attacks of September 11, 2001.[25] In its outline, Westboro Baptists' message is markedly similar to the message of Religious Right pastors and politicians. America, the New Jerusalem, the New Israel, like the historical Israel, has turned away from God: "[Americans] rapidly descended into irreversible apostasy; and, with no holy pattern to keep their spirits and doctrines in paths of righteousness, cunningly devised fables and darkest heresy completely took over. They must be nationally punished—so must America—for an example unto them that after should live ungodly."[26]

For Westboro Baptists, the death of service members is not a surprise but a fitting and logical response from an angry God who demands holiness from individuals and the nation. Every service member killed in battle was reared in a culture that despised God, says Tim Phelps, and, still, Americans have not humbled themselves before God and repented:

> You taught him that God was joking about all those sins, when he said you were going to pay for them. Well, now you know better. He cut that child [a deceased soldier] down before the child's life began. And here you are, railing against God for his hand of judgment, when what you should be doing is getting down on your knees and thanking him that he hasn't killed you yet. There's no hope for that kid. He's in hell.[27]

"You did this," Tim Phelps states baldly, blaming America for the death of its service members. "We warned you. You punished us for warning you . . . and now you're paying the price."[28]

Westboro Baptists complicate the relationship between sexual sin and national doom in one unique way: viewing themselves as prophets for contemporary America, they see public response to them as the same as public response to God, as Tim Phelps suggests when he says that America is "paying the price" for punishing Westboro Baptist Church. God sent Westboro Baptists to preach against America's sexual sin, and when America responds by ignoring or opposing the church, America will pay—through civilian deaths in crimes and accidents and through military deaths. Former member Sara Phelps explicitly cited attacks on Westboro Baptist Church in the 1990s, when, as described on the church's web site, an area man was found guilty of setting off a "4- to 6 inch 'explosive device' made of a one inch PVC pipe that was detonated with a fuse,"[29] as the source of God's choice to use IEDs to kill American soldiers and marines: "Ten years ago, the fags set off an IED at our church, and it says in the Bible, [the] Lord says, 'Vengeance is mine; I shall repay.' Ten years later, do you think it's a coincidence that American soldiers are getting blown up by IEDs? . . . When you start messing with the servants of the Most High God, God is going to kick your ass, period."[30] From this perspective, when bad things happen—when vengeance occurs—it is God repaying America for its sins. Indeed, says Fred Phelps, "it's no surprise to me that God's picking off these miserable brats." The logic is clear: because America attacked Westboro Baptist Church, God is using the same weapon—IEDs—to attack America. Indeed, killing American soldiers is God's chosen way of punishing America precisely because it strikes at Americans' hopefulness about their future, their children, and their security:

> You can't hardly imagine a more fitting way to severely punish a people than to begin to blow the cream of their young manhood and woman-hood to smithereens in Iraq, and the forum, the venue to preach that, is the funeral of some soldier, some young American soldier who's been blown to smithereens by an IED. It's as though the Lord God said, "You raised him for the devil and hell [and] I'm giving him back to you in a bodybag. You partook as part of that evil nation that set off a bomb, an IED, at my servant's church. That is not a minor matter."[31]

Westboro Baptist Church's vision of itself as the lone remnant of the true apostolic church on earth enables it to see itself as central in God's interaction with the world. At the same time, the belief that God has a special purpose and thus ensures the success of that mission is held by many religious leaders beyond Westboro Baptist Church. The difference between them and Westboro Baptist Church's confidence that God protects it from its enemies is that Westboro Baptists define their enemies not as liberal politicians, atheists, or others are viewed as inimical to conservative Christianity but as America itself, embodied in its soldiers. Targeting the military dead as enemies is perceived as simply too uncivil—in the sense of both *rude* and a threat to *American civilization*—for the Religious Right, as for many Americans, to tolerate.

CIVIL LIBERTY VERSUS CIVILITY

Pickets at military funerals and at the scenes of national tragedy have sparked the greatest outrage from opponents of Westboro Baptist Church. As Justice Ruth Bader Ginsberg asked during Margie Phelps's oral arguments in *Snyder v. Phelps*, "Why should the First Amendment tolerate exploiting this bereaved family when you have so many other forums for getting across your message?"[32] To the general public, criticism of the dead at the moment of their death or while they are being mourned is reprehensible. However, Westboro Baptist Church argues that its message is precisely most potentially valuable to its audience at that moment, for when people are emotionally vulnerable, they are more open to hearing the truth of God.[33]

*Snyder v. Phelps* illustrates the tension around military funeral pickets. In early March 2006, Matthew Snyder, a US Marine from York, Pennsylvania, was killed when he was ejected from a Humvee in a non-combat-related accident during a resupply mission, Operation Mighty Oak, in Iraq. According to the marines' account of the incident, the driver of Snyder's Humvee was out of formation at the time of the accident, ignored orders to fall back into formation, and was driving excessively fast. No one in the vehicle was wearing a seat belt, even though seat-belt use is stressed as a safety protocol. When the Humvee hit some potholes, the driver lost control of the vehicle, and Snyder, who was riding as gunner, was declared dead at the scene.[34] His body was returned for burial, and a funeral was held on March 10, 2006, at St. John's Catholic Church in Westminster, Maryland. Westboro Baptist Church picketed at a distance of 1,000 feet from the funeral site, holding signs that said, "Thank God for Dead Soldiers" and "Semper Fi Fags." Picketers were present prior to the funeral but left the site before the funeral began. At the time, Maryland had no laws limiting funeral pickets, and one passed in 2006 requires picketers to be only 100 feet from the funeral.[35] Thus, Westboro Baptists were much farther from the funeral than the law now requires, and at the time, they could legally have been as close as they liked.

The picket did not disturb the funeral service, though the funeral procession detoured to avoid potentially seeing it. As usual, Westboro Baptists did not use sound equipment to amplify their words. Though the

Margie Phelps "connects the dots" for those entering and exiting Arlington National Cemetery in 2010: because America tolerates homosexuality, God hates America and is destroying America by killing its soldiers. (Photograph by Rebecca Barrett-Fox. All rights reserved.)

tops of their signs were visible at the funeral site, the words and images were not, and Albert Snyder, the father of Matthew Snyder and the man who brought the case against Westboro Baptist Church, was not aware of the small protest at the time of the funeral. By the time the funeral started, the picketers were gone.

While watching the news that evening, Albert Snyder saw video coverage of Westboro Baptist Church's picket of his son's funeral and grew distressed. According to his lawyer, his stress contributed to worsening of his diabetes. A few months after the funeral, he completed an online search about the picket and found his way to God Hates Fags, where he read what the church terms an "epic" about his son—a kind of open letter connecting God's wrathful punishment with America's tolerance of homosexuality and other sins to Matthew Snyder's death. All of the information contained in the epic was publicly available information, some of it taken from Matthew Snyder's obituary, and thus church members had not violated Albert or Matthew Snyder's privacy by accessing it or republishing it.[36]

On June 5, 2006, Albert Snyder filed a civil claim against Westboro Baptist Church. Originally, he accused the church of committing the following torts:

- Defamation, which is the false written or spoken statement of fact that damages a person's reputation.[37]
- Intrusion on seclusion, which is defined as intentionally intruding, physically or otherwise, upon the solitude or seclusion of another or his private affairs or concerns, in a way highly offensive to a reasonable person.[38]
- Publicity given to private life, which Snyder claimed occurred through the publication of private facts, an "invasion of privacy [committed] by publishing private facts about an individual, the publication of which would be offensive to a reasonable person. Such a claim can only be successful, however, if the facts in question are not legitimately newsworthy."[39]
- Intentional infliction of emotional distress, which required Snyder to prove that defendants Fred Phelps, Shirley Phelps-Roper, and

Rebekah Phelps-Davis acted intentionally or recklessly, engaged in conduct that was extreme and outrageous, acted in ways that caused distress, or conducted themselves in ways that directly resulted in his severe emotional distress.

- Conspiracy to commit the above acts.

On October 15, 2007, the defendants' motion to dismiss the claims was granted in part. The court granted summary judgment for the Westboro Baptists on the invasion of privacy claim based on publication of private facts and the defamation claim. According to Shirley Phelps-Roper, the presiding judge noted that church members' assertion that Matthew Snyder's mother engaged in adultery was not defamation because, in contemporary America, it is simply not an insult to say that a woman slept with a man while she was married to another. This logic, stressed Shirley Phelps-Roper, was indicative of the moral decline of American law.[40] In its summary judgment, the court declared, "These comments—as extreme as they may be—they are taken in terms of religious expression. This is not the type of language that one is going to assume is meant as a statement of fact."[41] These words would become important later, when a group of state attorneys general supporting Snyder protested in an amicus brief that this logic would encourage the *most* outrageous statements, for the more extreme the words are—that is, the less likely they are to be understood as fact—the more protected they are.[42]

The summary judgment left the jury to consider only two charges, intrusion upon seclusion and the intentional infliction of emotional distress, as conspiracy "piggybacks" on the other claims, so if the court found church members to be liable for the first two torts, then the church members would also be found to have acted in a conspiracy to commit them. Further, only the first two torts were ones that could be remedied through monetary damages. The jury trial lasted from October 22 to October 31, 2007, and, in the end, the jury awarded Snyder $2.9 million in compensatory damages, $6 million in punitive damages for invasion of privacy, and $2 million for the intentional infliction of emotional distress.[43] On February 4, 2008, the judge reduced the punitive damages to $2.1 million, thus reducing the total award from $10.9 million to $5 million, suggesting a legal awareness that an appellate court, which would surely hear the case, would hesitate to use civil torts to limit free speech. Indeed, the Fourth Circuit Court of Appeals reversed the ruling entirely on September 24, 2008, and, to the outrage of many, required that Snyder pay Westboro Baptist Church's legal fees. In reversing the decision, the majority opinion wrote,

> Notwithstanding the distasteful and repugnant nature of the words being challenged in these proceedings, we are constrained to conclude that the Defendants' signs and Epic are constitutionally protected. To paraphrase our distinguished colleague Judge Hall, judges defending the Constitution "must sometimes share [their] foxhole with scoundrels of every sort, but to abandon the post because of the poor company is to sell freedom cheaply. It is a fair summary of history to say that the safeguards of liberty have often been forged in controversies involving not very nice people."44

Westboro Baptists agreed, noting in a post–Supreme Court blog, "That First Amendment is there for THAT speech—the speech that nobody wants to hear."45

Though the Fourth Circuit Court of Appeal's decision would neither stop future funeral pickets nor satisfy the public's desire to punish Westboro Baptist Church, legal experts were in increasingly frustrated agreement that, under the facts of this case, Westboro Baptist Church was probably in the legal, though certainly not moral, right. Indeed, many began to worry that, should the decision be heard by the Supreme Court, the rights of free speech, peaceable assembly, and freedom of religion would be under review. The Supreme Court agreed to hear the case in March 2010, and, on October 6, 2010, both sides appeared before the Court.

Many filing amicus briefs in the case expressed ambivalence. Fourteen amicus briefs were filed, with five supporting Snyder's side, six supporting Westboro Baptist Church's position, and three supporting neither side. Every brief, regardless of the legal position it supported, expressed empathy for Albert Snyder and appreciation for his son's sacrifice and condemned Westboro Baptist Church's actions. Though focusing on different aspects of the case, all of the briefs that supported Westboro Baptist Church's position drew attention to the potentially chilling effects that a

decision against the church would have on free speech.[46] Those supporting Snyder stressed the "sacrosanct" nature of funerals[47] and the outra-
geousness of church members' conduct, calling it "an affront of the most
egregious kind."[48] An amicus brief filed by the state of Kansas, home state
of the church, supported by forty-seven other states and the District of
Columbia, argued, "Traditions as old as humanity, much older than our
Constitution, demand such privacy; the First Amendment does not abro-
gate all history and cultural norms to protect the Phelpses' unprecedented
tactics."[49] The brief by the attorneys general contends that the sacred nature of funerals predates the Constitution and that the unthinkable act of
funeral pickets cannot upset that, despite the First Amendment.[50] This
amicus brief ignores the fact that it was Snyder who sought to silence religious speech because of its content; to silence Westboro Baptist Church
based on the content of its argument *would* be a violation of First Amendment rights. Indeed, the Supreme Court justices agreed in an 8-1 decision, with Justice Alito dissenting and Justice Breyer offering a concurring
opinion seeking a wider rule. Wrote Chief Justice Roberts,

> The "content" of Westboro's signs plainly relates to broad issues of
> interest to society at large, rather than matters of "purely private con-
> cern." . . . While these messages may fall short of refined social or po-
> litical commentary, the issues they highlight—the political and moral
> conduct of the United States and its citizens, the fate of our Nation,
> homosexuality in the military, and scandals involving the Catholic
> clergy—are matters of public import.

Further, he noted, any limitations on free speech around the scene of
a funeral would necessarily have to limit messages of support for the
mourners or be applied inconsistently. "A group of parishioners standing at the very spot where Westboro stood, holding signs that said 'God
Bless America' and 'God Loves You,' would not have been subjected to
liability. It was what Westboro said that exposed it to tort damages," he
commented.[51] Indeed, the thousands of counterpicketers who have appeared to provide an alternative message at funeral scenes, holding signs
just like the ones Justice Roberts imagined, have never been the subject of
legal action. What Westboro Baptist sought—and won—in *Snyder* was a

defense not only of its legal right to picket near funerals but a broader defense of free speech. Julie Francis, mother of Matthew Snyder and ex-wife of Albert Snyder, said so in an editorial printed in the *Baltimore Sun* a few days after the Supreme Court announced its ruling in favor of Westboro Baptist Church:

> I truly believe this is an issue of free speech. I do not like it, and I do not like the WBC, but it is free speech. . . . I am glad free speech has prevailed. It's been a tough road because it can be misconstrued by those who don't know me and think that I support those vile people. That has never been the case. I love my son: As a Marine, Matt was entrusted with defending and protecting our rights, our liberties, our Constitution. . . . I am glad the Supreme Court has ruled with the law, with the nation, with the Constitution. In America, you cannot take away the right of free speech, no matter how vile. I do believe our blessed Matt would feel the same way.[52]

Or, as Joshua Lawrence, founder of the Primitive Baptist tradition, said, "The price of this inestimable jewel, civil and religious liberty, was the price of blood."[53]

Expressing the majority opinion of the court, Chief Justice Roberts agreed that the protection of free speech best aligns with our national ideals:

> Speech is powerful. It can stir people to action, move them to tears of both joy and sorrow, and—as it did here—inflict great pain. On the facts before us, we cannot react to that pain by punishing the speaker. As a Nation we have chosen a different course—to protect even hurtful speech on public issues to ensure that we do not stifle public debate. That choice requires that we shield Westboro from tort liability for its picketing in this case.[54]

In contrast, Westboro Baptists themselves have been injured and their property damaged in the exercise of their right to preach this message. For example, when church members picketed in response to the deaths of twenty-nine miners from an explosion at the Upper Big Branch Mine in Montcoal, West Virginia, Shirley Phelps-Roper's hair was set on fire by a cigarette and she was spat upon, an action that resulted in an arrest for assault but a not-guilty verdict.[55] In another instance, a Nebraska man attacked church members with bear repellent at a church picket in Omaha, harming no church members but injuring sixteen others, including a police officer, and sending some to the hospital.[56] On November 15, 2010, two tires on the van that church members drove to a picket of a military funeral in McAlester, Oklahoma, were slashed during the picket, and no automotive shop in town would perform repairs.[57] On November 25, 2010, church members were attacked at a soldier's funeral in Harrisonville, Missouri, though police quickly regained control of the situation, which included hundreds of counterprotesters, many of whom surrounded the van carrying Westboro Baptists.[58] At the June 6, 2015, funeral of Beau Biden, Delaware politician and son of Vice President Joe Biden, a passerby threw hot coffee at church members, resulting in his arrest.[59] Despite claims that they have no right to picket and despite vigilante efforts to make them stop, Westboro Baptists continue their activism, viewing themselves primarily as religious activists but also as First Amendment defenders.[60]

Westboro Baptists care deeply about the First Amendment. In part this may reflect the legal training of many church members and the subsequent commitment of Phelps-Chartered to generally progressive legal causes, including criminal defense and work on behalf of racial minorities and indigenous people as well as women and children. In addition, the absolute predestination theology of the church dismisses "free will" and "free choice," so church members are encouraged to think of the freedom of religion not as a choice but as a duty. Fortunately, they say, God has given them the First Amendment to ensure that they can perform this duty: "The Lord God of Eternity set up this constitutional republic in its infancy knowing that when this nation would no longer endure sound scriptural doctrine, His servants on the ground were going to need certain tools in place to allow them to fulfill their duty to Him and to their fellow man."[61] In this view, God not only approves of the message of the church but provides the means for its delivery.

Westboro Baptist Church critics frequently suggest limiting freedoms of religion and speech in exchange for greater civility—or, more specifically, to silence this particular group of religious believers. For example, at a September 11, 2010, protest of the church's US flag and Koran burning, one protester who came to the event to show her displeasure with the destruction of a US flag declared that "if they have the right to burn the flag," which they do, provided they are doing so as part of an otherwise legal and peaceable protest, "then maybe we have too many constitutional rights."[62] Another protester, the father of a US Army soldier serving at the time in Afghanistan, agreed, saying that destroying the US flag is "treason," and church members should be punished accordingly.[63] Such sentiment is widespread. For example, Julie Banderas, host of Fox News Channel's *The Big Story*, lost her temper during an on-air exchange with Shirley Phelps-Roper on June 10, 2006, saying after a heated exchange, "These people should be arrested, and I understand the right to protest, but when you disgrace not only our fallen soldiers, but when you disgrace innocent young children, I swear. Lock 'em up. Throw away the key. Give 'em the death penalty. I think it's disgusting."[64] Here, Banderas intersperses her anger at Westboro Baptists' incivility ("I think it's disgusting") with legal judgments ("Lock 'em up. Throw away the key. Give 'em the death penalty") that are appropriate for criminal actions, even though Westboro Baptists did not break the law. Indeed, in the case of Matthew Snyder's funeral, church members were so attentive to the spirit of the law that they exceeded the letter of it, staying 1,000 feet away from the site of a *future* funeral (since they were not present during the actual funeral) when there was no law against any kind of funeral picketing in Maryland at the time.

Banderas, like many of the counterpicketers and other Westboro Baptist Church opponents interviewed for this research, expresses, at least in the heat of an argument, a willingness to see civil liberties curtailed in order to silence disagreeable opinion that is unpleasantly expressed. Nevertheless, she is unlikely to see herself—especially because she is a journalist—as advocating censorship. Kathleen C. Boone sees this contradiction repeatedly among religious fundamentalists: "Well-worn maxims of American culture—to each his own, everyone is entitled to his own opinion, don't tread on me—our fierce defense of individualism and personal freedoms seems to fall almost completely by the wayside in the fundamentalist world. Even more curiously, fundamentalists espouse Americanist sentiments without awareness of the contradiction."[65]

Banderas's tirade occurred in the midst of an argument with Shirley Phelps-Roper about military funeral pickets. Banderas sees herself as defending fallen servicemen and -women, but she does not see her willingness to use imprisonment or capital punishment to silence criticism of military deaths as antithetical to democracy or free speech. Though neither Banderas nor all counterprotesters who would withdraw Westboro Baptist Church's First Amendment rights are fundamentalist religious believers or claim to be patriots, the policy they espouse would threaten the Constitution to which they also claim to be committed. As Jonathan Phelps accused a counterprotester at an event at the University of Kansas's Lied Center, "You hate the Constitution"—a comment that further angered the man, a veteran.[66]

Indeed, church members characterize critics who would silence the church purely because of the content of its message as inconsistent hypocrites. "What about the First Amendment?" Fred Phelps asked an imaginary critic during a 2010 sermon as the church prepared to continue its court battle. "'To hell with the First Amendment!'" his imagined critic yells back.[67] This, clearly, is a reason for Westboro Baptists to mistrust the general public and state and federal lawmakers who would revoke their right to speak because of the content of their words.

Courts have been more careful than members of the public in protecting free speech, freedom of religion, and the freedom to peaceably assemble. In July 2010, US District Judge Richard G. Kopf reminded Westboro Baptist Church opponents that the church's destruction or disrespectful use of an American flag, even at a military funeral, is protected speech and cannot be cause for arrest. Asked Judge Kopf of those government officials involved in Shirley Phelps-Roper's arrest for flag desecration at a military funeral in Nebraska, "Recognizing your duty of candor to the tribunal, and following *Johnson* and *Eichman* [1989 and 1990 Supreme Court cases that had already established the legality of flag desecration], am I not bound to restrain future enforcement of the Nebraska flag statute at least as applied to the plaintiff and members of her church so long as they otherwise act peacefully while desecrating the American or Nebraska flag during their religiously motivated protests?"[68] The frustration that Judge Kopf expressed in this memo was likely a result of both the ugliness of the church's behavior and the failure of Nebraska's legal system to adhere to laws that guarantee free speech regardless of content.[69] As the officers and lawyers who arrested and prosecuted Shirley Phelps-Roper ought to have known, the arrest was unwarranted and would possibly result in a countersuit—as it did, costing Nebraska taxpayers money. Given the legal training of so many of its members, Westboro Baptists are unlikely to break the law, even as their opponents would like to create more restrictive laws to limit their ability to preach their message.

In the meantime, many opponents respond to Westboro Baptist Church with their own uncivil words and acts. Frequently opponents are baited into uncivil or even embarrassing actions by the taunts of Westboro Baptists, who have, over nearly twenty years of pickets, developed tough skins, self-calming techniques in order to avoid being goaded into fighting back illegally, and a large vocabulary of insults aimed at infuriating opponents. For example, a group of three young men, each in their late teens or early twenties, protested the church's burning of the Koran on September 11, 2010. As Shirley Phelps-Roper, carrying a sign that declared "God Hates Muslims," crossed the street outside the church in order to speak to some Muslims who were also picketing the event, one young man intervened, stepping directly in front of Shirley and standing nose to nose with her. Heaving his own sign into the air, he obstructed her path. Taking a step back, Shirley turned to her brother and said, "Jon, get a load of this lady over here."

Looking around, the young man, who had shoulder-length hair, was bewildered. There was no woman at the scene.

Shirley Phelps-Roper repeated her call to her brother, who came to the scene with a camera. At the second instance of being called a woman, the young man replied hotly, "I'm not a woman."

Shirley Phelps-Roper continued to egg him on by speaking about but not to him. "John, get a picture of the little lady with the pink shoes."

Looking down at his shoes—which were, indeed, bright pink sneakers—the young man grew furious as he recognized that she was casting doubts on his sex. "I'm a man! Look at this! I've got a cock!" Promptly he unzipped his pants and wagged his penis in front of the audience of church members, church protesters, and media. The police officer who had been patrolling the area was not present at that moment, but church members could legally have reported this young man for public indecency. Instead, they merely scoffed at him, making jokes about the size of his penis in order to further humiliate and anger him. Here, church members used a bullying tactic learned on the grade school playground—humiliating a man by calling him a woman—and the protester, who likely saw himself as an ally of both women and gay people, responded exactly as they anticipated: with his own incivility. "They're the experts" at hurtful, in-your-face confrontation, shunned son Nate Phelps noted in an interview for the documentary *Fall from Grace*, as this young man learned.[70]

Such responses are not uncommon. In this research, more than 75 percent of the comments that counterpicketers or passersby made to Westboro Baptists contained profanity; this included responses delivered at two military funerals and at the entrance of Arlington National Cemetery, where visitors are reminded by signs to maintain the dignity of the space with silence or quiet voices. Many of the oral criticisms directed at church members involved calling them "faggots," "fags," "dykes," "lesbians," "lesbos," "buttfuckers," or "cocksuckers"—all homophobic insults. These words were yelled out of car windows and shouted and spoken by passersby, and they were used among counterpicketers even when Westboro Baptists were not within earshot. It is likely that some users of homophobic insults chose these words because they assume that insults about sexuality would be most hurtful to antigay religionists. Others may have chosen them because they sincerely believe that at least some Westboro Baptists are gay and closeted. However, most epithets seemed to be spoken in moments of sheer anger, without awareness of the rhetorical purpose of those particular words, and follow-up interviews with people who used them were met with unhelpful explanations: "I said it because he's a faggot"; "She's got to be a lesbian. Look at how ugly she is." That homophobic words were so often and mindlessly chosen—for example, those words never appeared on a sign held by a counterpicketer, suggesting that those who planned what words they would say did not choose homophobic ones—indicates that such insults are latent in the culture, familiar as mean and useful in degrading others.

Similarly homophobic insults have been spray-painted on Westboro Baptist Church repeatedly. In May 2010, vandals spray-painted, among other words and images, "cunt," references to anal sex, and a 3-foot-tall penis on the garage and exterior wall of the church building. In contrast to previous instances of vandalism, the church this time resisted a city ordinance that requires the removal of public nuisances that are visible from the public right-of-way or easement. The city, recognizing the church's First Amendment right to free speech, granted the request to leave the graffiti, which the city would otherwise remove. The purpose of leaving the graffiti was to show to the community, "in as much as we've been telling this nation that they are a rebellious, good-for-nothing group," according to Shirley Phelps-Roper, that Topekans and their youth are uncivil, violent bullies.[71] In this way, Westboro Baptist Church activism reveals willingness among some of those who oppose it to use misogynistic, violent, and homophobic language. In addition to their own uncivil words and deeds, Westboro Baptists reveal an incivility and, in particular, homophobia already present in contemporary America.

The tension between civil liberties and civility has rarely been as taut as it was in Snyder v. Phelps, and efforts to suppress incivility through the courts via intimidation or vandalism are unlikely to silence Westboro Baptists. "Think you've got us scared?" Fred Phelps asked of an imaginary public in a sermon. "Wrong!" His audience of church members responded with confident laughter at their enemies.[72] Further, the curtailment of civil liberties for Westboro Baptists means limiting the civil liberties of all Americans. As University of Maryland law professor Mark Graber, in response to Snyder v. Phelps, noted, "We risk silencing the best social outcasts as well as the worst when we give juries the power to determine whether speech meets constitutional standards and allow them to award unlimited damages."[73] The result might be silence from Westboro Baptist Church, but it would also mean silencing those whose religiously motivated words made Americans horrified by slavery and Jim Crow laws. This is an unacceptable loss in a democratic society. An erosion of the wall of separation between church and state, a wall that now protects the right of Westboro Baptists to practice their unpopular religion, would give other religious fundamentalists the opportunity to define the status quo. Note

Martin E. Marty and R. Scott Appleby, "The success of fundamentalisms in reimagining the nation and remaking the state have occurred primarily if not exclusively in states in which the public-private distinction . . . has not been written into the constitution and protected by laws and judicial rulings. . . . In politics in which some form of church-state separation has been adopted, fundamentalism seems less likely to dictate the course of national self-definition."[74] In this framework, the Religious Right, which seeks to reclaim the world for God and, in doing so, to bring secular law in line with religious belief, is more of a threat to democracy, in that it would seek to continue to define the nation as "pure, not pluralist," than the world-renouncing Westboro Baptist Church, which has no hope of purifying the nation. And in that battle, the Religious Right has a powerful weapon: the Christian, heteronormative war hero.

## THE CHRISTIAN, HETERONORMATIVE WAR HERO

Westboro Baptist Church's decision to picket military funerals and attack the nation's sacred symbols—and, to a much lesser extent, members' pickets of funerals of gay people and gay cultural events—has elicited outrage and led to widespread and extraordinary efforts to curtail their civil liberties. This response is in large part because of the manner in which Westboro Baptist Church has engaged the American heteronormative religious nationalist ideal—and, perhaps, because in its engagement Westboro Baptist Church calls attention to the constructed nature of this ideal. As Benedict Anderson has argued, this ideal is epitomized in the American citizen-soldier, one who is willing "not so much to kill, as to die willingly"[75] for the nation. The nation itself is defined, in part, by fraternity, "the deep, horizontal comradeship" that gives its members "the image of their communion."[76] The citizen-soldier is a figure that affirms the masculinist, militaristic, imperialist, and heterosexist aspects of popular American Christianity[77]—aspects that have been perceived by believers as under attack for centuries.

Central to efforts to repel these perceived attacks is the citizen-soldier, both a metaphoric and literal figure for conservative Christians. Christian men who are not in the military nonetheless use militaristic language to describe their roles in the church and in their families. They are "modern-day knights," and both men and women are "prayer warriors."[78] Metaphors of military service appear throughout conservative Christian discourse, from Sunday school curricula to Christian music (from the children's song "I'm in the Lord's Army" to hymns such as "Onward, Christian Soldiers" to Christian pop). The relationship goes two ways, too, as gun manufacturers and survivalist groups appeal to Christian conservatives by means such as writing scriptural verses on assault weapons ("Blessed be the Lord my Rock, who trains my hands for war, my fingers for battle," Psalm 144:1).[79] The military has purchased gun sights with references to scriptures from Matthew, John, 2 Corinthians, and Revelation. [80]

In addition, conservative believers—men and women alike—attribute a kind of holiness to actual military servicemen (and, more reluctantly, -women) that sets them apart from civilians because they are viewed as doing God's duty.[81] Churches pray for members of the military, sponsor service members while they are abroad by sending care packages, and work to reintegrate them into civilian life when they return. Groups such as Military Ministry, an outreach of the conservative Campus Crusade for Christ, seek not only to support current Christians serving in the military but also to strategically use the structure of the military to "[transform] the nations of the world through the militaries of the world."[82] The US military, then, becomes a force for Christianizing the globe. In order to fulfill this mission, the group works to "stop the unraveling of the military family," "build Christian military leaders and influence our nation for Christ as a result," "wage Christian outreach, discipleship and training on the Internet to military members across the world," and "change continents for Christ" through the conversion and support of indigenous military leaders worldwide.[83] These goals of defending "traditional family," creating a Christian nation, and creating a Christian world align with broader Religious Right views of a "pure, not pluralist" world. The "Christianization" of the military has been a strategic goal of Religious Right groups since 9/11, argues Jeff Sharlet in his coverage of the issue for *Harper's* magazine:

What men such as these have fomented is . . . not a conspiracy but a cultural transformation, achieved gradually through promotions and prayer meetings, with personal faith replacing protocol according to the best intentions of commanders who conflate God with country. They see themselves not as subversives but as spiritual warriors— "ambassadors for Christ in uniform," according to Officers' Christian Fellowship; "government paid missionaries," according to Campus Crusade's Military Ministry.[84]

As evidenced in blogs such as *A Christian Marine's Journey*[85] and *Christian Military Wives*,[86] conservative believers within the military and their supporters view their military service as part of their larger duty to God. The overlap of Christianity and the military has come under increasing criticism, especially during a war being fought in places of historic tension between Christians and Muslims.[87]

This coalescence of military service and Christianity occurs not just among those in active duty but also in their home-front communities. Writes Tony Perkins about his military service, "Every generation of my family has served in the military," and, for him, becoming a marine was one of the most important moments of his life—"besides giving my heart to Jesus Christ and meeting and marrying my wife."[88] Here, Perkins highlights the family tradition of military service and orders it only under his faith—which centers on his born-again conversion experience—and his marriage. Religion, family, and military service—or, more precisely, born-again Christianity, heterosexual marriage, and US military service— are the top three meaningful aspects of his life.

The citizen-soldier uses his Christian belief to defend military action around the world, often by depicting national enemies as threats to Christianity.[89] The military, in turn, becomes a defender of Christianity.[90] This version of Christianity is adamantly heterosexist.[91] Liberal religious believers point out that lost amid this continued defense of Christianity, heterosexism, and nationalism at home and the promotion of Christianity, heterosexism, and American culture abroad are traditional Christian concerns for the alleviation of poverty, sickness, and suffering.[92] A civil theology that melds nationalism and religion has two negative consequences, argues Glenn T. Miller in *Religious Liberty in America: History and Prospects*: "Not only does such a perspective contribute to a national self-righteousness—as it did in the early national period—but the divine mission all too easily becomes a mundane secular goal."[93] Yet that secular goal—in this case, the reversal of gay rights advances—has been central to the culture wars from the 1970s onward and has real-life consequences for gay Americans.

Until the repeal of DADT, the citizen-soldier, whether dead or alive, was thus always constructed as straight, male, and religious—and always as a hero.[94] When President George W. Bush signed legislation limiting picketing in federal cemeteries in response to the military funeral pickets of Westboro Baptist Church, the legislation was titled "The Respect for America's Fallen Heroes Act," making clear in the title two things: first, that members of the military deserve special protection from funeral picketing—protection not available to the gay citizens targeted by Westboro Baptist Church for years—and second, that a soldier becomes a hero when he dies, no matter how he lived or how he died. For example, Pat Tillman, the former professional football player who joined the military in 2002, was killed by friendly fire, and Matthew Snyder was killed in a collision that resulted when the driver of his Humvee failed to follow orders. Albert Snyder, Matthew Snyder's father, was publicly critical of the military and the war, expressing doubt that his son's death was meaningful in securing America.[95] Regardless, in this scheme, death makes one a hero, and military service erases "class, regional, and ethnic differences and creates a 'national masculinity' embodied in the individual soldier."[96]

This notion of the fallen serviceman as the ideal citizen (male, straight and thus presumably procreative, Christian, and heroic) is, in part, why pickets of the funerals of the war dead are so offensive to Americans and, in particular, to conservative religious believers, who value straightness and Christianity so highly. When the city of Casper, Wyoming, responded to Westboro Baptist Church's promise to picket Matthew Shepard's funeral by attempting to hastily pass a law banning funeral protests, the American Center for Law and Justice (ACLJ), a conservative Christian legal defense organization, filed a brief expressing concern that such a ban would infringe upon Westboro Baptist Church's religious freedoms, saying there should be "no funeral exception to the First Amendment."[97] When, a few years later, the state of Missouri attempted to pass a similar law in response to Westboro Baptist Church's military

Bekah Phelps-Roper stomps on the American flag at an October 2010 picket at Arlington National Cemetery while a US flag, with its red and white stripes replaced with rainbow stripes, is upside down behind her. (Photograph by Rebecca Barrett-Fox. All rights reserved.)

funeral picketing, the ACLJ took the opposite position, this time filing a friend-of-the-court brief arguing against the right of Westboro Baptist Church to protest.[98] What had changed? Only the presumed sexuality of the deceased and his identity as a soldier.[99]

"No more arresting emblems of the modern culture of nationalism exist than cenotaphs and tombs of Unknown Soldiers," notes Anderson.

"Void as these tombs are of identifiable mortal remains or immortal souls, they are nonetheless saturated with ghostly national imaginings."[100] The empty tomb is meaningful because it houses the ideal of the citizen-soldier, unencumbered with factual details about the cause of death or the kind of life lived. "The Tomb's scene of interpellation can have very powerful effects, for it permits the mourning subject to transform a particular loss—real or imagined—into the general loss suffered by the nation,"[101] so all citizens grieve—and thus all citizens are harmed by funeral pickets.

Pickets at military funerals are consequently condemned as attacks on the American ideal of the straight, Christian hero who died defending the nation—regardless of whether the dead person was, in fact, straight or Christian or was actually defending the nation at the time of death. In contrast, pickets at the funerals of gay people are, if unkind or ineffective or embarrassing to those who share the names "Baptist" or "Church" with Westboro Baptist Church, defended as exercises in free speech. Scenes of military funeral pickets capture public attention in particular, Westboro Baptist Church has found, because military funeral pickets—and flag desecration—hit an emotional nerve. "We found their idol," Shirley Phelps-Roper says of military funeral pickets and flag desecration.[102] Not only do these, of all the outrageous acts the church performs, inspire the most fury, but they are also the ones that are most directly aimed at the heterosexist religious nationalism that informs the Religious Right's definition of America. Indeed, the very term "flag desecration" indicates that holiness that has been assigned to the flag. In another example, Stephen McAllister, University of Kansas law professor, solicitor general of Kansas, and coauthor of an amicus brief supporting Snyder's position before the Supreme Court, titled a presentation in support of Snyder "Is Nothing Sacred?"[103] But, in the court of law, the answer is clear: no. The state has no authority to decide which objects are sacred.

Precisely because flags and military funerals are experienced as sacred objects and sacred events by many religious believers, Westboro Baptist Church has selected these objects and events for use in the preaching of its message. Indeed, its use of these objects is ideally suited to its theological purposes of shattering idols, calling sinners' attention to their worship of "false gods," and sharing God's message of doom for the nation. Steve

Jonathan Phelps stands in front of the Supreme Court as Snyder v. Phelps is heard inside, October 5, 2010. A US flag, a POW flag, and a gay pride flag hang from his waistband. Jonathan entertained questions from the blocks-long line of court watchers who hoped to catch a glimpse of the oral arguments. (Photograph by Rebecca Barrett-Fox. All rights reserved.)

Drain explains why he drags the flag at pickets, saying, "I do it so that it can be a springboard into conversation about idolatry. . . . The fact is these people have more respect and reverence for a piece of cloth that's colored in a certain way than they do for the word of God."[104] Whether or not Drain is correct, the church's engagement with these objects and activism at military funerals has prompted the greatest public outrage.

The emotional intensity of the public response to Westboro Baptist Church's desecration of objects, symbols, and ritual events widely perceived to be sacred is made intelligible by James A. Aho's explanation that "political drama is far more trenchant than textbook recitation in instilling messages of national, cultural, and racial identity[, for] drama represents a people's legends and myths not just to the ear, but to all the senses."[105] Westboro Baptists, with their colorful signs, parodies of patriotic songs, vulgar language, and flag trampling, catch the eye and ear of all who encounter them. They engage patriotic symbols—ones made sacred by a civil theology that views America as blessed from its creation but in spiritual decay—in ways that inflame their audiences. Their actions, though, are justified by the same texts that other conservative believers use to defend and extend their own converging views of religion and patriotism. Westboro Baptists have every reason to feel confident that they are fulfilling God's mission for them: "Should we not take heart, Beloved[?] We have more than abundant evidence . . . to believe that our Father placed us upon this hill; and ordered His holy light to shine; and no power on earth or in Hell can hide that light."[106]

This is the same biblical metaphor that drove early Puritan settlers and drives contemporary Christian reformers. The hyper-Calvinism of Westboro Baptists further emboldens them, though, for a strong belief in predestination produces independent spirits. This theology "fears no man, though seated on a throne, because it fears God, the only real sovereign."[107] With God for them, Westboro Baptists fear no Supreme Court decision, physical assaults from outsiders, or the defection of their own children. In a religious narrative that announces that God rules now and will save his people, the success of the church mission is guaranteed.

Westboro Baptist Church's confidence is derived from the same source as Religious Right groups' confidence: the belief that God has a unique role for America in world history; that God wants American law and culture to follow biblical edicts, as interpreted in conservative Protestant theology; that Christians have a duty to make their culture conform to this model; and that God will bless them and give them victory in the war for America's soul. As argued in chapter 4, the Religious Right sees the fight against legalized homosexuality and gay rights as central in that war. Westboro Baptist Church, then, although it does not identify as part of the Religious Right and is indeed rejected by other Religious Right groups, is not so much distinct from the Religious Right as a fringe element of it, positioned at the most politically conservative and tactically offensive point on the antigay religious spectrum.

*The misery he had was a longing for home;*
*it had nothing to do with Jesus.*
　　Flannery O'Connor, *Wise Blood*[1]

With the death of founding pastor Fred Phelps, many hoped that Westboro Baptist Church would be dismantled, perhaps in an implosion as members fought for power; perhaps with a whimper as members realized that their beloved "Gramps" had not lived to see the return of Jesus, as they had hoped; perhaps with a relieved sigh as a family caught in the spell of a physically and psychologically abusive cult leader was finally able to escape his grip. The church's failure to fold suggests that the popular depictions of the church as dependent upon its founder were erroneous.

Indeed, the church started more than a year before Fred Phelps's death to prepare for a shift in leadership structure, moving from a single preacher/pastor to a set of elders, all men, who would preach in turn. Already serving alongside Fred Phelps in addressing the spiritual needs of the congregation, the elders now moved to the pulpit, each working to develop his preaching voice in distinction from but aligning with the leader they were losing. Around the same time, the public information officer position changed hands, with longtime spokesperson Shirley Phelps-Roper departing from that role, which was adopted by Steve Drain. Rumors

circulated that Shirley Phelps-Roper had been "deposed" from her powerful position as spokesperson as the new elder system was implemented,
but no evidence suggests that she had ever expected to step into the pulpit,
an idea that had always been unthinkable in the congregation. Instead of
leaving the position because of thwarted ambitions, she left the position
because, according to Steve Drain, she had served well and faithfully in it
and deserved a break.[2]

With the transition in leadership did come one break in the church:
some high-profile members who had been reared in the picketing church
left.

❖ Westboro Baptist church includes participants with three different sets
of memories: those present at the founding, when there was no need to
preach against homosexuality because same-sex attraction was so culturally taboo that the church and the greater public were already in accord;
those who came of age as the church rose to infamy; and those born into
a church already famous for its antigay activism. Each generation has lost
some of its members, with three of Fred Phelps's thirteen children, daughter Dorotha and sons Mark and Nate, rejecting the church as they entered
adulthood in the 1970s and 1980s and before the church began its antigay
activism and a fourth, Katherine Phelps-Griffin, and a son-in-law whose
wife remains in the church leaving since the picketing began. Of the adult
children who remain, nearly all had left the congregation at some point
prior to its turn toward antigay activism, only to return. Fred Phelps's
youngest children were in their midtwenties and his oldest grandchildren
young teens when the church began its antigay activism. Of those who
are old enough to leave, nearly twenty have gone since the start of antigay
picketing—and most have left since the start of antimilitary picketing. At
the same time, dozens more children have been born into the church, with
all those who are currently children, teens, or adults in their early twenties
having no memory of life before the pickets. Since Fred Phelps left the
pulpit, three weddings have occurred within the church and new individuals and families have joined, promising more children for the future.

Religious groups entering their second generation are vulnerable to
instability, and those on the margins of the religious landscape may be

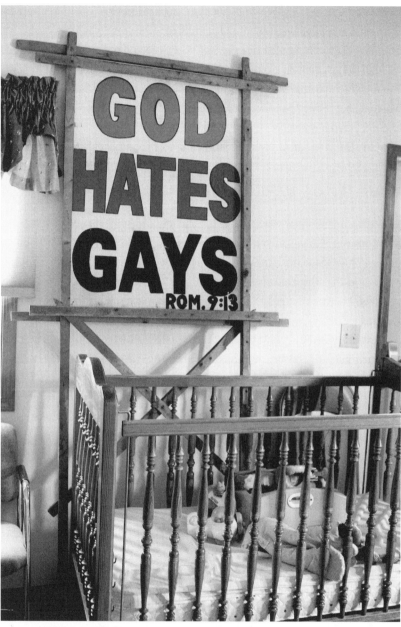

An early Westboro Baptist Church sign, from before the church had standardized its message to "God Hates Fags" or perfected its sign-making ability, decorates the wall beside the crib in the nursery. (Photograph courtesy of Ailecia Ruscin. All rights reserved.)

more susceptible to instability as power is transferred and as the first generation of people born in the group come to adulthood. Unlike their parents, they did not chose to join, having been born into the group, but such strong socialization means that unchoosing it in young adulthood, the first opportunity they may have to do so, feels impossible. Both those who go and those who stay, though, change the religion as it adapts to meet the needs of new members. In her study of coming of age in unconventional religious movements, *Perfect Children: Growing Up on the Religious Fringe*, Amanda van Eck Duymaer van Twist notes, "The birth of a second generation puts pressure on existing practices, dynamics, and resources."[3] Groups can respond by culling their membership to exclude those who disagree, refining their message to increase tension with the outside world, adapting to internal pressures that drive people out, accommodating outside influences that draw people away, revising their theology to account for the group's failures and changes, or disbanding.

Over its more than sixty years of existence, Westboro Baptist Church has used a variety of such strategies. Shortly after founding the church as an extension of East Side Baptist Church, Fred Phelps began to refine his message, relentlessly preaching against fraternal organizations, for example, in ways that drove people away. Over time, the church became more and more restrictive. For example, at its founding, women were not required to wear hair coverings during services, though they are now. When Libby Phelps-Alvarez left the group in 2009 at age twenty-five, she cited the church's new prohibition against two-piece swimwear as one motivation for her departure. The problem was not so much the prohibition itself as the fact that it evidenced the church's growing policing of church members' lives.

Indeed, since the mid-2000s, as the church began to focus on national tragedies and predict national destruction, its theology has grown more prescriptive and more hateful, the result of "extreme updates to WBC doctrine" that, says Libby, "further chipped away at my faith."[4] What church elders describe as the members' duty to watch out for each other in order to detect signs of spiritual weakness and bolster each other is described by ex-members as simply being under surveillance. For example, ex-member Megan Phelps-Roper, who left in 2013 at age twenty-seven along with her nineteen-year-old sister Grace, recalled in an interview that if a person is considering leaving, "they take your phone away, they take your computer away" so that external voices of doubt and criticism are silenced and you are under constant surveillance.[5] Megan was quick to note that this was not physical abuse—but such abuse is not necessary when church members have internalized the idea that the church speaks for God and is thus as omnipresent as God. Admits Libby, "It may sound foolish or paranoid, but I became convinced they were godlike and were somehow able to observe me at all times."[6] Megan echoes the sentiment. "We were both terrified after leaving," she reports of the feelings that she and Grace experienced. "I was afraid we were going to hell. Many times when we were driving, I thought God was going to kill us."[7] Even worse than the prospect of death was the prospect of hell. "The hottest places in hell" are for ex–church members because they know the truth but reject it.[8] The fear that he would "burn in what the Bible calls 'the Lake of Fire'" was why Zach Phelps-Roper returned to the church "not once, not twice, but four or five times (I lost count) before I finally left them forever."[9]

In addition to growing more restrictive toward members over time, the church became increasingly hateful toward outsiders. As it approached its day at the Supreme Court in 2010, the tone of its work changed. "We actually started praying for people to die," shares Libby.[10] Her cousin Zach, who left in February 2014, shared in a Reddit "Ask Me Anything" forum that "when I was at Westboro, I did pray for these people to die: President Barack Obama; Lady Gaga; Albert [Snyder, of *Snyder v. Phelps*]; George W. Bush; and many, many other people."[11] During this time, the church released an imprecatory prayer for America, beseeching God to "remember her iniquities, O LORD, for her sins have reached unto heaven!" The prayer asks, "Avenge thy servants on her O LORD GOD that we may rejoice."[12]

This focus on the this-worldly destruction of Westboro Baptist Church critics unsettled some people in the church. For Megan, who had been one of the junior leaders of the church and had pioneered much of its social media outreach, the church's increasingly constrictive theology was worrisome but hard to break free of. She recognized at one point that there was no evidence that anyone could introduce to church members that would change their minds; if you told them that you loved them, they would say that you are a liar or delusional.[13] "For the most part, it is a *tight* argument," she reflected in a 2015 interview with atheist writer Sam Harris.[14] In fact, "once you accept the premises, it's almost impossible to argue yourself out of that paradigm."[15] For her, though, the tightness also meant that if there was a chip in the wall of theology, the whole thing could crack. That chip happened in July 2012.

Megan had been corresponding with David Abitbol, the founder of a blog called *Jewlicious*, a grassroots outreach to Jewish young adults, on the issue of sexuality and forgiveness. Megan argued that gay people should be executed based on passages in Leviticus, a text shared by Christians and Jews. In response, Abitbol directed her attention to a Christian scripture—Jesus's instruction to the religious leaders of his day that the one of them without sin should "cast the first stone" in executing an adulteress. Of course, in that gospel passage, the leaders realize that all have sinned, and so they drop their stones and walk away, while Jesus tells the woman to "go and sin no more." When church members had been confronted with that text previously, as was common, they would point out that they were hurling words, not stones. But in her conversation with Abitbol, Megan realized that, by promoting the government imposition of death for same-sex sex acts, they were encouraging others to "cast the first stone." In effect, they were advocating for cutting off the opportunity for repentance. One of the women in the church had had a child out of wedlock, Abitbol noted. Wasn't the punishment for that also stoning? Megan protested that this was different from homosexuality because gay people do not repent. But, Abitbol pointed out, no one repents if you execute them.

Megan Phelps-Roper was a long way from executing someone herself, but the point was made, perhaps more so because her mother, with whom Megan was very close, had given birth to her first son, Megan's half-brother, prior to marrying Megan's father. For months, from July to November, Megan wrestled with the church's twin demands that people repent of their sins and that gay people should be executed. Church elders dismissed her concerns as getting "wrapped around the axle," caught up in theological details that could only prevent her from obeying God. She was reminded by her mother, for whom she had served as a right hand in the organization of pickets, that "the heart is deceitful above all things, and desperately wicked" (Jeremiah 17:9), so she could not trust her own judgments or interpretations of the Bible.[16] Still, she hung on, hoping, like Martin Luther, to reform the church from the inside. "We didn't want to leave; we wanted the church to be right,"[17] she shared, because for all their lives it had been right—had, even if it had been loud, at least claimed to be inspired by love. But to wish people dead before they could repent? That seemed to clash with the church's demand that repentance was a duty. By the fall of 2012 she realized "there wasn't anything else we could on the inside."[18] She consulted with Grace, and the two took steps to depart.

For Megan, who had so stridently advocated for the church's theology, and Grace, the months before they left were harder than the months after they left because they were living with doubt, not merely about what the church taught but with the thought that if the church was wrong in one area, its claim to hold the truth had to necessarily be wrong, too. The church itself had increasingly stressed that the elect would be in agreement on all things; there was no room for dissent, even over the smallest issues. There was no way for the church to move, and the tension was impossible. Megan articulated the choice she faced: "I either have to lose *everything* or go along with this thing I don't believe."[19] Living a lie was not possible for her—and her family did not want that, either, for her doubts could influence her cocongregants and would certainly make them look like hypocrites in their ministry.

For other ex-members who grew up in Westboro Baptist Church as it developed its antigay activism, the reasons for leaving were less intellectual. For some, like Libby, the feeling of personal oppression helped them to understand the pain that the church was causing others. In multiple interviews as well as in her memoir, *Banished: Surviving My Years in the Westboro Baptist Church*, Lauren Drain claims that, though she had long questioned church teachings, she was kicked out because her parents disapproved of an innocent online relationship she had with a man who had asked her some questions about the church.[20] Her parents, in contrast, accused Lauren of multiple and repeated transgressions of church teachings about cross-gender relationships, and Lauren notes in her memoir that she had previously visited a boy in his home without her parents' knowledge, a clear violation of the rules. They also claimed that she had used their credit card to purchase a plane ticket for a visit to the man whom Lauren had met online. Regardless of the exact reason for her departure, what is clear is that Lauren had, with or without warning, crossed a line and found that the church was far more involved in her personal relationships than she preferred.

Zach, Megan and Grace's brother, was suffering physically from a back injury when he recognized that he no longer wanted to be part of the church. He stresses the connection between his injury and his deconversion, but the link is still not clear, even to him. "I just know that I see things different from them now," he says.[21] Perhaps the physical pain, and certainly his professional work as a nurse in a women's prison, brought him to a greater understanding for the need for compassion for others.

Westboro Baptist Church deliberately cultivates an image of the outside world as evil. Writes Libby,

> I was warned against the outside world: again and again, in sermons and private conversations, I was told that people outside of WBC were sinners, alcoholics, drug addicts, lost souls with no moral compass. So I was terrified of what lurked beyond the protective walls my family had carefully erected around me—especially of gay people, because according to the WBC, homosexuals were the absolute worst group of people in the world. . . . My only view of life outside WBC was that it was an orgy of sin. That absolutely everyone was bound for eternal damnation.[22]

Too often the world outside the church confirmed this image as counterprotesters screamed profanities, physically attacked picketers, and continually harassed church members. At the 2011 Gay Pride Day parade in nearby Lawrence, Kansas, for example, a young teen from the church was separated from her group of picketers and followed down the sidewalk by some college-aged men, who continually blocked her path, screaming at her, an experience that clearly shook her and likely confirmed to her the vitriol of the world outside the church. Violence is not directed just at individual church members, of course. On October 5, 2010, the day *Snyder v. Phelps* was heard by the Supreme Court, for example, an envelope containing white powder was delivered to Phelps-Chartered. Though the powder was determined not to be anthrax, the intention of intimidation was clear. In another case, authorities suspected that Mark Uhl, a Liberty University student, may have intended to use homemade bombs against church members who were picketing at Jerry Falwell's funeral in 2007.[23] The violence of responses works to show, to those inside the church, that outsiders will not welcome them.

The reality of leaving, though, is often quite different. Now that a sizable number of young adults have left the church, a chain of people can assist with the exit. Support comes from strangers, too. After he left the church, for example, Zach was suffering from significant depression. When he finally made his departure public, he found many people reaching out to him in support, including a mental health nurse whom he credits with helping him rethink religion, as, postdeparture, he had continued to be afraid for the fate of his soul. As he slowly moved to spiritual peace, he says, he remembered Isaiah 48:22: "'There is no peace,' saith the Lord, 'unto the wicked.'" But, months after leaving, "I realized I was actually starting to find peace, even though Westboro would say I was wicked. I realized, OK, Westboro was literally wrong."[24]

For Megan and Grace, the embrace of the outside world was warm. In the model that Zach would follow, they kept quiet about their departure for several months, announcing it in February 2014, shortly before their grandfather's death. They soon found themselves the subject of media scrutiny and worked hard to avoid sensationalism, even as they recognized that their faces and names would forever be associated with the church. They began a listening tour, visiting people they had previously picketed, apologizing but also, more, learning. Articulate writers and speakers, they have spoken and written in limited settings, keeping their words about their family discreet and nondefensively stressing the positive aspects of growing up in the church in order to help people understand how it could be appealing to those inside. Both have worked to apply the lessons they learned to other contexts. Zach hopes to travel in "an endeavor to promote unconditional love worldwide," specifically opposing the church but also more broadly advocating for peace.[25] Megan, who works at a title company in North Dakota, has spoken about connections between kinds of religious extremism, as has her atheist activist uncle Nate

Phelps. Grace, a student in Topeka, has used her considerable talent in photography to work with Planting Peace, the organization that launched Equality House, a gay rights center located directly across the street from the church, to document the plight of gay homeless youth in Jamaica.[26] Libby, a physical therapist in nearby Lawrence, Kansas, has volunteered with Equality House, and both Libby and Lauren Drain have worked with the NoH8 campaign. Lauren now works as a personal trainer, maintains an active online presence in the personal training world, and competes in bodybuilding competitions. Lauren is married, and Libby, her sister Sara (who has maintained a lower profile), and her cousin Josh have married and had children; Megan lives with her boyfriend.

If the psychological part of leaving is exhausting, even with the relatively good outcomes for recent ex-members, the practical part is relatively easy. They are not unceremoniously kicked out of the family home, though the cut is still relatively swift. A liaison from the church is assigned to each person so that any paperwork—for example, related to health insurance—is handled appropriately. Ex-members are given a chance to find housing, and some leave with a car. The goal, from the church's perspective, is not to hurt the person but simply to say good-bye to someone who does not want to be there. Even in cases when people want to remain—Lauren Drain, for example, begged not to be disfellowshipped and promised to change if she could be permitted to stay—if the church recognizes, in their behavior, that they are not committed to the cause, then they are disfellowshipped. The situation is painful for parents, some of whom continued to choke up in personal interviews even months after the departure of their adult children. Indeed, that Shirley Phelps-Roper moved from her position as media contact around the same time that her daughters left was not particularly surprising, as the loss of her daughters was personally difficult, former members shared. For years, Megan, in particular, had worked alongside her "madre," as she affectionately called her mother, mentor, and friend. Megan, named after Shirley's own mother, was being groomed for a future role as a matriarch in the group. To lose that relationship so publicly was a challenge, even for a woman used to presenting an emotionally controlled face. Yet in response to every interview question about her departed children, Shirley Phelps-Roper brings the conversation back to God's standard: of course human relationships are important—but they are so far less important than our relationship to God. Very quickly, "you have to decide: Do you serve God or the child?"[27] Human feelings about such matters are fleeting in the expanse of eternity—and they distract from the mission of the church. Although the church stresses that members must be "on guard" and always watching against sin taking root in their families, ultimately, God has predestined some for salvation and others for damnation. This does not mean that Westboro Baptists cannot have relationships with ex-members, but the reality, say church members, is that they have no reason to have contact with them. "They don't want to live the way I want to live. They honestly don't want to be in communion with me. They don't honestly want to be in touch with us," explains Margie Phelps.[28]

Though ex-members may agree with the first two of Margie Phelps's claims, they disagree with the last one. Lauren Drain dedicated her memoir to her younger siblings still in the church, and Josh Phelps has expressed his desire for his parents to meet his children. Grace includes this subtitle on her Instagram account: *J'adore ma sœur et ma famille. J'aime voyager* (I love my sister and my family. I like to travel). Megan states her commitment to the principle that "human beings are more important than ideology" in expressing her desire to connect with her family again.[29] At least some ex-members continue to follow church members online and in social media and to include past photos of happier family times in their own online writing. Wrote Megan in her official announcement of her and her sister's departure, "We dearly love our family. They now consider us betrayers, and we are cut off from their lives, but we know they are well-intentioned. We will never not love them."[30] And the love was mutual: "I felt loved and treasured and valued and cared for" during her time in the church, Megan explains, a sentiment repeated in every interview I conducted with a second-generation member.[31] Indeed, says Sam Phelps-Roper, an elder in the congregation, the challenge for many ex-members is to leave a such a loving community; some, he says, hang on too long, past the time when they know that they "do not love the doctrines of this place," because they are so well treated.[32]

The love for each other did not stop with disfellowship, even if the communication has ended, and ex-members continue to hope for positive changes for those within the church. If church members could reject their restrictive interpretations of biblical texts, says Megan, "they would be doing amazing, incredible things that would change the world for the better."[33] Indeed, before his antigay picketing, Fred Phelps already had an entry in the Kansas State Historical Society for his civil rights work. Upon his death, son Nate Phelps reflected on the loss his father's life represented, saying, "I will mourn his passing, not for the man he was, but for the man he could have been."[34] Zach claims that a transformation did happen and that his grandfather had a change of heart about gay people in response to the presence of Equality House across the street. In a story that Zach shared on Facebook on May 22, 2014, and that was later picked up in multiple outlets, he wrote:

> Fred W. Phelps, my grandfather, came out in support of the Equality House before he was voted out of WBC. Specifically, on the day that he was excommunicated, he stood outside of the front door of the church (but not within anyone's earshot but a few members of WBC who happened to be in the immediate vicinity). . . . I say, he spoke words to this effect to the Equality House: "You are good people." I feel like he had a change of heart after my grandmother nearly passed away, and he felt the pangs of loss. . . . He waited for news of her every day and night while she was in intensive care. I think this triggered a chain reaction whereby he developed great empathy for others . . . which would explain why he would support Planting Peace's anti-suicide and anti-bullying platforms, and their charities across the world. . . . I love my grandfather! And I believe people DO change, if they are inspired enough![35]

Zach's story, though, has been denied by church members, with Steve Drain stating explicitly in regard to a change of Fred Phelps's heart that "what he [Zach] said is not true."[36] During Fred Phelps's stay in hospice prior to his death, Drain was a regular visitor and saw "not any kind of evidence that he had changed his mind on the biblical standards of homosexuality."[37] On the matter of Phelps's alleged excommunication, the church is unwilling to speak, noting that it does not comment on the spiritual state of participants. What is clear is that Phelps remained in his home, which is part of the church, as long as he was able, and during his time in hospice he was tended to by church members. His photo not merely remains part of the church's online presence but is highlighted on many web sites, and his sermons and news broadcasts remain available through the web site. The church arranged for his interment at an undisclosed location, not, Sam Phelps-Roper says without a trace of irony, because his grandfather would have cared if people came to mock his gravesite—an idea that probably "would have him laughing in his grave"—but because of the disruption that visitors and vandals would have on mourners at nearby gravesites.[38] This act of compassion and respect is just one of the apparent contradictions of a church that can both tenderly love and shun its members.

Ex-members must work hard to both move on and make sense—which may mean making amends—of their experiences. They must be careful, too, about not appearing self-pitying. No matter what their church did to them, it did far worse to others. In an interview with Anderson Cooper, Libby was unexpectedly confronted by a mother of a fallen soldier whose funeral her family had picketed since her departure; it was only during this part of the interview, after she had talked about her own experiences, that Libby shed tears.[39] Most ex-members are able to situate the church's actions in the much broader problem of homophobia that leads to real suffering and even death among queer people. In reflecting on her experience documenting the lives of homeless queer teens in Jamaica, Grace drew from her own experiences: "My heart hurt for them. I know what that's like, being rejected by your family for not going along with their beliefs. There's an irony there that I couldn't ignore: that I share a fate with the very people I was taught to dehumanize so fiercely."[40] Of course, the few ex-members of Westboro Baptist Church are unable to stop their church from either the inside or the outside, much less undermine homophobia and the structural inequality facing queer people. Unless the broader culture rejects the theology that links homosexuality and national doom, those who remain in Westboro Baptist Church—with the legal right to preach their message won by their predecessors, their own training in media and technology, and their growing-up years spent on the picket line—will continue to tap into latent antigay religious sentiment.

Indeed, reflects Tim Phelps, son of Fred Phelps and himself father to ten children, he and his siblings and children are "battle worn, battle tried"; "We were weaned on this, so you've got some rabid . . . generation of children."[41] The death of the patriarch, then, will not dissuade the church, for Westboro Baptist Church is from a tradition where church conflict is "a drama of doctrine as much as it is a clash of wills and passions."[42]

The goal of opponents, then, should not be to silence church members—for not only does that goal seem unlikely to be met, but it endangers the First Amendment—but to give no aid or comfort to the message, to reject its underlying theology. Nate Phelps, in encouraging residents of Topeka in their fight against his father, instructed them to ensure that church members' "seeds of hate will fall on barren soil."[43] To create that "barren soil," the larger culture must reject not only Westboro Baptist Church's message but the Religious Right's similarly antigay theology and policy. This task requires more than ignoring the church's message of national doom because of homosexuality; it requires countering it wherever it appears—and most importantly when it takes sanctuary in churches more palatable than Westboro Baptist Church.

# NOTES

## INTRODUCTION

1. A transcript of the debate, hosted by Fox News, is available at http://www .foxnews.com/politics/2011/09/22/fox-news-google-gop-2012-presidential -debate.

2. As reported in Michael Muskal, "GOProud, a Gay-Rights Group, Condemns Santorum's Debate Comments," *LA Times*, September 23, 2011, http://articles .latimes.com/2011/sep/23/news/la-pn-rick-santorum-dadt-debate20110923.

3. Peter Montgomery, "Gay Bashing the Religious Right's Forever Issue," *Religion Dispatches*, October 7, 2011, http://www.religiondispatches.org/dispatches /guest_bloggers/5237/gay-bashing_the_religious_right%E2%80%99s_forever _issue.

4. Family Research Council, "DADT Defeat Doesn't Mean Conservative Surrender," *Washington Update*, December 20, 2010, http://www.frc.org/washington update/dadt-defeat-doesnt-mean-conservative-surrender.

5. CNN, "Anti-gay Stance Hits YouTube," March 10, 2008, http://www.cnn .com/video/#/video/us/2008/03/10/ dnt.ok.lawmaker.anti.gay.kwtv.

6. Pierre Bynum, "Don't Ask Don't Tell," *Prayer Team*, September 21, 2011, http://www.frc.org/prayerteam/prayer-targets-david-wilkerson-economy-israel -un-jerusalem-prayer-values-voter-summit-dadt (italics in the original).

7. Proverbs 13:34. This passage is taken from the King James translation.

8. Fred Phelps, sermon, September 11, 2011, http://godhatesfags.com/sermons /outlines/Sermon_20110911.pdf.

9. The phrase is taken from Jesus's words in Matthew 5:14. John Winthrop encouraged early Puritan settlers with the comparison between their new city and Jesus's "city upon a hill" in the sermon "A Model of Christian Charity," in a *Life and Letters of John Winthrop*, 2nd ed., edited by Robert C. Winthrop, vol. 2 (Boston: Little, Brown, 1866), 18–20.

10. Westboro Baptist Church, "Perpetual Memorial to Matthew Shepard," God Hates Fags, http://www.godhatesfags.com/library/memorials/matthewshepard memorial.html. The play *The Laramie Project*, now commonly performed by high schools and picketed by members of Westboro Baptist Church, includes Phelps as a character (Moisés Kaufman, *The Laramie Project*, Dramatists Play Service, 2001).

11. Westboro Baptist Church, "God's Wrath against America Revealed," God Hates America, http://www.godhatesamerica.com/godswrath.html.

12. Westboro Baptist Church, "Fag Nation," America Is Doomed, http://www.americaisdoomed.com.

13. The first picket at the funeral of a soldier was held on June 15, 2005, at the funeral of army Spc. Carrie L. French. Remembers church spokesperson Shirley Phelps-Roper, "I recall perfectly the first soldier funeral, because it was one of the few things that we have done that I actually thought through and realized was going to leave a mark. I knew we were stepping off into the middle of HUGE Doomed [A]merican idols." E-mail to the author, May 1, 2009.

14. As of September 2015, forty-six states had passed legislation limiting funeral pickets.

15. The bill became US law 109-228 on January 3, 2006.

16. Patriot Guard Riders, "Our History," http://www.patriotguard.org/Home/OurHistory/tabid/145/Default.aspx.

17. The original order of judgment was filed November 5, 2007, in the US District Court for the District of Maryland. The full text of the decision, in favor of Albert Snyder, is available online at http://www.citmedialaw.org/sites/citmedialaw.org/files/2007-11-05-Order%20of%20Judgment.pdf. The September 24, 2009, reversal of that decision by the appellate court is available at http://www.pace.ca4.uscourts.gov/opinion.pdf/081026.P.pdf. The Supreme Court decision is available at http://www.supremecourt.gov/opinions/10pdf/09-751.pdf.

18. Fred Phelps, Jr., interview with the author, May 6, 2011.

19. HR1627, Honoring America's Veterans and Caring for Camp Lejeune Families Act of 2012, passed into law July 18, 2012, and is available at Congress's web site, https://www.congress.gov/bill/112th-congress/house-bill/1627.

20. For an overview of the legal battle to limit funeral picketing on the state level, see David Levie, Zachary Navit, and Kara Tappan, "Special Report: Constitutionality of State Funeral-Picketing Laws since Snyder v. Phelps," First Amendment Center, February 11, 2014, http://www.firstamendmentcenter.org/special-report-constitutionality-of-state-funeral-picketing-laws-since-snyder-v-phelps.

21. Shirley Phelps-Roper, e-mail to the author, October 19, 2008.

22. Westboro Baptist Church, "Past Picket Locations," God Hates Fags, http://www.godhatesfags.com/ picketlocations.html.

23. Steve Drain, director, Hatemongers. Originally titled Fred: The Movie, it was created in 2000. The film can be downloaded at http://www.hatemongers.com/clips.html.

24. Shirley Phelps-Roper, interview with the author, July 30, 2009.

25. Annie Gowan, "Holy Hell," Washington Post, November 12, 1995, http://infoweb.newsbank.com.www2.iib.ku.edu:2048/iw-search/we/InfoWeb?p

_product=NewsBank&p_theme=aggregated5&p_action=doc&p_docid
=0EB28567A53ABC9A&d_place=WPIW&f_subsection=sSTYLE&f_issue=1995
–11–12&f_publisher.

26. Paul Froese and Christopher D. Bader, *America's Four Gods: What We Say about God—and What That Says about Us* (New York: Oxford University Press, 2010), 176.

27. Shirley Phelps-Roper, interview with the author, July 30, 2008.

28. Mark Memmot, "9-Year-Old to Westboro Baptist Church: God Hates No One," *The Two-Way*, May 16, 2012, http://www.npr.org/blogs/thetwo-way/2012/05/16/152821271/9-year-old-to-westboro-baptist-god-hates-no-one.

29. Westboro Baptist Church, "'God Loves Everyone'—The Greatest Lie Ever Told!" God Hates Fags, http://www.godhatesfags.com/written/reports/200603 31_god-loves-everyone-lie.pdf.

30. Examples include Angel Action, a counterprotest first used at Matthew Shepard's funeral, in which activists shielded grieving family members from the sight of Westboro Baptists by wearing large angel wings, and the Million "Fag" March, an annual picket at or near Westboro Baptist Church in Topeka that draws activists holding signs that parody the signs of Westboro Baptist Church members. For a more thorough discussion of counterprotests, see Rebecca Barrett-Fox, "Standing Up to (Some Kinds of) Hate: Ambivalence in Community Responses to Westboro Baptist Church," paper presented at the annual meeting of the American Sociological Association, Chicago, IL, August 22–25, 2015.

31. Richard Land, president of the Ethics and Religious Liberty Commission of the Southern Baptist Convention, called pickets at the funerals of soldiers "grotesque assault[s] on . . . bereft family members [that are] nothing less than verbal pornography and obscenity [that are] not, and should not, be protected under the First Amendment," declaring that "for this group of misguided zealots to do their despicable deeds in the name of God is blasphemous." He also reassured his audience, "Let there be no doubt. This man is not a Southern Baptist, and his 'church' is not a Southern Baptist church." Such a statement serves more as an effort to distance Land's Southern Baptist Convention from Westboro Baptist Church than to inform, for Westboro Baptist Church does not claim to be a Southern Baptist Church. Instead, it identifies as a primitive or "old school" Baptist church, and any well-informed reader of the *Christian Post*, in which Land's article appeared, would recognize the difference. Richard Land, "Verbal Terrorism," *Christian Post*, November 7, 2007, http://www.christianpost.com/Opinion/Columns/2007/11/verbal-terrorism-07/index.html.

32. For example, after *Snyder v. Phelps* was decided, at the lower court level, in favor of the plaintiff, Westboro Baptist Church published a press release declaring,

"Thank God for the $10.9 Million Verdict!" According to the press release, the initial verdict in *Snyder v. Phelps*, which was later reduced to $5 million by a federal court that found the original amount to be excessive, guarantees God's future punishment of America, which would or would not be recalled if the appellate court's decision was upheld by the Supreme Court. The writer of the press release quotes from 2nd Thessalonians 1, which says, "Seeing it is a righteous thing with God to recompense tribulation to them that trouble you"—in other words, that God will repay America with "tribulation" for its "persecution" of Westboro Baptist Church. Westboro Baptist Church, "Thank God for the $10.9 Million Verdict!" God Hates Fags, October 31, 2007, http://www.godhatesfags.com/written/fliers /archive/20071031_thank-god-for-verdict.pdf.

33. Steve Drain, interview with the author, April 16, 2015.

34. Timothy Phelps, "WBC v. The World," Sign Movies, January 30, 2013, http://www.signmovies.com.

35. Westboro Baptist Church, "America's Gone a Whoring from God," God Hates Fags, May 6, 2007, http://www.godhatesfags.com/written/sermons/out lines/Sermon_20070506.pdf .

36. Cynthia Burack, "Getting What 'We' Deserve: Terrorism, Sexuality, and the Christian Right," *New Political Science* 25, no. 3 (2005): 345.

37. Kathleen M. Blee, *Inside Organized Racism: Women in the Hate Movement* (Berkeley: University of California Press, 2002), 21.

38. Roger Friedland, "Money, Sex, and God: The Erotic Logic of Religious Nationalism," *Sociological Theory* 20, no. 3 (November 2002): 388.

39. Estranged son Nate Phelps has suggested that if his father found a Bible verse that he thought justified it, Westboro Baptist Church could become violent, either toward outsiders or toward members. *The Standard*, television series, hosted by Peter Klein (2010; Vancouver: VisionTV), http://vimeo.com/ 10584739. At a minimum, the church maintains significant power over the lives of the individuals involved in it.

40. Blee, *Inside Organized Racism*, 11.

41. Robert N. Minor, *When Religion Is an Addiction* (St. Louis, MO: Humanity Works!, 2007), 1.

42. In his dissent in *Snyder v. Phelps*, Justice Alito, the lone dissenter, argued that the words on the church's signs amount to "fighting words" (those "that by their very utterance inflict injury or tend to incite an immediate breach of the peace [though they] . . . are no essential part of any exposition of ideas, and are of such slight social value as a step to truth that any benefit that may be derived from them is clearly outweighed by the social interest in order and morality" [*Chaplinksy*

v. *New Hampshire*, 1942]). Justice Roberts, writing the majority opinion, disagreed, finding that because the words of the church address issues of public concern, such as politics, even though they address these issues through examples of individuals, they do not meet the definition of "fighting words."

43. Sam Phelps-Roper, interview with the author, May 6, 2011.

44. Blee, *Inside Organized Racism*, 21.

45. Faye Ginsburg, "Preface," *Contested Lives: The Abortion Debate in an American Community* (Berkeley: University of California Press, 1998), xxxiv.

46. Ibid.

47. Blee, *Inside Organized Racism*, 2.

48. Westboro Baptist Church, "Contact Us," God Hates America, http://www .godhatesamerica.com/contact.html.

49. James L. Peacock and Ruel W. Tyson, Jr., *Pilgrims of Paradox: Calvinism and Experience among the Primitive Baptists of the Blue Ridge* (Washington, DC: Smithsonian Institution Press, 1989), 221.

50. Sydney E. Ahlstrom, "Introduction," *Theology in America: The Major Protestant Voices from Puritanism to Neo-Orthodoxy*, edited by Sydney E. Ahlstrom (Indianapolis, IN: Bobbs-Merrill, 1967), 13.

51. Rosalie H. Wax, *Doing Fieldwork: Warnings and Advice* (Chicago: University of Chicago Press, 1971), 3–4.

52. "About Us," God Hates Fags, http://www.godhatesfags.com/wbcinfo /aboutwbc.html.

CHAPTER 1. THE HISTORY OF WESTBORO BAPTIST CHURCH

1. Steve Tompkins, "Phelps' Work Raises Hopes, and Questions," *Wichita Eagle*, February 13, 1983. Bob Jones University did not admit African American students until 1971 and had a ban on interracial dating until 2000. "Bob Jones U. Apologizes for Racism," *CBS News*, November 21, 2008, http://www.cbsnews.com /stories/2008/11/21/national/main4625581.shtml.

2. Nate Phelps, interview by Walt Bodine and Gina Kaufman, *Walt Bodine Show*, KCUR, June 14, 2010, http://archive.kcur.org/kcurViewDirect.asp?PlaylistID=7469.

3. "Repentance in Pasadena," *Time*, June 11, 1951, http://www.time.com/time /magazine/article/0,9171,814897,00.html.

4. Jonathan Phelps, e-mail to Calvary Baptist Church in Sterling, Colorado, November 4, 2009.

5. Joe Taschler and Steve Fry, "The Transformation of Fred Phelps," *Topeka Capital-Journal*, August 3, 1994, http://cjonline.com/indepth/phelps/stories/0803 94_phelps01.shtml.

6. Abigail Phelps, interview with the author, November 4, 2009.

7. Unfortunately, the denominational affiliation of the man who baptized Fred Phelps is unknown, other than to say that he was "Baptist." For Primitive Baptists, this is a reason to reject claims that Fred Phelps was a Primitive Baptist, as they believe that only those who have been baptized by a Primitive Baptist can be called Primitive Baptists. In this view, neither Fred Phelps nor anyone he baptized is a Primitive Baptist. If they wanted to be, they would need to be rebaptized by a Primitive Baptist minister.

8. Joe Taschler and Steve Fry, "The Gospel According to Fred," *Topeka Capital-Journal*, August 3, 1994, http://cjonline.com/indepth/phelps/stories/080394_phelps04.shtml.

9. Shirley Phelps-Roper, e-mail to the author, June 30, 2010.

10. Joe Taschler and Steve Fry, "Fate, Timing Kept Phelps in Topeka," *Topeka Capital-Journal*, August 3, 1994, http://cjonline.com/indepth/phelps/stories/080394_phelps13.shtml.

11. Joe Taschler and Steve Fry, "Phelps' Law Career Checkered," *Topeka Capital-Journal*, August 3, 1994, http://cjonline.com/indepth/phelps/stories/080394_phelps16.shtml.

12. Ibid.

13. Quoted in Jean Van Delinder, "Brown v. Board of Education of Topeka: A Landmark Case Unresolved Fifty Years Later, Part 2," Prologue: The Journal of the National Archives 36, no. 1 (Spring 2004), http://www.archives.gov/publications/prologue/2004/spring/brown-v-board-2.html.

14. Joe Taschler and Steve Fry, "As a Lawyer, Phelps Was Good in Court," *Topeka Capital-Journal*, August 3, 1994, http://cjonline.com/indepth/phelps/stories/080394_phelps17.shtml.

15. *Wecker v. Kansas Power and Light*, 1986; *Fisher v. Southwest Bell*, 1986; *Hinman v. Rogers*, 1987.

16. Taschler and Fry, "As a Lawyer, Phelps Was Good in Court."

17. Tompkins, "Phelps' Work Raises Hopes, and Questions."

18. Ibid.

19. Gregory S. Boyd, "Fred Waldron Phelps, Sr.," report provided to ABC News's *20/20* (Wichita, KS: Gay Services Bureau, 1992), Bruce McKinney Collection at the Kenneth Spencer Research Library, University of Kansas, Lawrence (hereafter Spencer Research Library).

20. Tompkins, "Phelps' Work Raises Hopes, and Questions."

21. Taschler and Fry, "Phelps' Law Career Checkered."

22. Notes the court in *State of Kansas v. Fred W. Phelps, Sr.* (1979), "The trial

became an exhibition of a personal vendetta by Phelps against Carolene Brady. His examination was replete with repetition, badgering, innuendo, belligerence, irrelevant and immaterial matter, evidencing only a desire to hurt and destroy the defendant. The jury verdict didn't stop the onslaught of Phelps. He was not satisfied with the hurt, pain, and damage he had visited on Carolene Brady."

23. In that case Judge Keith Anderson sentenced Phelps to ten days in jail for direct contempt of court relating to the improper questioning of JoAnn Norwood in a case about bad checks. Boyd, "Fred Waldron Phelps, Sr."

24. *State v. Phelps*, 1979.

25. Ibid.

26. Actually, the justices were divided. All agreed that Phelps should be disbarred from practice in the state. A minority added that he should have been disbarred from practice in federal court, too.

27. *State v. Phelps*, 1979.

28. Al Polczinski, "Fred Phelps Sr.," *Wichita Eagle*, July 15, 1990.

29. Southern Poverty Law Center, "Fred Phelps Timeline," *Intelligence Report* 101 (Spring 2001), http://www.splcenter.org/get-informed/intelligence-report /browse-all-issues/2001/spring/a-city-held-hostage/fred-phelps-timel.

30. Polczinski, "Fred Phelps Sr."

31. Ibid.

32. Tompkins, "Phelps' Work Raises Hopes, and Questions."

33. Polczinski, "Fred Phelps Sr."

34. Ibid.

35. Westboro Baptist Church, "FAQ: Are You Associated with a Militia, Aryan Nation, Nazi, KKK, or Any Other Similar Group?" God Hates Fags, http://www .godhatesfags.com/faq.html.

36. Fred Phelps, letter to the editor, *Topeka Capital-Journal*, March 8, 1998, Kansas Collection at Spencer Research Library (italics in original).

37. Tompkins, "Phelps' Work Raises Hopes, and Questions."

38. Southern Poverty Law Center, "A City Held Hostage," *Intelligence Report* 101 (Spring 2001), http://www.splcenter.org/get-informed/intelligence-report /browse-all-issues/2001/spring/a-city-held-hostage.

39. Joe Taschler and Steve Fry, "Faxes, Pickets, Politics Carry Phelps' Message," *Topeka Capital-Journal*, August 3, 1994, http://cjonline.com/indepth/phelps /stories/080394_phelps21.shtml.

40. Shirley Phelps-Roper, e-mail to the author, August 26, 2010.

41. Ibid.

42. Incumbent governor John Carlin lost the 1990 Democratic primary with

79,406 votes to Joan Finney's 81,250 votes; Fred Phelps received 11,634 votes. "Election Statistics: 1990 Kansas Election Results," Kansas Secretary of State, http://www.kssos.org/elections/elections_statistics.html.

43. Ibid.

44. Election Statistics: 1992 Kansas Election Results," Kansas Secretary of State, http://www.kssos.org/elections/ elections_statistics.html.

45. Fred Phelps, open letter to Joan Wagnon, August 7, 1992, Kansas Collection, Spencer Research Library.

46. "Topeka Mayor—Primary," Our Campaigns, http://www.ourcampaigns .com/RaceDetail.html?RaceID=569791.

47. "Election Statistics: 1998 Kansas Election Results," Kansas Secretary of State, http://www.kssos.org/elections/ elections_statistics.html. His running mate was Abe Ibrahim, a Palestine-born immigrant to Topeka who had served as an intelligence officer in the US military. Jim McClean, "Sawyer, Miller Make Unconventional Choices to Fill Out Gubernatorial Tickets," *Topeka Capital-Journal*, June 11, 1998, http://cjonline.com/stories/061198/ gov_govcandidates.shtml.

48. Election Statistics: 1998 Kansas Election Results," Kansas Secretary of State, http://www.kssos.org/elections/elections_statistics.html.

49. Michael A. Jones-Correa and David L. Leal, "Political Participation: Does Religion Matter?" *Political Research Quarterly* 54, no. 4 (December 2001): 765. See also Clyde Wilcox and Leopoldo Gomez, "Religion, Group Identification, and Politics among American Blacks," *Sociological Analyses* 51, no. 3 (Autumn 1990): 271–285.

50. Southern Poverty Law Center, "Fred Phelps Timeline."

51. Jodi Wilgoren, "Vote in Topeka Today Hangs on Gay Rights and a Vitriolic Local Protester," *New York Times*, March 1, 2005, http://www.nytimes.com /2005/03/01/national/01topeka.html?pagewanted=1.

52. "*Time* Article Focuses Debate," *Topeka Capital-Journal*, February 22, 2005, http://cjonline.com/stories/022205/loc_articlefocus.shtml.

53. Wilgoren, "Vote in Topeka Today Hangs on Gay Rights and a Vitriolic Local Protester."

54. "Support in Unlikely Places," *Advocate*, April 12, 2005, 21.

55. In Shawnee County, where Topeka is located, voters approved of a ban on same-sex marriage 31,322 to 15,135. Overall, the vote to amend the state constitution to define marriage as between one man and one woman passed by 70 percent. "Election Statistics: 2005 Constitutional Amendment Results by County," Kansas Secretary of State, http://www.kssos.org/elections/elections_statistics.html.

56. "Election Summary Report," *Shawnee County*, March 4, 2005, https://www .snco.us/election/prev/20050301-primary.htm.

57. Tim Hrenchir, "City Race Gets *Time* Coverage," *Topeka Capital-Journal*, February 12, 2005, http://cjonline.com/ stories/021205/loc_councilrace.shtml.

58. Wilgoren, "Vote in Topeka Today Hangs on Gay Rights and a Vitriolic Local Protester."

59. Roy Bragg, "Topeka Has Little Love for Hateful Preacher," *San Antonio Express-News*, April 10, 2005, http://nl.newsbank.com/nl-search/we/Archives?p _product=SAEC&p_theme=saec&p_action=search&p_maxdocs=200&s_disp string=Topeka%20AND%20date(4/9/2005%20to%204/12/2005)&p_field_date -0=YMD_date&p_params_date-0=date:B,E&p_text_date-0=4/9/2005%2to%20 4/12/2005)&p_field_advanced-0=&p_text_advanced-0=(Topeka)&xcal_numdocs =50&p_perpage=25&p_sort=YMD_date:D&xcal_useweights=no.

60. Shirley Phelps-Roper, interview with the author, July 30, 2008.

61. Brad Sears, "Kansas—Sexual Orientation and Gender Identity Law and Documentation of Discrimination," Documenting Discrimination on the Basis of Sexual Orientation and Gender Identity in State Employment series, the Williams Institute, University of California–Los Angeles School of Law, September 2009, http://escholarship.org/uc/item/05g290fb;jsessionid=4FE0B56ABECE5A1A04 A813933208008D#page-1.

62. Fred Phelps, sermon, February 14, 2010, http://www.godhatesfags.com /sermons/outlines/Sermon_20100214.pdf.

63. For example, in his commentary on the church, *Philadelphia Inquirer* columnist and talk show host Michael Smerconish describes "how disturbed [Fred Phelps's] fiery eyes left me," saying that Phelps reminded him "more of Lucifer" than "a man of God." Smerconish, "Head Strong: Free (and Hateful) Speech vs. the Right to Gather," *Cleveland Plain Dealer*, March 19, 2010, http://www.cleveland .com/opinion/index.ssf/2010/03/free_and_hateful_speech_vs_the.html.

64. For an example of this in writing, see James Petigru Boyce's 1887 *Abstract of Systematic Theology*, which is basically a list of biblical passages "proving" Calvinist principles of election (Escondido, CA: Den Bulk Christian Foundation, 1996).

65. John G. Crowley, "The Primitive or Old School Baptists," in *The Baptist River: Essays on the Many Tributaries of a Diverse Tradition*, edited by W. Glenn Jonas, Jr. (Macon, GA: Mercer University Press, 2006), 178.

66. Ibid.

67. Fred Phelps, sermon, February 7, 2010, http://www.godhatesfags.com /sermons/outlines/Sermon_20100207.pdf.

68. Kathleen C. Boone, *The Bible Tells Them So: The Discourse of Protestant Fundamentalism* (Albany: State University of New York Press, 1989), 13.

69. For a fuller articulation of how proof-texting has been used to support

antigay interpretations of the Bible, see L. William Countrymen, "The Bible, Heterosexism, and the American Public Discussion of Sexual Orientation," in *God Forbid: Religion and Sex in American Public Life*, edited by Kathleen M. Sands (New York: Oxford University Press, 2003), 167–185.

70. Shirley Phelps-Roper, e-mail to the author, June 28, 2010.

71. Crowley, "The Primitive or Old School Baptists," 179.

72. Ibid.

73. Peter J. Thuesen, *Predestination: The American Career of a Contentious Doctrine* (New York: Oxford University Press, 2009), 6.

74. Shirley Phelps-Roper, e-mail to the author, May 12, 2010.

75. Boone, *The Bible Tells Them So*, 13.

76. Megan Phelps-Roper, interview with the author, July 17, 2010. Notably, Megan and her sister Grace left Westboro Baptist in the spring of 2013.

77. Ibid.

78. Shirley Phelps-Roper, e-mail to the author, August 10, 2010.

79. The King James translation of Romans 1:18–32 reads, "For the wrath of God is revealed from heaven against all ungodliness and unrighteousness of men, who hold the truth in unrighteousness; Because that which may be known of God is manifest in them; for God hath showed it unto them. For the invisible things of him from the creation of the world are clearly seen, being understood by the things that are made, even his eternal power and Godhead; so that they are without excuse: Because that, when they knew God, they glorified him not as God, neither were thankful; but became vain in their imaginations, and their foolish heart was darkened. Professing themselves to be wise, they became fools, And changed the glory of the uncorruptible God into an image made like to corruptible man, and to birds, and four-footed beasts, and creeping things. Wherefore God also gave them up to uncleanness, through the lusts of their own hearts, to dishonour their own bodies between themselves: Who changed the truth of God into a lie, and worshipped and served the creature more than the Creator, who is blessed for ever. Amen. For this cause God gave them up unto vile affections: for even their women did change the natural use into that which is against nature: And likewise also the men, leaving the natural use of the woman, burned in their lust one toward another; men with men working that which is unseemly, and receiving in themselves that recompense of their error which was meet. And even as they did not like to retain God in their knowledge, God gave them over to a reprobate mind, to do those things which are not convenient; Being filled with all unrighteousness, fornication, wickedness, covetousness, maliciousness; full of envy, murder, debate, deceit, malignity; whisperers, Backbiters, haters of God, despiteful, proud,

boasters, inventors of evil things, disobedient to parents, Without understanding, covenant-breakers, without natural affection, implacable, unmerciful: Who, knowing the judgment of God, that they which commit such things are worthy of death, not only do the same, but have pleasure in them that do them."

80. Westboro Baptist Church, "FAQS: How Do I Join You?" God Hates Fags, http://www.godhatesfags.com/faq.html.

81. William N. Eskridge, Jr., "Body Politics: *Lawrence v. Texas* and the Constitution of the Disgust and Contagion," *Florida Law Review* 57, no. 5 (2005): 1020 (italics in original).

82. Ibid., 1023.

83. Martin A. Monto and Jessica Supinski, "Discomfort with Homosexuality: A New Measure Captures Differences in Attitudes toward Gay Men and Lesbians," *Journal of Homosexuality* 61, no. 6 (2014): 912.

84. Westboro Baptist Church, "FAQ: Doesn't the Bible Say That God Loves Everyone?" God Hates Fags, http://www.godhatesfags.com/faq.html#Hate.

85. Shirley Phelps-Roper, e-mail to the author, August 9, 2010.

86. Ibid.

87. A few years later another University of Kansas film student, K. Ryan Jones, made a documentary about the church titled *Fall from Grace*. Jones, who did not join the church, and Drain, who did, should not be confused.

88. The participant's name has been changed.

89. The participant's name has been changed.

90. Fred Phelps, sermon, July 18, 2010, http://www.godhatesfags.com /sermons/outlines/Sermon_20100718.pdf.

91. John G. Crowley, *Primitive Baptists of the Wiregrass South: 1815 to the Present* (Gainesville: University Press of Florida, 1998), 167.

92. Jael Phelps, interview with the author, October 4, 2008.

93. Shirley Phelps-Roper, e-mail to the author, September 28, 2006.

94. Bertram Wyatt-Brown, *The Shaping of Southern Culture: Honor, Grace, and War, 1760s–1880s* (Chapel Hill: University of North Carolina Press, 2011), 107.

95. Shirley Phelps-Roper, e-mail to the author, March 15, 2010

96. Sam Phelps-Roper, interview with the author, July 17, 2010.

97. Tim Phelps, interview with the author, March 10, 2010.

98. Sam Phelps-Roper, interview with the author, July 17, 2010.

99. Group interview with the author, July 17, 2010.

100. Shirley Phelps-Roper, e-mail to the author, September 28, 2006. She has expressed this attitude after the departure of her children who have left the congregation since then.

101. Ibid.

102. Ibid.

103. Shirley Phelps-Roper, e-mail to the author, May 10, 2010.

104. Joe Taschler and Steve Fry, "Life in a War Zone," *Topeka Capital-Journal*, http://www.culteducation.com/group/1226-westboro-baptist-church/22008-life -in-a-war-zone-.html.

105. The King James translation of Matthew 18:15–19 reads, "Moreover if thy brother shall trespass against thee, go and tell him his fault between thee and him alone: if he shall hear thee, thou hast gained thy brother. But if he will not hear thee, then take with thee one or two more, that in the mouth of two or three witnesses every word may be established. And if he shall neglect to hear them, tell it unto the church: but if he neglect to hear the church, let him be unto thee as an heathen man and a publican. Verily I say unto you, Whatsoever ye shall bind on earth shall be bound in heaven: and whatsoever ye shall loose on earth shall be loosed in heaven. Again I say unto you, That if two of you shall agree on earth as touching any thing that they shall ask, it shall be done for them of my Father which is in heaven."

106. Shirley Phelps-Roper, e-mail to the author, April 1, 2010.

107. Robert Wuthnow Robert and Matthew P. Lawson, "Sources of Christian Fundamentalism in the United States," in *Accounting for Fundamentalisms: The Dynamic Character of Movements*, The Fundamentalism Project, vol. 4, edited by Martin E. Marty and R. Scott Appleby (Chicago: University of Chicago Press, 1994), 40.

108. Nate Phelps, public presentation at the Topeka Performing Arts Center, April 24, 2010.

109. Emmanual Sivan, "The Enclave Culture," in *Fundamentalisms Comprehended*, The Fundamentalism Project, vol. 5, edited by Martin E. Marty and R. Scott Appleby (Chicago: University of Chicago Press, 1991), 56.

110. Taschler and Fry, "Life in a War Zone."

111. Sivan, "The Enclave Culture," 18.

112. Justin Kendall, "Dead to Fred," *The Pitch*, November 9, 2006, http:/www .pitch.com/content/printVersion/158048.

113. Ibid.

114. Shirley Phelps-Roper, interview with the author, July 30, 2009.

115. Kendall, "Dead to Fred."

116. Ibid.

117. Justin Kendall, "The New Fred," *The Pitch*, November 2, 2006, http://www .pitch.com/kansascity/the-new-fred/Content?oid=2183486.

118. Leo Booth, *When God Becomes a Drug: Breaking the Chains of Religious Addiction and Abuse* (Los Angeles: Jeremy P. Tarcher, 1991), 112.

119. Steve Drain, interview with the author, April 16, 2015. From a predestination perspective, Ham's wickedness does not cause him to go to hell; instead, his rejection by God, which occurred before the start of time, caused him to be wicked.

120. Fred Phelps, sermon, March 14, 2010, http://www.godhatesfags.com /sermons/outlines/Sermon_20100314.pdf.

121. Shirley Phelps-Roper, e-mail to the author, September 28, 2006.

122. Nathan Dinsdale, "Father Knows Best," *Santa Fe Reporter*, April 20, 2005, http://www.altweeklies.com/aan/father_knows_best/ Story?oid=145872.

123. Westboro Baptist Church, "The Night America Bombed Westboro Baptist Church with an IED (Improvised Explosive Device) in a Cowardly Move to Stop WBC's Anti-Gay Gospel Preaching—Thereby Bringing Down the Unmitigated and Irreversible Wrath of God upon this Evil Nation, Manifesting Itself in the Daily Bloody IED-Deaths of American Soldiers in Iraq and Other Places," August 20, 1995, http://www.godhatesfags.com/bombing.

124. Fred Phelps, sermon, March 28, 2010, http://www.godhatesfags.com /sermons/outlines/Sermon_20100328.pdf.

125. Fred Phelps, sermon, February 14, 2010, http://www.godhatesfags.com /sermons/outlines/Sermon_20100214.pdf.

126. Shirley Phelps-Roper, e-mail to the author, March 13, 2010.

127. Gabriel A. Almond, Emmanual Sivan, and R. Scott Appleby, "Fundamentalisms: Genus and Species," in *Fundamentalisms Comprehended*, The Fundamentalism Project, vol. 5, edited by Martin E. Marty and R. Scott Appleby (Chicago: University of Chicago Press, 1991), 405–414.

128. Sam Harris, "Leaving the Church: An Interview with Megan Phelps-Roper," *Waking Up with Sam Harris*, July 2, 2015, http://www.samharris.org/blog /item/leaving-the-church.

129. Shirley Phelps-Roper, e-mail to the author, June 28, 2010.

130. Shirley Phelps-Roper, e-mail to the author, April 6, 2005.

131. Dinsdale, "Father Knows Best."

CHAPTER 2. THE THEOLOGY OF WESTBORO BAPTIST CHURCH

1. James L. Peacock and Tim Pettyjohn, "Fundamentalisms Narrated: Muslim, Christian, and Mystical," in *Fundamentalisms Comprehended*, The Fundamentalism Project, vol. 5, edited by Martin E. Marty and R. Scott Appleby (Chicago: University of Chicago Press, 1991), 123.

2. Sydney E. Ahlstrom, "Introduction," in *Theology in America: The Major Protestant Voices from Puritanism to Neo-Orthodoxy*, edited by Sydney E. Ahlstrom (Indianapolis, IN: Bobbs-Merrill Company, 1967), 12.

3. James L. Peacock and Ruel W. Tyson, Jr., *Pilgrims of Paradox: Calvinism and Experience among the Primitive Baptists of the Blue Ridge* (Washington, DC: Smithsonian Institution Press, 1989), 98.

4. Ibid., xvii–xviii.

5. For example, Shirley Phelps-Roper's youngest sons, Jonah and Noah, appeared on ABC's television newsmagazine *20/20* in 2007, articulating the church's antigay theology. When asked if children are "too young" to be exposed to such strong language and images, Shirley Phelps-Roper said clearly, "No, they're not young. . . . They're never too young to hear [the Word of God]." John Stossel, Ruth Chenetz, and Patrick McMenamin, "'America's Doomed': Freedom of Speech or Unlawful Hate Mongering?" *20/20*, November 2, 2007, http://abcnews.go.com/2020/story?id=3812344&page=1.

6. Bertram Wyatt-Brown, *The Shaping of Southern Culture: Honor, Grace, and War, 1760s–1880s* (Chapel Hill: University of North Carolina Press, 2011), 109.

7. Peacock and Tyson divide Primitive Baptists into three categories: Progressives, who have adopted Arminian theology, Sunday school, and musical instruments; Old Regulars, who are Calvinist and reject the innovations of the Progressives; and Absoluters, who defend a "hyper-Calvinism" that includes a stricter biblical logic, a belief that "everything in time and nature is predetermined," and double predestination—that is, the belief that God actively chooses both to elect some people and damn others (*Pilgrims of Paradox*, 120). Westboro Baptists are best described as Absoluters, though they do permit musical accompaniment. Primitive Baptists are also known as Old Baptists; Particular Baptists (because they believe that election is only for "particular" people, in contrast to General Baptists, who believe that salvation is available to all); or "Hardshells," a pejorative nickname used among Primitive Baptists themselves but not welcome from outsiders.

8. "Despite modern denials by certain Baptists that Baptists are Protestants, the matrix of the Baptist movement had been powerfully shaped by the Protestant Reformation, and some have even claimed that the Baptists are the truly thoroughgoing Reformers." James Leo Garrett, Jr., *Baptist Theology: A Four Century Study* (Macon, GA: Mercer University Press, 2009), 6–7.

9. Unlike other contemporary Anabaptist groups such as the Amish and Mennonites, however, most Baptists are not pacifists, and many Baptist groups have abandoned traditional Radical Reformers' arguments for a strict separation of church and state, as Baptist leadership in Religious Right organizations suggests.

10. John G. Crowley, "The Primitive or Old School Baptists," in *The Baptist River: Essays on the Many Tributaries of a Diverse Tradition*, edited by W. Glenn Jonas,

Jr. (Macon, GA: Mercer University Press, 2006), 159. Because Fred Phelps was not clearly baptized by a Primitive Baptist minister, Primitive Baptists believe that he was not a Primitive Baptist and thus that all the baptisms he completed are invalid.

11. At the same time that they claim to follow only the example of the earliest church, Primitive Baptists, like all Baptists, "adhere to the Trinitarian and Christological doctrines formulated by the first four ecumenical councils [First Council of Nicea in 325, First Council of Constantinople in 381, Council of Ephesus in 431, and Council of Chalcedon in 451] and expressed in the earliest Christian creeds" and thus have, in fact, adopted theological claims explicitly articulated many centuries after the establishment of the earliest churches (Garrett, *Baptist Theology*, 21).

12. Crowley, "The Primitive or Old School Baptists," 162.

13. For a history of this tension, see Carla Gardina Pestana, *Quakers and Baptists in Colonial Massachusetts* (New York: Cambridge University Press, 1991).

14. James R. Mathis, *The Making of the Primitive Baptists: A Cultural and Intellectual History of the Antimission Movement, 1800–1840* (New York: Routledge, 2004), 96.

15. Glenn T. Miller, *Piety and Intellect: The Aims and Purposes of Ante-Bellum Theological Education* (Atlanta, GA: Scholars Press, 1990), 297.

16. *The Articles of the Synod of Dort and Its Rejection of Errors: With the Events Which Made Way for that Synod*, translated and edited by Thomas Scott (Utica, NY: William Williams, 1831), available via Google Books.

17. Peter J. Thuesen, *Predestination: The American Career of a Contentious Doctrine* (New York: Oxford University Press, 2009), 81.

18. Ibid., 97.

19. Wyatt-Brown, *The Shaping of Southern Culture*, 117.

20. Generally used derogatorily, "hyper-Calvinism" is an interpretation of Calvin's theology that concludes that the message of salvation should not be offered to the nonelect, argues that God hates the nonelect, and stresses the secret over the revealed will of God.

21. Hyper-Calvinism was best articulated by John Gill (1697–1771), a self-taught British Baptist who argued against "free offers of grace"—that is, preaching the gospel message to the nonelect. Called "the only man that ever hunted and drove out Arminianism from the explanation of every verse in the Bible" by nineteenth-century Primitive Baptists Cushing Biggs Hassell and Sylvester Hassell in *History of the Church of God, from the Creation to A.D. 1885; Including Especially the History of the Kehukee Primitive Baptist* (Middleton, NY: Gilbert Beebe's Sons, 1886), 499, he is much admired by Westboro Baptists, though the church has found flaws with some of his claims, such as his argument that marriage to non-Christians is

acceptable. Joseph Hussey's 1707 *God's Operations of Grace but No Offers of His Grace* (London: D. Bridge, 1707; electronic resource by Farmington Hills, MI: Thomson Gale, 2003) is also foundational to the "no-offers" version of Calvinism espoused by hyper-Calvinists.

22. Peter J. Thuesen documents how the lightning rod, invented by Ben Franklin, divided believers, with some suggesting that "the new technology interfered with God's sovereign judgments and might draw even greater wrath from on high." New Englanders' efforts to control lightning, "the perfect image of an undomesticated providence," was punished, some argued, with an earthquake in Cape Anne, Massachusetts, in 1755. In response to the earthquake, pastor Thomas Prince noted that the prevalence of lightning rods in Boston was, no doubt, the reason why the city was so badly shaken, warning, "O! there is no getting out of the mighty Hand of God!" Thuesen, *Predestination*, 88–89, quoting Prince, *Earthquakes the Works of God, and Tokens of His Just Displeasure* (Boston, 1755). To this day, many Amish subgroups prohibit the use of lightning rods on their barns and houses. John A. Hostetler, *Amish Roots: A Treasury of History, Wisdom, and Lore* (Baltimore, MD: Johns Hopkins University Press, 1992), 87.

23. Indeed, Thomas Jefferson, writing to John Adams in a letter dated April 11, 1823, described Calvin's God as "a daemon of malignant spirit," *Jefferson's Extracts from the Gospels: "The Philosophy of Jesus" and "The Life and Morals of Jesus,"* edited by Dickinson W. Adams and Ruth W. Lester (Princeton, NJ: Princeton University Press, 1983), 410.

24. Wyatt-Brown, *The Shaping of Southern Culture*, 1027.

25. Although Arminianism, as articulated by Dutch theologian Jacobus Arminius, predates Methodism and although some Methodists are Calvinists, Arminianism probably has its strongest presence in Methodism.

26. "The Kehukee Declaration," *Essential Baptist Principles*, http://www.essential baptistprinciples.org/ resolutions/kehukee_declaration.htm.

27. Mathis, *The Making of the Primitive Baptists*, 67.

28. Thuesen, *Predestination*, 103.

29. Peacock and Tyson, *Pilgrims of Paradox*, 88.

30. As Wyatt-Brown notes, "Modernity in the ways of worship and faith had to be stoutly resisted or they would disgrace their perception of God Himself" (*The Shaping of Southern Culture*, 109).

31. In *Predestination*, Thuesen traces the battles over predestination among twentieth-century mainstream Baptists, with special attention devoted to the turnover at Baptist seminaries over the issue (172–208).

32. The exception to this is the "No-Hellers," Primitive Baptist Universalists

who are Calvinists yet believe that they will enter heaven. They are found in Pennsylvania, Tennessee, Kentucky, Virginia, and West Virginia. Howard Dorgan, *In the Hands of a Happy God* (Knoxville: University of Tennessee Press, 1997). Among the few who identify as Primitive Baptist Universalists is bluegrass musician Ralph Stanley, who was baptized in his seventies and now attends Slate Creek Primitive Baptist Church in Buchanan County, Virginia. Ralph Stanley with Eddie Dean, *Man of Constant Sorrow: My Life and Times* (New York: Gotham, 2009), 394.

33. Timothy P. Weber, "The Two-Edged Sword: The Fundamentalist Use of the Bible," in *The Bible in America: Essays in Cultural History*, edited by Nathan O. Hatch and Mark A. Noll (New York: Oxford University Press, 1982), 116.

34. Hassell and Hassell, *History of the Church of God*, estimated that in 1885 Primitive Baptists numbered about 100,000 members in 3,000 churches (630). Elmer T. Clark, *Small Sects of America*, rev. ed. (New York: Abingdon Press, 1937), estimated 65,000 in 1937 (203). No Primitive Baptist leader would speak on record, but all estimated the current number to be no more than 40,000 to 50,000.

35. Here Lawrence refers to the story of Hagar, Abram, and Sarai (whose names will soon be changed to Abraham and Sarah) that begins in Genesis 16. Abram, who was not able to produce a son with his wife, Sarai, impregnated her maidservant Hagar, who bore Ishmael. Abram was unwilling to wait for God's promise of a son through his wife, though God later delivered on this promise, blessing the aged Abram and Sarai with Isaac. Lawrence is encouraging the developing Primitive Baptist churches not to attempt to increase the church through means outside God's will, as Abram tried to secure himself a son with Hagar, but to wait for God's plan to bear fruit, as it did with the birth of Isaac.

36. Joshua Lawrence, "Address to the Particular Baptist Churches of the 'Old School' in the United States (1832)," in *Antirevivalism in Antebellum America: A Collection of Religious Voices*, edited by James D. Bratt (New Brunswick, NJ: Rutgers University Press, 2006), 77–78.

37. Primitive Baptists distinguish between "close" communion, in which Primitive Baptists from different congregations in good standing take communion together, and "closed" communion, in which only members from a congregation can take communion in that church.

38. Mathis, *The Making of the Primitive Baptists*, 149.

39. John G. Crowley, *Primitive Baptists of the Wiregrass South: 1815 to the Present* (Gainesville: University Press of Florida, 1998), 163.

40. Mathis, *The Making of the Primitive Baptists*, 150.

41. Nancy T. Ammerman, "Accounting for Christian Fundamentalisms: Social Dynamics and Rhetorical Strategies," in *Accounting for Fundamentalisms: The*

*Dynamic Character of Movements*, The Fundamentalism Project, vol. 4, edited by Martin E. Marty and R. Scott Appleby (Chicago: University of Chicago Press, 1991), 168.

42. Fred Phelps, sermon, February 7, 2010, http://www.godhatesfags.com/sermons/outlines/Sermon_20100207.pdf (emphasis in original).

43. Garrett, *Baptist Theology*, 209.

44. "Primitive Baptist Creeds of Faith," Primitive Baptist Web Station, http://www.pb.org/creeds.html.

45. Of course, Primitive Baptists are not the only Christians who adhere to these texts. The brand of Calvinism that they espouse is linked to biblical inerrancy and fundamentalism across denominations (Thuesen, *Predestination*, 192–193).

46. Although all Primitive Baptists espouse some form of Calvin's ideas about predestination, not all describe themselves as Calvinists. According to the web site of West San Antonio Primitive Baptist Church, "We embrace the biblical doctrines of salvation (soteriology) commonly known as Calvinism, but are distinguished from 'reformed' churches by our insistence that these principles pre-date the reformation and are explicitly taught throughout the scriptures." For this reason, the church says, "we prefer to describe our teaching as 'Calvinistic' to avoid the presumptions that usually attend the Calvinist label." "Are Primitive Baptists Calvinists?" Frequently Asked Questions, West San Antonio Primitive Baptist Church, http://www.westsapb.org/faq.htm. Because labeling Primitive Baptists as Calvinists denies their authenticity as direct descendants of the first-century church, some are insulted by the terminology. Elder Michael N. Ivey complains that "incorrect identification of Primitives as Calvinists is a common trap most religious historians seem to fall into." "A Welsh Succession of Primitive Baptist Faith and Practice," the Primitive Baptist Web Station, http://www.pb.org/pbdocs/chhist5.html. However, even those who find the term "Calvinism" problematic subscribe to the five points of Calvinism as put forth by John Calvin, though they do not agree with him on some other positions, most notably infant baptism and church-state relations. Further, some Primitive Baptists accuse Calvin of theological points about predestination different from those they hold; thus, for example, Liberty Primitive Baptist Church (South Smithville, GA) claims that Calvin argued for absolute predestination in all things, not just salvation, and double predestination (God's choice not only to elect some to salvation but to damn those who are not elect) but claims that these two beliefs are not in line with Primitive Baptist belief. "Ten Reasons Why Primitive Baptists Are Not Calvinist," Liberty Primitive Baptist Church, http://www.libertypbc.org/docs/Articles_Sermons/Ten%20Reasons%20Primitive%20Baptist%20are%20not%20Calvinist.pdf.

However, a study of other Primitive Baptist confessions of faith shows that at least some Primitive Baptist churches believe in absolute predestination and double predestination.

47. See, for example, the web sites of Ebenezer Primitive Baptist Church of Faith and Order (Westover, AL), http://www.ebenezerpbc.org/index.php?option =com_content&view=article&id=48:qa&catid=34:articles, and Bethlehem Primitive Baptist Church (Echola, AL), http://www.bethlehempbc.org/about-primitive -baptists.

48. William A. Scott, *Historical Protestantism: An Historical Introduction to Protestant Theology* (Englewood Cliffs, NJ: Prentice-Hall, 1971), 37.

49. Samuel Willard, "What Is the Duty That God Requires of Man?" Sermon CXLVII, Question XXXIX, from *Compleat Body of Divinity* (Boston: B. Green and S. Kneeland, 1726; electronic resource by Farmington Hills, MI: Thomas Gage, 2003).

50. Scott, *Historical Protestantism*, 37.

51. Ibid.

52. Jonathan Edwards, "God Glorified in Man's Dependence," Selected Writings of Jonathan Edwards, edited by Harold P. Simonson (New York: Frederick Ungar Publishing, 1970), 51–52.

53. Seventeenth-century Scottish Calvinist Hugh Binning explains in his essay on predestination that the apostle Paul, in Romans 9:15, in response to the charge that God is unkind in predesting Esau for hell and Jacob for heaven while the twins were still in Rebekah's womb, says that the apostle did not deny the human interpretation of this unconditional election as unfair but instead quoted from God's words to Moses: "I will have mercy on whom I will have mercy, and I will have compassion on whom I will have compassion." Says Binning, "That is the supreme rule of righteousness, and hitherto must we flee, as the surest anchor of our hope and stability." "Of Predestination (I)," in *The Works of the Pious, Reverend, and Learn'd Mr. Hugh Binning* (Glasgow: John Robb and Robert Duncan, 1768; electronic resource by Farmington, MI: Thomas Gage, 2003).

54. Thuesen, *Predestination*, 5.

55. This is the central thesis of Edwards's "God Glorified in Man's Dependence," 45–64.

56. Writes Elder Tim McCool, "This verse of scripture is often taken out of context to attempt to prove that Jesus died for all the inhabitants of the world. Taken in context, Jesus is making a factual point to Nicodemus, a Jew who erroneously believed that eternal salvation was limited to the physical nation of the Jews. Jesus explained to Nicodemus that God so loved the world (Greek *kosmos*—created

order), and NOT just the Jews, that He gave His only begotten Son. The purpose of His Son being given was that *whosoever*—which is a definitive group and not mankind in general—believeth on him should not perish but have eternal life." "Questions & Answers about Primitive Baptists," Lexington Primitive Baptist Church, http://www.lexpbc.org/Q24.html. Westboro Baptists make a similar case against extending John 3:16 to all of humanity in "FAQ: Doesn't the Bible Say That God Loves Everyone?" God Hates Fags, http://www.westborobaptistchurch.com /mobile/faq.html.

57. Crowley, "The Primitive or Old School Baptists," 164.

58. Says Crowley, "Belief in regeneration as a prerequisite to understanding Primitive doctrine made proselytizing, even of one's children, seem presumptuous, if not useless." *Primitive Baptists of the Wiregrass South*, 167.

59. John Calvin, *The Institutes of the Christian Religion*, from *The Protestant Reformation*, edited by Hans J. Hillerbrand (New York: Harper Torchbooks, 1968), 202.

60. Fred Phelps, sermon, March 28, 2010, http://www.godhatesfags.com /sermons/outlines/Sermon_20100328.pdf.

61. God's "great project," writes Hugh Binning in "Of Predestination (I)," "is not simply to manifest the glory of his goodness, but of his gracious and merciful goodness, the most tender and excellent of all; and therefore man must be miserable, sinful, and vile, that the riches of his grace may appear in choosing and saving such persons."

62. For example, Sara Phelps denounced her sister Libby Phelps, who left the church in 2009, in an interview captured on video and posted online, "Talking to the Phelps Fam about Beatings, Libby, and Why Standards Seem to Have Changed," http://www.youtube.com/watch?v=GhOESGugXH8. Sara Phelps has since then herself left the congregation.

63. Fred Phelps, sermon, February 7, 2010, http://www.godhatesfags.com /sermons/outlines/Sermon_20100207.pdf.

64. Westboro Baptist Church, "FAQ: Why Do You Have Signs Saying 'Thank God for 911,' 'Thank God for AIDS,' 'Thank God for Katrina,' 'Thank God for IEDs,' 'Thank God for Dead Soldiers,' and Otherwise Thanking God for Things that Humans Think Are Bad?" God Hates Fags, http://www.westborobaptist church.com/mobile.faq.html.; quoting John Gill's exposition of Psalm 58:10.

65. Fred Phelps, sermon, February 7, 2010, http://www.godhatesfags.com /sermons/outlines/Sermon_20100207.pdf.

66. Binning encouraged the Calvinist who questions the doctrine of predestination to "ponder that well, who thou art who disputest; who God is, against whom thou disputest—and if thou have spoken once, thou wilt speak no more—what

thou art, who is as clay formed out of nothing; what he is, who is the former; and hath not the potter power over the clay?" "Of Predestination (II)," in *The Works of the Pious, Reverend, and Learn'd Mr. Hugh Binning.*

67. Binning, "Of Predestination (I)," warns people not to question God's will regarding predestination, saying, "Predestination is a mystery, indeed, into which we should not curiously and boldly inquire beyond what is revealed; for then a soul must needs lose itself in that depth of wisdom, and perish in the search of unsearchableness." Predestination "is rather to be admired than conceived."

68. In contrast, the infralapsarian (or postlapsarian or sublapsarian) view of unconditional election argues that God elected people after the fall. Otherwise, infralapsarians argue, God would have been the author of original sin.

69. Jonathan Edwards, "Sinners in the Hands of an Angry God," *Selected Writings of Jonathan Edwards*, 97.

70. Rebekah Phelps-Davis, interview with the author, March 14, 2010.

71. Shirley Phelps-Roper, e-mail to the author, June 28, 2010.

72. A second but less common debate occurred between those who defended the traditional view that election was absolute and unconditional and those who believed that, though election to eternal salvation is unconditional, obedience to God's commandments in this life can result in "conditional time election," a respite from the anxiety of worrying about one's election. Crowley, *Primitive Baptists of the Wiregrass South*, 135–136.

73. Or, as Binning writes in "On Predestination (II)," "May he [God] not do with his own as he pleases? Because he is merciful to some souls, shall men be displeased, and do well to be angry? Or, because he, of his own free grace, extends it, shall he be bound by a rule to do so with all? Is he not both just and merciful, and is it not meet that both be showed forth? If he punish thee, thou canst not complain, for thou deserves it; if he show mercy, why should any quarrel, for it is free and undeserved grace. By saving some, he shows grace; by destroying others, he shows what all deserve."

74. Edwards, "God Glorified in Man's Dependence," 51.

75. Westboro Baptist Church, "Each Human Is Like Clay," *Vine*, August 8, 2015, https://vine.co/v/ewjqvLxijZw. Romans 9:21–24 says, "Hath not the potter power over the clay, of the same lump to make one vessel unto honor, and another unto dishonor? What if God, willing to show his wrath, and to make his power known, endured with much long-suffering the vessels of wrath fitted to destruction: And that he might make known the riches of his glory on the vessels of mercy, which he had afore prepared unto glory, Even us, whom he hath called, not of the Jews only, but also of the Gentiles?" Paul's point, according to Westboro

Baptist Church, is that God, as the creator of each person, can make each person for the purpose he chooses. Some people he makes "fitted to destruction" simply to illustrate this majestic power and mercy to those he has selected to save.

76. Thuesen, *Predestination*, 45–72.

77. Ibid., 67.

78. Max Weber, *The Protestant Ethic and the Spirit of Capitalism*, translated by Talcott Parsons (Mineola, NY: Dover, 2003).

79. For such introspection in the life of Jonathan Edwards, see George Marsden's *Jonathan Edwards: A Life* (New Haven, CT: Yale University Press, 2004).

80. Zach Phelps-Roper, interview with the author, June 27, 2015.

81. Mathis, *The Making of the Primitive Baptists*, 132.

82. Peter Iver Kaufman, *Prayer, Despair, and Drama: Elizabethan Introspection* (Urbana: University of Illinois Press, 1996), 20.

83. Westboro Baptist Church, "FAQ: If God Hates Homosexuals as a Group, Why Do You Sometimes Aim Signs at Individual People, Not at the Group? How Can You Say That an Individual Is in Hell?" God Hates Fags, http://www.god hatesfags.com/faq.html#Join.

84. Westboro Baptist Church, "FAQ: Are You a Sinner? If So, Does This Mean You Will Burn in Hell, or Are You Better Than These People?" God Hates Fags, http://www.godhatesfags.com/faq.html#Join.

85. Fred Phelps, sermon, March 14, 2010, http://www.godhatesfags.com /sermons/outlines/Sermon_20100314.pdf.

86. Fred Phelps, sermon, February 21, 2010, http://www.godhatesfags.com /sermons/outlines/Sermon_20100221.pdf.

87. Samuel Willard, "What Is Effectual Calling?," Sermon CXV, Question XXXI, from *Compleat Body of Divinity*.

88. Cotton Mather, *Free Grace Maintained and Improved* (Boston: B. Green, 1706; electronic resource by Farmington Hills, MI: Thomas Gale, 2003).

89. John Cotton, *An Exposition of First John* (Jay P. Green, Sr., 2003), 484.

90. Writes Binning in "Of Predestination (II)," "His eternal counsel of life is so far from loosing the reins to men's lusts, that it is the only certain foundation of holiness; it is the very spring and foundation from whence our sanctification flows by an infallible course."

91. In "What Is Effectual Calling?," Puritan preacher Samuel Willard noted three responses of those who "come within the sound of the Gospel": (1) those who "stop their ears, and turn their backs on it"; (2) those who "give external entertainment to the Gospel, and make a profession of Faith and Repentance, and so become members of a visible Church, and enjoy the external priviledges of

it; but yet their hearts were never thoroughly changed, nor they broken off from their sins"; and (3) those in whom "the habits of Sanctification . . . are wrought in Effectual Vocation, which are afterwards carried on in progressive Holiness."

92. Binning, "Of Predestination (II)."

93. Matthew 25:12.

94. Justin Kendall, "Dead to Fred," *The Pitch*, November 9, 2006, http:/www .pitch.com/content/printVersion/158048.

95. Scott, *Historical Protestantism*, 40.

96. Thuesen, *Predestination*, 3.

97. Peacock and Tyson, *Pilgrims of Paradox*, 28.

98. Boone, *The Bible Tells Them So*, 11.

99. Peacock and Tyson, *Pilgrims of Paradox*, 29.

100. Ibid., 97.

101. Wyatt-Brown, *The Shaping of Southern Culture*, 126.

102. Westboro Baptist Church, "FAQ: Who Are You, What Do You Do, and Why Do You Do It?" God Hates Fags, https://www.westborobaptistchurch.com /mobile/faq/html.

103. For example, the Phelps family is frequently referred to as "the Phelps clan" in news reports. The rhetorical association between the groups prompted Ku Klux Klan, LLC (incorporated in 2003 in Arkansas), to release the following statement on its web site: "The Ku Klux Klan, LLC. has not or EVER will have ANY connection with The 'Westboro Baptist Church.' We absolutely repudiate their activities." "News Release," KKK Homepage, http://kukluxklan.bz. Even here, the racist group uses quotation marks to undermine the authority of Westboro Baptist Church to call itself a church.

104. The church property and the homes that adjoin it are commonly described as a "compound," conjuring comparisons both to the Branch Davidians of Waco, Texas, and to the Fundamentalist Latter-Day Saints' Yearning for Zion Ranch near Eldorado, Texas.

105. For example, the May 10 and May 17, 2015, sermons were explications of Edwards's "Sinners in the Hands of an Angry God." Jonathan Phelps, "God Is Angry with the Wicked Every Day," May 10, 2015 (Part I), and May 17, 2015 (Part II), God Hates Fags, http://www.godhatesfags.com/sermons/outlines/Sermon _20150510.pdf.

106. See, for example, the level of detail about marital sex acts in Tim and Beverly LaHaye's *The Act of Marriage: The Beauty of Sexual Love* (Grand Rapids, MI: Zondervan, 1998) or Oral Roberts's unwittingly hilarious attempt to define appropriate sex as only vaginal-penis contact, undated sermon, http://www.youtube

.com/watch?v=_-BxqfAM1Ag. Of course, not all evangelicals adopt such stringent rules about appropriate sexual contact between opposite-sex married adults, as Kelsey Burke shares in her ethnography of online Christian sex-toy stores and sex web sites, *Christians under Covers: Evangelicals and Sexual Pleasure on the Internet* (Berkeley: University of California Press, 2016.)

107. Sam Phelps-Roper, interview with the author, August 13, 2005.

108. Shirley Phelps-Roper, e-mail to the author, September 28, 2006.

109. Fred Phelps, "The Charge Given to the Married by the Church of the Lord Jesus Christ: On the Occasion of the Marriage of Brent D. Roper and Shirley L. Phelps (Members of the Westboro Baptist Church) on November 25, 1983," God Hates Fags, November 25, 1983, http://www.godhatesfags.com/sermons/19831125_brent-roper-shirley-phelps-wedding.pdf.

110. Rebekah Phelps-Davis, interview with the author, March 14, 2010.

111. *The Most Hated Family in America*, television documentary, written by Louis Theroux and directed by Geoffrey O'Conner (London: BBC, 2007).

112. Joe Taschler and Steve Fry, "Faxes, Pickets, Politics Carry Phelps' Message," *Topeka Capital-Journal*, August 3, 1994, http://cjonline.com/indepth/phelps/stories/080394_phelps21.shtml.

113. Gay Catholics who are in same-sex relationships are sometimes denied communion. Laurie Goodstein, "Gay and Transgender Catholics Urge Pope Francis to Take a Stand," *New York Times*, July 28, 2015, http://www.nytimes.com/2015/07/29/us/gay-and-transgender-catholics-urge-pope-francis-to-take-a-stand.html?_r=0. Gay Protestants may be publicly kicked out of their churches, may be quietly asked to leave their congregations, or may simply face such hostility that they cannot return. Bernadette C. Barton, *Pray the Gay Away: The Extraordinary Lives of Bible Belt Christians* (New York: New York University Press, 2012).

114. Jennifer Glass and Philip Levchak, "Red States, Blue States, and Divorce: Understanding the Impact of Conservative Protestantism on Regional Variation in Divorce Rates," *American Journal of Sociology* 119, no. 4 (2014): 1034. See also Barna Group, "New Marriage and Divorce Statistics Released," *Barna*, March 31, 2008, https://www.barna.org/barna-update/family-kids/42-new-marriage-and-divorce-statistics-released#.VncrrbYrJaQ.

115. Lucinda Borkett-Jones, "'Many Women in Church Have Had an Abortion but It's the Last Place They Can Talk about It," *Christian Post*, May 19, 2015, http://www.christiantoday.com/article/many.women.in.church.have.had.an.abortion.but.its.the.last.place.they.can.talk.about.it/54193.htm.

116. Susan Crawford Sullivan, *Living Faith: Everyday Religion and Mothers in Poverty* (Chicago: University of Chicago Press, 2011), 61.

117. An unknown number of pastors, for example, were implicated in infidelity when hackers shared data from the web site Ashley Madison (which has the slogan "Life Is Short. Have an Affair") in the summer of 2015, including high-profile evangelists such as R. C. Sproul, Jr. R. C. Sproul, Jr., "Judgment and Grace," *Jesus Changes Everything*, August 31, 2015, http://rcsprouljr.com/blog/general/judgment-and-grace.

118. David Roach, "Lifeway Research Finds Pastors Divided on When to Perform Weddings," *LifeWay*, June 28, 2011, http://www.lifeway.com/Article/LifeWay-Research-pastors-divided-when-to-perform-weddings.

119. Stephanie Samuel, "Southern Baptist Convention to 'Disfellowshipped' Church Pastor: Denomination's Failings Regarding Divorce Are Not an Opportunity for Gay Marriage," *Christian Post*, October 25, 2014, http://www.christianpost.com/news/southern-baptist-convention-to-disfellowshipped-church-pastor-denominations-failings-regarding-divorce-are-not-an-opportunity-for-gay-marriage-128618/#hAQwXFeK7Ju42WZ9.99.

120. David Roach, "SBC Not 'Third Way' on Divorce," *Baptist Press*, October 23, 2014, http://www.bpnews.net/43583/sbc-not-third-way-on-divorce.

121. Sarah Kaplan and James Higdon, "The Defiant Kim Davis, The Ky. Clerk Who Refuses to Issue Gay Marriage Licenses," *Washington Post*, September 2, 2015, http://www.washingtonpost.com/news/morning-mix/wp/2015/09/02/meet-kim-davis-the-ky-clerk-who-defying-the-supreme-court-refuses-to-issue-gay-marriage-licenses.

122. Shirley Phelps-Roper, e-mail to the author, May 12, 2010.

123. Robert N. Minor, *When Religion Is an Addiction* (St. Louis, MO: Humanity-Works!, 2007), 64.

124. For example, after a churchwide study session on the parable of the persistent in Luke 18 on Sunday, July 4, 2010, a child in upper elementary school was responsible for demonstrating his knowledge of Revelation 9, taken from the King James translation, to Shirley Phelps-Roper. Although church members are supposed to memorize scripture, mere rote recitation is insufficient to demonstrate mastery. For this reason, Shirley interrupted the child after nearly every verse of the twenty-one-verse chapter to quiz him on the meaning of words, ask him to explain why the writer chose to repeat a phrase, or ask for a cross-reference. After he ably answered each of her concerns, the child quickly picked up his recitation at the verse where he had been interrupted.

125. Shirley Phelps-Roper, e-mail to the author, May 12, 2010.

126. Thuesen, *Predestination*, 215.

127. Rick Warren, *The Purpose Driven Life* (Grand Rapids, MI: Zondervan, 2002).

128. Morgan Lee, "Russell Moore: Westboro Baptists Are Not Baptist; Think 'Book of Mormon' Play to LDS Church," *Christian Post*, March 24, 2014, http:// www.christianpost.com/news/russell-moore-westboro-baptist-are-not-baptists -think-book-of-mormon-broadway-play-to-lds-church-116588. For another typical argument refuting Westboro Baptist Church's claim to be either Baptist or a church, see Norris Burke, "Inaccurate Labels Bring False Assumptions," *Star Gazette*, March 4, 2015, http://www.stargazette.com/story/news/connections/faith /2015/03/04/norris-burkes-column/24372981.

129. Cynthia Burack, "Compassion Campaigns and Antigay Politics: What Would Arendt Do?" *Politics and Religion* 2 (April 2009): 31–53.

130. Binning, "On Predestination (I)."

131. Joe Taschler and Steve Fry, "Phelps Flock: Afterlife Is Prearranged," *Topeka Capital-Journal*, August 3, 1994, http://cjonline.com/indepth/phelps/stories /080394_phelps18.shtml.

132. Richard Baxter, "Directions for Hating Sin," in *The Practical Works of Richard Baxter*, vol. 1 (London: George Virtue, 1838), 89.

133. Fred Phelps, sermon, February 21, 2010, http://www.godhatesfags.com /sermons/outlines/Sermon_20100221.pdf.

134. Westboro Baptist Church, "FAQ: How Do You Feel about People Who Confess and Realize Their Sins?," God Hates Fags, http://www.westborobaptist church.com/mobile/faq.html.

135. Cynthia Burack, "Contesting Compassion: Love Wins Out in the Ex-Gay Movement." Paper presented at the Western Political Science Association, Albuquerque, NM, March 16–18, 2006, http://www.allacademic.com//meta/p_mla _apa_research_citation/0/9/7/6/0/pages97608/p97608-1.php.

136. Westboro Baptist Church, "FAQ: Have Any Homosexuals Repented as a Result of Your Picketing?" God Hates Fags, http://www.westborobaptistchurch .com/mobile/faq.html#Repent.

137. Nathan Dinsdale, "Father Knows Best," *Santa Fe Reporter*, April 20, 2005, http://www.altweeklies.com/aan/father_knows_best/ Story?oid=145872.

138. Westboro Baptist Church, "FAQ: 'Do You Ever Pray for the Salvation of Those You Feel Are Condemned?,'" God Hates Fags, http://www.godhatesfags .com/faq.html#Condemned.

139. The church quotes John 17:9, in which Jesus says, "I pray for them [the elect]: I pray not for the world, but for them which thou has given me; for they are thine." The church understands Matthew 5:44 ("Pray for them who despitefully use you, and persecute you") as a recognition that there are elect outside the church who do need to hear its message, just as Saul of Tarsus, before his conversion, was an enemy of Christians. Ibid.

140. Ben Phelps, @ChristianQuotes, @FagsDoomNations, Twitter, August 23, 2015, https://twitter.com/search?f=tweets&q=Preaching%20has%20a%20 two-fold%20puprose%3A%20it%20saves&src=typd.

141. Steve Drain, interview with the author, April 16, 2015.

142. Ibid.

143. Roy Bragg, "Topeka Has Little Love for Hateful Preacher," *Express-News* (San Antonio, TX), April 10, 2005, http://nl.newsbank.com/nl-search/we/Archives ?p_product=SAEC&p_theme=saec&p_action=search&p_maxdocs=200&s_disp string=Topeka%20AND%20date(4/9/2005%20to%204/12/2005)&p_field_date -0=YMD_date&p_params_date-0=date:B,E&p_text_date-0=4/9/2005%20to%204 /12/2005)&p_field_advanced-0=&p_text_advanced-0=(Topeka)&xcal_numdocs =50&p_perpage=25&p_sort=YMD_date:D&xcal_useweights=no.

144. Steve Drain, interview with the author, April 11, 2010.

CHAPTER 3. THE MEANS, MINISTRIES, AND MISSION
OF WESTBORO BAPTIST CHURCH

1. David Ehrenstein, "Kinder, Gentler Homophobia," *Advocate*, April 6, 2006, http://www.advocate.com/article.aspx?id=43756.

2. Clara S. Lewis artfully argues that, in the 1990s and 2000s, public discourse around hate (including antigay) crimes both expressed public outrage at the brutality of such crimes as the murder of Matthew Shepard and helped to distance the public from those events as perpetrators were stigmatized as people who do not share a community's values rather than as products of deeply embedded structures of prejudice and hate. Lewis, *Tough on Hate? The Cultural Politics of Hate Crimes* (New Brunswick, NJ: Rutgers University Press, 2013).

3. Don't Ask, Don't Tell was repealed by President Obama in 2011. DOMA, which aims to "define and protect the institution of marriage," according to the text of the bill, became public law 104-199 on September 21, 1996, and became null with the US Supreme Court's 2015 *Obergefell v. Hodges* decision, which recognized the legality of same-sex marriages in all states.

4. *Hatemongers*, VHS, directed by Steve Drain (2000), http://www.hatemongers .com/clips.html.

5. Allegations of Gage Park as a "cruisy area" were supported by excerpts from *Bob Damron's Address Book, '92*, a listing of gay-friendly establishments and places where casual gay sex was available (as reprinted in a letter to Mayor Butch Felker and Police Chief Bob Weinkauf from Westboro Baptist Church, dated August 31, 1992). Further, Max Movsovitz, a gay man who agreed to consensual oral sex with an undercover police officer in a case that Movsovitz and gay rights activists hoped would overturn Kansas antisodomy laws, was arrested in Gage Park

in 1995, furthering the impression that Gage Park was an area where gay sex was common. See Deb Taylor, "Nightmare in Gage Park," *Liberty Press*, October 1998, http://www.debtaylor.com/deb/articles/maxnew.html.

6. Joe Taschler and Steve Fry, "Faxes, Pickets, Politics Carry Phelps' Message," *Topeka Capital-Journal*, August 3, 1994, http://cjonline.com/indepth/phelps/stories /080394_phelps21.shtml.

7. Annie Gowan, "Holy Hell: Fred Phelps, Clergyman, Is on a Crusade," *Washington Post*, November 12, 1995, https://www.washingtonpost.com/lifestyle/style /holy-hellfred-phelps-clergyman-is-on-a-crusade/2014/03/20/afoa3e52-b06b -11e3-a49e-76adc9210f19_story.html.

8. See, for example, Westboro Baptist Church, "Declare Independence from Gay Oppression," press release, July 1, 1991.

9. Jael Phelps, interview with the author, April 18, 2010.

10. Kansas's statute 1969 21-3505 made same-sex anal or oral intercourse a misdemeanor punishable by a fine of up to $1,000 and six months in jail. The law, unlike many other states' antisodomy laws, applied only to same-sex couples and, unlike *any* other state's laws, did not provide exemptions for minors. The law was at the center of *Matthew R. Limon v. State of Kansas*, a 2000 case that led to the imprisonment of eighteen-year-old Matthew R. Limon, a teenager with slight mental retardation who already had two similar charges against him, for performing consensual oral sex on a fellow male resident, age fourteen, at a home for teens with mental impairments. Had Limon been found guilty of the same crime with a fourteen-year-old girl, he would have received a maximum of fifteen months in prison, but, under Kansas law, he was originally sentenced to more than seventeen years. By the time the ACLU won an appeal of the case, Limon had already served five years of his original sentence. At the original trial, Attorney General Jared Maag, representing the state, defended the state's right to punish same-sex couples engaging in consensual oral or anal contact without making the same acts between members of opposite sex illegal by saying that the law was aimed at promoting "traditional sexual roles." "The state argued the reasons for different punishments of similar sex acts was to promote marriage, encourage procreation and prevent the spread of sexually transmitted diseases," reported Scott Rothschild, "Judge Ridicules Underage Sex Law," *Lawrence Journal-World*, December 3, 2003, http://www2.ljworld.com/news/2003/dec/03/judge_ridicules_underage. Kansas's law, like Texas's, was struck down by the US Supreme Court in 2003, with Justice O'Connor making a special note that, even if states could make anal sex illegal, applying the law only to same-sex couples violated the equal-protection guarantee of the Constitution.

11. *The Most Hated Family in America*, television documentary, written by Louis Theroux and directed by Geoffrey O'Conner (London: BBC, 2007).

12. The church requested payment of $96,740.21 for costs related to the case; see Andy Marso, "Marine's Dad Vows to Defy Westboro Church on Court Costs, Lawyer Says," Fox News, March 9, 2011, http://www.foxnews.com/politics/2011 /03/09/marines-dad-vows-defy-westboro-church-court-costs-lawyer-says.

13. Nathan Dinsdale, "Father Knows Best," *Santa Fe Reporter*, April 20, 2005, http://www.altweeklies.com/aan/father_knows_best/Story?oid=145872.

14. Gabriel A. Almond, Emmanual Sivan, and R. Scott Appleby, "Fundamentalisms: Genus and Species," in *Fundamentalisms Comprehended*, The Fundamentalism Project, vol. 4, edited by Martin E. Marty and R. Scott Appleby (Chicago: University of Chicago Press, 1991), 402.

15. Moreover, correcting misrepresentations would require a lot of time, as they are common in reports about Westboro Baptist Church. Fred Phelps did, however, address inaccurate reporting on the church at the start of many of his sermons as well as in public and private letters to his opponents. For example, he took issue with Mark Enoch's reporting, from October 12, 1991, in Topeka's *Capital-Journal*, especially his failure to understand the "age-old theological dispute between Calvinists and Arminians," though he expressed no confidence in Enoch's ability to understand theology, saying, "You are too morally depraved even to comprehend this old-time gospel I preach." Fred Phelps, letter to Mark Enoch, October 31, 1991.

16. Shirley Phelps-Roper, interview with the author, July 30, 2008.

17. Steve Drain, "Our Commission: Saturation," Sign Movies, January 18, 2014, http://www.signmovies.com.

18. Ibid.

19. Taschler and Fry, ""Faxes, Pickets, Politics Carry Phelps' Message."

20. Ibid.

21. Donna Minkowitz, "Dancing on Your Grave," POZ, December 1994/January 1995, http://www.poz.com/articles/2106_13378.shtml.

22. Taschler and Fry, "Faxes, Pickets, Politics Carry Phelps' Message."

23. Jael Phelps, interview with the author, April 18, 2010.

24. Rebekah Phelps-Davis, interview with the author, July 18, 2010.

25. Taschler and Fry, "Faxes, Pickets, Politics Carry Phelps' Message."

26. For a history of public response to the web site, see "Hate, American Style," *Wired*, July 2, 1997, http://www.wired.com/culture/lifestyle/news/1997/07/4872.

27. For example, the church maintains numerous Twitter accounts that allow it to "tweach" its message in no more than 140 characters. Just as the founders of

Twitter hope to saturate the world with their technology, argues Fred Phelps, Jr., so, too, is the mission of Westboro Baptist Church "to preach to the world," as "that is the primary reason we exist"; see Fred Phelps, Jr., "Tweaching," Sign Movies, December 14, 2013, http://www.signmovies.com. In church-produced videos titled "Tweaching" and "Vines," Sign Movies, February 8, 2014, http://www.sign movies.com, Fred Phelps, Jr., walks viewers through the ways the church uses social media to share its message and provides directions for how viewers can access them.

28. Shirley Phelps-Roper, e-mail to the author, April 1, 2010.

29. Fred Phelps, sermon, February 7, 2010, http://www.godhatesfags.com /sermons/outlines/Sermon_20100207.pdf.

30. Westboro Baptist Church, "Is Hell Too Harsh?" *Spare Not* blog, November 11, 2011, http://blogs.sparenot.com/workmen/2011/11/11/is-hell-too-harsh-2.

31. Jonathan Phelps, interview with the author, April 18, 2010.

32. The King James translation of Zechariah 1:21 says, "Then said I, What come these to do? And he spake, saying, These are the horns which have scattered Judah, so that no man did lift up his head: but these are come to fray them, to cast out the horns of the Gentiles, which lifted up their horn over the land of Judah to scatter it."

33. Steve Fry, "Picketers Defend Their Duty to Preach," *Topeka Capital-Journal*, November 28, 1995.

34. Brent Roper, "Love Thy Neighbor Equals Rebuke," Sign Movies, http:// www.signmovies.com/videos/signmovies/index.html.

35. Steve Drain, interview with the author, April 16, 2015.

36. The Fourth Circuit Court of Appeals decision can be found at http://pacer .ca4.uscourts.gov/opinion.pdf/081026.P.pdf; internal citations omitted.

37. The impression that America devalues fundamentalist beliefs is widely espoused in conservative Christian rhetoric. Summit Ministries, for example, claims that "today countless Christian youth have fallen victim to the popular ideas of our modern world. Most have adopted these ideas into their own worldview, while still others go on to renounce their Christian faith altogether." The organization offers classes and camps that train young people to counter the influences of Marxism, feminism, and cultural relativism; see "About," Summit Ministries, http://www.summit.org/about.

38. *The Most Hated Family in America*.

39. Ibid.

40. For example, Margie Phelps received an award from the state for her outstanding work in corrections in 2005; see Alex Friedmann, "Hate-Filled Religious

Fanatics Find a Home in Kansas Corrections," *Prison Legal News*, December 2006, https://www.prisonlegalnews.org/11027_displayArticle.aspx.

41. Lizz Phelps, ninth daughter of Fred and Margie Phelps, was a lawyer for the sheriff's department before returning to school to earn an MA in public administration. She now works for the state in ensuring compliance with Medicaid for people with mental health impairments and disabilities. Margie Phelps, fourth child of Fred and Margie Phelps, works in corrections in addition to consulting for the family law firm. Brent Roper, husband of Shirley Phelps-Roper, is director of human resources for the National Association of Insurance Commissioners and has written textbooks on the use of computers in law offices (*Using Computers in the Law Office* [Florence, KY: Cengage, 2007]) and the management of law offices (*Practical Law Office Management* [Florence, KY: Cengage, 2006]).

42. For example, Ben Phelps, son of Fred Phelps, Jr., and Betty Phelps, made a $500 donation to the 2002 campaign of Kansas attorney general Phil Kline. In 2006, when Kline's then-opponent Paul Morrison noted that Kline had accepted the contribution, Kline promptly donated $500 to the Patriot Guard Riders, a motorcycle brigade that stages counterprotests at military funerals where Westboro Baptists picket. See Scott Rothschild, "Kline Makes Donation to the Patriot Guard Riders," *Lawrence Journal-World*, August 16, 2006, http://www2.ljworld.com /news/2006/aug/16/kline_makes_donation_patriot_guard.

43. "Repentance in Pasadena," *Time*, June 11, 1951, http://www.time.com/time /magazine/article/0,9171,814897,00.html.

44. Westboro Baptist Church, "Filthy Manner of Life," God Hates America, http://www.godhatesamerica.com/filthymanneroflife.html.

45. Gerard A. Brandmeyer and R. Serge Denisoff, "Status Politics: An Appraisal of the Application of a Concept," *Pacific Sociological Review* 12, no. 1 (Spring 1969): 5–11.

46. For a time, Westboro Baptist Church had a relationship with a small church in Indiana that held similar beliefs, but that church dissolved amid leadership problems.

47. For an interesting defense of Westboro Baptist Church's theology and right to espouse it, see *The Right to Be Wrong*, a blog maintained by Canadian Alyzza Martin, http://www.therighttobewrong.net. Despite Canada's 2002 law against discrimination based on sexual orientation (C-415) and the nation's 2003 law making hate speech a criminal offense, known as the Fred Phelps law (C-250), Martin defends the right of the church to engage in funeral pickets. She identifies as a Christian, but, because of her theology, she would never be accepted by Westboro Baptist Church. Texts of the Canadian law are available at "House

Publications—Private Members' Bills," Parliament of Canada, http://www2.parl .gc.ca/HouseBills/BillsPrivate.aspx?language=E&Parl=37&Ses=1#C-415.

48. William R. Hutchison, *Religious Pluralism in America: The Contentious History of a Founding Ideal* (New Haven, CT: Yale University Press, 2003), 219.

49. John G. Crowley, "The Primitive or Old School Baptists," in *The Baptist River: Essays on the Many Tributaries of a Diverse Tradition*, edited by W. Glenn Jonas, Jr. (Macon, GA: Mercer University Press, 2006), 181.

50. Westboro Baptist Church, "Welcome Depraved Sons and Daughters of Adam," God Hates Fags, http://www.godhatesfags.com.

51. According to 4 USC § 8 (a), "The flag should never be displayed with the union down, except as a signal of dire distress in instances of extreme danger to life or property"; see US Government Publishing Office, http://www.gpo.gov /fdsys/pkg/USCODE-2011-title4/pdf/USCODE-2011-title4-chap1-sec8.pdf.

52. Westboro Baptist Church, "FAQ: What Are You Trying to Accomplish?" God Hates Fags, http://www.westborobaptistchurch.com/mobile/faq.html.

53. Gabriel A. Almond, Emmanual Sivan, and R. Scott Appleby, "Explaining Fundamentalisms," in *Fundamentalisms Comprehended*, The Fundamentalism Project, vol. 5, edited by Martin E. Marty and R. Scott Appleby (Chicago: University of Chicago Press, 1991), 429.

54. James L. Peacock and Ruel W. Tyson, Jr., *Pilgrims of Paradox: Calvinism and Experience among the Primitive Baptists of the Blue Ridge* (Washington, DC: Smithsonian Institution Press, 1989), 99.

55. Shirley Phelps-Roper, interview with the author, July 30, 2008.

56. Shirley Phelps-Roper, interview with David Pakman, *Midweek Politics Radio*, March 11, 2010, http://www.midweekpolitics.com/shirley-phelps-roper.

57. Cynthia Burack and Jyl J. Josephson, "Origin Stories," in Cynthia Burack, *Sin, Sex, and Democracy: Antigay Rhetoric and the Christian Right* (Albany: State University of New York Press, 2008), 89.

58. Quoted, from "Eternity of Hell Torments," in Peter J. Thuesen, *Predestination: The American Career of a Contentious Doctrine* (New York: Oxford University Press, 2009), 85.

59. "Thank God for 9/11," Sign Movies, http://www.signmovies.net/videos /signmovies/index.html.

60. Fred Phelps, "A Message to Topeka from Fred Phelps," *Topeka Capital-Journal*, January 4, 2002, http://cjonline.com/indepth/phelps/stories/phelps_letter.shtml.

61. Westboro Baptist Church, "Manifesto of Westboro Baptist Church," God Hates Fags, http://www.godhatesfags.com/written/WestboroBaptistChurchinfo /tulip.html.

62. This position is expressed in Westboro Baptists' signs that say "AIDS = DEATH," a slogan that mimics ACT-UP's "SILENCE = DEATH" slogan. The stance was held by other Christians as well, though. For example, in 1987, the first time the question was asked by Pew Research, 60 percent of white evangelicals agreed that "AIDS might be God's punishment for immoral sexual behavior." Currently 38 percent of white evangelicals agree with this statement, whereas 23 percent of the general public does. Pew Research Center for the People & the Press, "23% See AIDS as God's Punishment for Immorality," Databank, http://pewresearch.org /databank/dailynumber/?NumberID=311.

63. Asked Ronald Reagan on April 2, 1987, "When it comes to preventing AIDS, don't medicine and morality teach the same lessons?" Gerald M. Boyd, "Reagan Urges Abstinence for Young to Avoid AIDS," New York Times, April 2, 1987, http:// www.nytimes.com/1987/04/02/us/reagan-urges-abstinence-for-young-to-avoid -aids.html. Echoing Reagan's position that AIDS-related deaths were an appropriate punishment for "unnatural" behavior, his communications director, Pat Buchanan, called AIDS "nature's revenge on gay men"; see David W. Webber, "John Roberts's Queer Reasoning on AIDS," Nation, September 26, 2005, http:// www.thenation.com/article/robertss-queer-reasoning-aids.

64. Argued Pat Robertson on a 1995 episode of The 700 Club, "[Homosexuals] want to come into churches and disrupt church services and throw blood all around and try to give people AIDS and spit in the face of ministers," as quoted in People for the American Way, "Gays as Enemies of Faith," Anti-Gay Politics and the Religious Right, 1998, http://www.pfaw.org/media-center/publications/anti -gay-politics-and-the-religious-right#deathpenalty.

65. Westboro Baptist Church members articulate this position in "Death Penalty for Fags," an undated video featuring Ben Phelps available at Sign Movies. Peter J. Peters, who preaches racist, anti-Semitic Christian Identity theology through his Scriptures for America radio show, has articulated this position in "Intolerance of, Discrimination against, and the Death Penalty for Homosexuals Is Prescribed in the Bible" (LaPorte, CO: Scriptures for America, 1992). Gene Robinson, an openly gay and sexually active Episcopal priest who now serves as bishop of New Hampshire, recalls his horror when, during an appearance on a radio call-in show, a self-identified Christian calmly explained to him why he supported the biblical mandate for executing those who engage in same-sex contact. When Robinson was nominated to be bishop in 2003, he received numerous death threats, including some that invoked these passages; see For the Bible Tells Me So, DVD, directed by Daniel Karslake (New York: First Run Features, 2009). Since his consecration, Robinson has continued to face such threats and wears a bulletproof vest during

some public appearances; see "Williams Criticized by Gay Bishop," *BBC News*, April 30, 2008, http://news.bbc.co.uk/2/hi/uk_news/7374662.stm.

66. "Vote Randall Lt. Governor," undated flier. In 1992, then–Senate candidate Mike Huckabee, who was a Republican presidential primary candidate in 2008, responded to an Associated Press questionnaire about HIV/AIDS policy by saying, "We need to take steps that would isolate the carriers of this plague. . . . It is the first time in the history of civilization in which the carriers of a genuine plague have not been isolated from the general population, and in which this deadly disease for which there is no cure is being treated as a civil rights issue instead of the true health crisis it represents." Though Huckabee has since said that he was not suggesting a quarantine, his endorsement of "isolation" was certainly interpreted that way by listeners. Associated Press, "Huckabee AIDS Comment Alarms Victim's Mom," MSNBC, December 11, 2007, http://www.msnbc.msn.com/id/22197928.

67. The dehumanization of gay people is repeated in Westboro Baptist Church rhetoric, with gay men and women compared to animals, called "beasts" and "brutes" and, in particular lesbians, "mutts." The Southern Baptist Convention likewise disallows the consideration that same-sex activity or desire are natural human behavior, saying, "God, the Creator and Judge of all, has ruled that homosexual conduct is always a gross moral and spiritual abomination for any person, whether male or female, under any circumstance, without exception" (Southern Baptist Convention, "Resolution on Domestic Partner Benefits," June 1997, http://www.sbc.net/resolutions/615), that "even desire to engage in a homosexual sexual relationship is always sinful, impure, degrading, shameful, unnatural, indecent and perverted" (Southern Baptist Convention, "Resolution on Homosexual Marriage," June 1996, http://www.sbc.net/resolutions/614/resolution-on-homosexual-marriage), and that the "homosexual lifestyle" is both "sinful and dangerous both to the individuals involved and to society at large" (Southern Baptist Convention, "On Same Sex Marriage," June 2003, http://www.sbc.net/resolutions/search/results.asp?query=gay at.

68. Westboro Baptist Church, fax, August 11, 1993.

69. Jodi Wilgoren, "Vote in Topeka Hangs on Gay Rights and a Vitriolic Local Protester," *New York Times*, March 1, 2005, http://www.nytimes.com/2005/03/01/national/01topeka.html.

70. Dinsdale, "Father Knows Best."

71. Ibid.

72. Fred Phelps, letter to editor Jeff Yarbrough, *Advocate*, October 26, 1993, Kansas Collection at the Kenneth Spencer Research Library, University of Kansas, Lawrence.

73. Ibid.

74. Ibid.

75. Westboro Baptist Church, "The O'Reilly Factor," parody, Sign Movies, http://www.signmovies.com/videos/news/index.html.

76. "Speaking Out," *Advocate*, January 25, 1994, 88.

77. "Grieving Family Forced to Deal with Phelps," *Topeka Capital-Journal*, August 3, 1994, http://cjonline.com/indepth/phelps/stories/080394_phelps06.shtml.

78. Michael Dorgan and Miranda Ewell, "San Francisco Mourns Loss of Friend and Hero: Shilts' Funeral Interrupted by Protesters," *Mercury News* (San Jose, CA), February 23, 1994, http://www.lexisnexis.com/hottopics/lnacademic/?.

79. Shirley Phelps-Roper, e-mail to the author, October 13, 2008.

80. Cynthia Burack, "From Doom Town to Sin City: Chick Tracts and Antigay Politics," *New Social Science* 28, no. 2 (June 2006): 175.

81. Steve Drain, interview with the author, April 16, 2015.

82. Elizabeth Phelps, e-mail to the author, October 26, 2010. For example, the church has picketed at the Cotton Bowl twice, the Fiesta Bowl once, and a Big 12 championship game; sporting events at the University of Kansas, Kansas State University, and in Nebraska; an ice-skating competition; and professional baseball and hockey games. Online discussion with Shirley Phelps-Roper, Charles Hockenbarger, Elizabeth Phelps, Fred Phelps, Jr., and Steve Drain, October 26, 2010.

83. Sara Phelps, "Ever Burn," parody of "Telephone" by Lady Gaga, Westboro Baptist Church Music Videos, Sign Movies, http://www.signmovies.com/videos/music/index.html.

84. Lady Gaga, Twitter, July 17, 2010, http://twitter.com/ladygaga/status/18791306606.

85. Lady Gaga, "At the Risk of Drawing Attention to a Hateful Organization," Facebook, July 17, 2010, http://www.facebook.com/note.php?note_id=417876234034&id=10376464573.

86. Westboro Baptist Church, "Westboro Baptist Church to Picket Whoremonger in Training Justin Bieber at the Sprint Center," press release, God Hates Fags, July 2, 2010, http://downloads.westborobaptistchurch.com/listDirectory/linklokurl.php?linklokauth=ZGxpbmRleC5waHA%2FZGlyPUZsaWVyXoFyY2hpdmUvLDEyODQwNjQxNDQsNzUuMzkuMTM4LjE5NywwLDEsTExfMCwsZmYzZGIyMTNhMDA3ZjJhZDhiNTllYjQwOTA3MWMzNjU%3D/dlindex.php?dir=Flier_Archive.

87. Peter Toon, *The New Dictionary of Theology* (Leicester, England: IVP, 1988), 324.

88. Westboro Baptist Church, "FAQ: Do You Ever Pray for the Salvation of Those You Feel Are Condemned?" God Hates Fags, http://www.godhatesfags.com/faq.html#Condemned.

89. Westboro Baptist Church, "FAQ: Why Don't You Leave It up to God and Stop Wasting Your Time Telling People That They Are Wrong?" God Hates Fags, http://www.godhatesfags.com/faq.html#Wrong.

90. Westboro Baptist Church, "Jesus Was a Jew—and You Killed Him," Jews Killed Jesus, http://www.jewskilledjesus.com.

91. Westboro Baptist Church, "Naughty Figs," Jews Killed Jesus, http://www.jewskilledjesus.com.

92. Ibid.

93. Ibid.

94. Westboro Baptist Church, "Come Together Good Figs," parody of the Beatles' "Come Together," God Hates Fags, http://www.godhatesfags.com/audio/index.html.

95. Westboro Baptist Church, "Sweden's Filthy Manner of Life," God Hates Sweden, http://www.godhatessweden.com/filthymanneroflife.html.

96. Westboro Baptist Church, "Naughty Figs."

97. Shirley Phelps-Roper, interview with the author, July 18, 2010.

98. Westboro Baptist Church, "Priests Rape Boys," Priests Rape Boys, http://www.priestsrapeboys.com.

99. Ibid.

100. Westboro Baptist Church, "All Parishioners of the Roman Catholic Church Are Pedophile Rape Enablers," Priests Rape Boys, http://www.priestsrapeboys.com/parishioners.html.

101. Ibid. (emphasis in original).

102. Abigail Phelps, interview with the author, November 4, 2009.

103. Westboro Baptist Church, "Other Christian 'Churches' Have Gone Awhoring after Strange Gods," Priests Rape Boys, http://www.priestsrapeboys.com/otherchurches.html.

104. Steve Drain, "Beast Watch: Lying False Prophets Are to Blame," Beast Obama, February 17, 2010, http://www.beastobama.com/beastwatch/index.html.

105. Ibid.

106. Ibid.

107. Ibid.

108. Steve Drain, "Your Pastor Is a Whore," Sign Movies, http://www.signmovies.com/videos/signmovies/index.html.

109. Westboro Baptist Church, "Open Letter to Primitive Baptist Churches,"

December 10, 2009, http://www.westborobaptistchurch.com/letters/20091210
_open-letter-to-primitive-baptist-churches.pdf.

110. Steve Drain, "Fag Church," Sign Movies, http://www.signmovies.com
/videos/signmovies/index.html

111. Ibid.

112. Ibid.

113. Drain, "Beast Watch: Lying False Prophets Are to Blame."

114. Ibid.

115. Drain, "Fag Church."

116. Drain, "Beast Watch: Lying False Prophets Are to Blame."

117. Joshua Kors, "'God Hates Fags': Q & A with Pastor Fred Phelps," *Huffington Post*, August 10, 2010, http://www.huffingtonpost.com/joshua-kors/god
-hates-fags-qa-with-pa_b_689430.html.

118. Westboro Baptist Church, "God's Wrath Revealed," GodSmacks blog,
http://blogs.sparenot.com/index.php/godsmacks.

119. Drain, "Beast Watch: Lying False Prophets Are to Blame."

120. Westboro Baptist Church, "God's Wrath Revealed against America," God
Hates America, http://www.godhatesamerica.com/godswrath.html.

121. Westboro Baptist Church, "FAQ: Why Do You Have Signs Saying 'Thank
God for 911,' 'Thank God for AIDS,' 'Thank God for Katrina,' 'Thank God for
IEDs,' 'Thank God for Dead Soldiers,' and Otherwise Thanking God for Things
That Humans Think Are Bad?" God Hates Fags, http://www.godhatesfags.com
/faq.html#Thank_God.

122. Thuesen, *Predestination*, 83.

123. Peacock and Tyson, *Pilgrims of Paradox*, 47.

124. Dick Snider, "Time for Topekans to Fight Fred Phelps' Fire with Fire,"
*Topeka Capital-Journal*, October 20, 1995.

125. "Katrina: Wrath of God?" *Morning Joe*, October 5, 2005, http://www.ms
nbc.msn.com/id/9600878.

126. "Hurricane Katrina Destroys New Orleans Days before 'Southern Decadence,'" Repent America, press releases, August 31, 2005, http://www.repent
america.com/pr_hurricanekatrina.html.

127. Alan Cooperman, "Where Most See a Weather System, Some See Divine
Retribution," *Washington Post*, September 4, 2005, http://www.washingtonpost
.com/wp-dyn/content/article/2005/09/03/AR2005090301408.html.

128. Thomas Foxcroft, "The Earthquake, a Divine Visitation: A Sermon
Preached to the Old Church in Boston, January 8, 1756" (Boston: S. Kneeland,
1756).

129. Thuesen, *Predestination*, 181.

130. Drain, "Beast Watch: Lying False Prophets Are to Blame."

131. Ibid.

132. Sara Phelps, interview with the author, April 18, 2010. She has since left the church.

133. John Gill, *Body of Divinity* (London, 1769), 387–388; available through Eighteenth Century Collections Online, http://gdc.gale.com/products/eighteenth-century-collections-online.

134. Dinsdale, "Father Knows Best."

135. Westboro Baptist Church, "FAQ: Why Don't You Leave It up to God and Stop Wasting Your Time Telling People That They Are Wrong?'"

CHAPTER 4. COBELLIGERENTS IN ANTIGAY ACTIVISM: WESTBORO BAPTIST CHURCH AND THE RELIGIOUS RIGHT

1. John Hagee, *What Every Man Wants in a Woman* (Lake Mary, FL: Charisma House, 2005), 68.

2. James Dobson, *Marriage Under Fire: Why We Must Win This Battle* (Sisters, OR: Multnomah, 2004), 41.

3. Paul Cameron, "The Psychology of Homosexuality," Family Research Institute, http://www.familyresearchinst.org/2009/02/the-psychology-of-homosexuality.

4. Pat Robertson, warning the city of Orlando against hosting "gay days" at Disney World, *The 700 Club*, June 6, 1998.

5. Jimmy Swaggart, telecast of sermon, September 12, 2004, http://www.spike.com/video-clips/e9nl1z/jimmy-swaggart-would-kill-a-homosexual.

6. Charles Worley, responding to President Barack Obama's statement of support for same-sex marriage, in a May 13, 2012, sermon. Full video coverage is available on YouTube courtesy of Catawba Valley Citizens against Hate, "Local Pastor Calls for Death of 'Queers & Homosexuals'—Part 2," May 22, 2012, https://www.youtube.com/watch?v=TaMBDigNOco.

7. Steven Anderson, sermon, November 30, 2014, at Faithful Word Baptist Church, Tempe, AZ. An excerpt of the sermon is available at "Sermons from Faithful Word Baptist Church," http://www.faithfulwordbaptist.org/page5.html.

8. Swaggart told the Associated Press, "If it's an insult, I certainly didn't think it was, but if they are offended, then I certainly offer an apology." Associated Press, "Swaggart Apologizes after Remarking about 'Killing' Gay Men," USA Today, September 22, 2004, http://usatoday30.usatoday.com/news/nation/2004-09-22-swaggart-remark_x.htm.

9. Faithful Word Baptist Church, http://www.faithfulwordbaptist.org.

10. Herbert H. Haines, *Black Radicals and the Civil Rights Mainstream, 1954–1970* (Knoxville: University of Tennessee Press, 1988), 7.

11. Fred Phelps, sermon, April 11, 2010, http://www.godhatesfags.com /sermons/outlines/Sermon_20100411.pdf.

12. Fred Phelps, sermon, March 28, 2010, http://www.godhatesfags.com /sermons/outlines/Sermon_20100328.pdf.

13. Fred Phelps, sermon, February 21, 2010, http://www.godhatesfags.com /sermons/outlines/Sermon_20100221.pdf.

14. Quoted in Joe Taschler and Steve Fry, "The Gospel According to Fred," *Topeka Capital-Journal*, August 3, 1994, http://cjonline.com/indepth/phelps/stories /080394_phelps04.shtml.

15. C. J. Pruner and Minch Minchin, "Protesters Hold Rally, Counter-Rally," *Independent Florida Alligator*, April 19, 2010, http://www.alligator.org/news/local /article_b35e2dce-4b5c-11df-957c-001cc4c03286.html.

16. Cynthia Burack, "From Doom Town to Sin City: Chick Tracts and Antigay Politics," *New Social Science* 28, no. 2 (June 2006): 176.

17. In my research, I never encountered a single progay conservative Christian counterprotester. This phenomenon will be addressed in chapter 5 of this book.

18. Paul Froese, Christopher D. Bader, and Buster Smith, "Political Tolerance and God's Wrath in the United States," *Sociology of Religion* 69, no. 1 (2008): 41.

19. Ibid., 40.

20. Paul Froese and Christopher D. Bader, "God in America: Why Theology Is Not Simply the Concern of Philosophers," *Journal for the Scientific Study of Religion* 46, no. 4 (2007): 478.

21. Fred Phelps, sermon, February 14, 2010, http://www.godhatesfags.com /sermons/outlines/Sermon_20100214.pdf.

22. Cynthia Burack and Jyl J. Josephson, "Origin Stories," in Cynthia Burack, *Sin, Sex, and Democracy: Antigay Rhetoric and the Christian Right* (Albany: State University of New York Press, 2008), 74.

23. Jean Hardesty, *Mobilizing Resentment: Conservative Resurgence from the John Birch Society to the Promise Keepers* (Boston: Beacon, 1999), 118.

24. See, for example, Christian sex guides, which entered the publishing market in the 1970s in response to secular sex manuals. These include Ed Wheat and Gaye Wheat, *Intended for Pleasure: Sex Technique and Sexual Fulfillment in Christian Marriage* (Grand Rapids, MI: Fleming H. Revel, 1997); Tim and Beverly LaHaye, *The Act of Marriage: The Beauty of Sexual Love* (Grand Rapids, MI: Zondervan, 1998); Kevin Lehman, *Sheet Music: Uncovering the Secrets of Sexual Intimacy in Marriage*

(Carol Stream, IL: Tyndale 2003); and, more recently, Mark Driscoll and Grace Driscoll, *Real Marriage: The Truth about Sex, Friendship, and Life Together* (Nashville, TN: Thomas Nelson, 2012). Christian gender manuals, which rely on traditional, dichotomous understandings of femininity and masculinity, likewise emerged in response to the feminist and men's movements of the 1960s and 1970s. Popular titles include Stu Weber, *The Tender Warrior: Every Man's Purpose, Every Woman's Dream, Every Child's Hope* (Sisters, OR: Multnomah, 2006); Robert Lewis, *Raising a Modern-Day Knight: A Father's Role in Guiding His Son to Authentic Manhood* (Carol Stream, IL: Tyndale, 1999); Pam Farrel and Doreen Hanna, *Raising a Modern-Day Princess: Inspiring Purpose, Value, and Strength in Your Daughter* (Carol Stream, IL: Tyndale, 2009); and Dennis Rainey, *Stepping Up: A Call to Courageous Manhood* (Little Rock, AR: Family Life, 2011).

25. Didi Herman, *The Antigay Agenda: Orthodox Vision and the Christian Right* (Chicago: University of Chicago Press,1997), 73.

26. Burack and Josephson, "Origin Stories," 90.

27. Ibid.

28. Ibid.

29. Ibid.

30. Ibid.

31. Steve Drain, interview with the author, April 16, 2015.

32. Ibid.

33. The Southern Poverty Law Center (SPLC) lists Westboro Baptist Church as one of six hate groups in Kansas under the heading "General Hate." The others fall under the headers "Neo-Nazi," "KKK," and "Racist Skinhead"; see "Hate Map," Southern Poverty Law Center, http://www.splcenter.org/get-informed /hate-map#s=KS. Notably, in 2011, the SPLC expanded its list of hate groups to include religiously affiliated groups such as the American Family Association, American Vision, Family Research Council, and the Family Research Institute that, in the SPLC's words, propagate "known falsehoods—claims about LGBT people that have been thoroughly discredited by scientific authorities—and repeated, groundless name-calling." However, "viewing homosexuality as unbiblical does not qualify organizations for listing as hate groups." Evelyn Schlatter, "18 Anti-Gay Groups and Their Propaganda," Intelligence Report, Winter 2010, Issue 140, http://www.splcenter.org/get-informed/intelligence-report/browse-all -issues/2010/winter/the-hard-liners. An online petition to ask the White House to declare the church a hate group was politely declined, as the White House explained that the government does not legally define groups this way; however, the White House recognized the sentiment behind the petition and noted that

President Obama had passed legislation protecting military funerals. Further, the White House pointed out that the popularity of the petition "shows just how strong the bonds that unite us can be"; "Here's What We Have to Say about the Westboro Baptist Church," White House, December 14, 2012, https://petitions.whitehouse.gov/petition/legally-recognize-westboro-baptist-church-hate-group-0.

34. Burack and Josephson, "Origin Stories," 90.

35. Ibid.

36. Martin E. Marty and R. Scott Appleby, "Introduction," in *Fundamentalisms and the State: Remaking Polities, Economies, and Militance,* edited by Martin E. Marty and R. Scott Appleby (Chicago: University of Chicago Press, 1991), 3.

37. Glenn T. Miller, *Religious Liberty in America: History and Prospects* (Philadelphia, PA: Westminster Press, 1976), 121.

38. Michael Cobb, *God Hates Fags: The Rhetorics of Religious Violence* (New York: New York University Press, 2006), 3.

39. Tony Perkins, "Help Change America This July 4th," letter to Family Research Council supporters, June 24, 2010.

40. "If My People, Who Are Called by My Name . . ." *Family Research Council Bulletin,* June 23, 2010.

41. Senator Robert Adley, "Sen. Adley Urges Citizens to Join Together for Statewide Day of Prayer Sunday," press release, June 16, 2010, http://senate.legis.state.la.us/adley/releases/2010/06-16-2010.pdf.

42. Brent Roper, comments at a Bible study attended by the author, July 18, 2010.

43. Shirley Phelps-Roper, comments at a Bible study attended by the author, July 18, 2010.

44. "Vote Randall Lt. Governor," press release, 1990.

45. Ibid.

46. For example, American Family Association leader Bryan Fischer called for the resignation of Republican presidential nominee Mitt Romney's national security and foreign policy spokesperson Richard Grenell, crowing that, in response to conservative Christian pressure, "There is no way in the world that Mitt Romney is going to put a homosexual activist in any position of importance in his campaign." Rebekah Metzler, "Conservative Radio Host High-Fives Romney Campaign for Canning Gay Adviser," *US News and World Report,* May 2, 2012, http://www.usnews.com/news/articles/2012/05/02/conservative-radio-host-high-fives-romney-campaign-for-canning-gay-adviser.

47. For an analysis of how America's ex-gay movement has framed debate about homosexuality in Uganda, see Susan E. Spivey and Christine M. Robinson,

"Genocidal Intentions: Social Death and the Ex-Gay Movement," *Genocide Studies and Prevention* 5, no. 1 (April 2010): 68–88.

48. Writes Paul Cameron of the Family Research Institute regarding Uganda's bill that makes repeat violators of the law against sodomy subject to execution, "Honorable people can differ on how severe should be the penalties for the various offenses catalogued in the Ugandan bill. But we find no warrant for considering this bill at odds with the historic values of either Christianity or democracy. . . . Many of its provisions would be welcome restorations to our own penal code." "The Ugandan Anti-Homosexuality Bill," Family Research Institute, December 2009, http://www.familyresearchinst.org/2010/02/dec-2009-the -ugandan-anti-homosexuality-bill.

49. Exodus International was an ex-gay Christian network primarily serving conservative evangelical Protestants. It closed in 2013, though local organizations affiliated with it have continued on in various forms.

50. Westboro Baptist Church, "FAQ: What Are You Trying to Accomplish?" God Hates Fags, http://www.westborobaptistchurch.com/mobile/faq.html.

51. Jerry Falwell, *Frontline* interview, PBS, 2000, http://www.pbs.org/wgbh /pages/frontline/shows/assault/interviews/falwell.html.

52. Ibid.

53. Michael Foust, "Night and Day: The Difference between Southern Baptists and Fred Phelps," *Baptist Press*, March 31, 2003, http://www.bpnews.net/bpnews .asp?id=15606.

54. Robert Stacy McCain, "Condemn Sin—and Sinner," *Insight on the News*, August 16, 1999, 32–33.

55. Elder David Montgomery, "Disclaimer," Primitive Baptist Online, September 9, 2008, http://primitivebaptist.info/mambo//index2.php?option=com _content&do_pdf=1&id=1434.

56. Elder Benjamin C. Winslett, "Fred Phelps and Westboro Baptist 'Church' Are *Not* Primitive Baptists," *Huntsville Patriot* blog, http://thehuntsvillepatriot .com/2010/04/fred-phelps-and-westboro-baptist-church-are-not-primitive -baptists (bold in original). Winslett's blog is devoted to right-wing politics and survivalist information.

57. Ibid.

58. Dana Fields, "Rights Debate Arises after Preacher Pickets AIDS Victims Funerals," *Indiana (PA) Gazette*, April 9, 1993, 3.

59. On the one hand, the use of musical instruments would be acceptable in Progressive Primitive Baptist churches, but Westboro Baptist Church's belief in absolute predestination would not. On the other hand, Primitive Baptist churches

that adhere to absolute predestination would not permit musical instruments. Likewise, Westboro Baptist Church's rejection of foot washing would be reason for disfellowshipping it from some Primitive Baptist associations but not others.

60. Winslett, "Fred Phelps and Westboro Baptist 'Church' Are Not Primitive Baptists."

61. In the King James version of the Bible, Hebrews 10:24 says, "And let us consider how we may spur one another on toward love and good deeds." Second Timothy 4:2 says, "Preach the word; be instant in season, out of season; reprove, rebuke, exhort with all long suffering and doctrine."

62. Westboro Baptist Church, "Open Letter to All Primitive Baptists from Westboro Baptist Church," God Hates Fags, http://www.westborobaptistchurch .com/written/letters/20091210_open-letter-to-primitive-baptist-churches.pdf.

63. "A Clergy Declaration in Response to the Environment of Hatred and Violence in Topeka, Kansas," press release, October 11, 1993, Wilcox Collection, Spencer Research Library, University of Kansas.

64. "Southern Baptists May Not Say 'God Hates Fags' as Fred Phelps Does but the Effect Is the Same," Soulforce, http://www.soulforce.org/pdf/sbcandphelps .pdf.

65. Surina Khan, "Calculated Compassion: How the Ex-Gay Movement Serves the Right's Attack on Democracy," Political Research Associates, 1998, http:// www.publiceye.org/equality/x-gay/X-Gay.html.

66. Carin Robinson and Clyde Wilcox, "The Faith of George W. Bush: The Personal, Practical, and Political," in *Religion and the American Presidency*, edited by Mark J. Rozell and Gleaves Whitney, The Evolving American Presidency series (New York: Palgrave MacMillan, 2007), 219.

67. Cobb, *God Hates Fags*, 3.

68. Burack, "From Doom Town to Sin City," 171.

69. Fred Phelps, sermon, April 11, 2010, http://www.godhatesfags.com /sermons/outlines/Sermon_20100411.pdf.

70. Steve Drain, interview with the author, April 16, 2015.

71. Foust, "Night and Day."

72. Tate Hausman, "The GOP's 'Kinder, Gentler' Gay Bashing," *Albion Monitor*, August 3, 1998, http://www.albionmonitor.com/9808a/copyright/gopgay attack.html.

73. For example, the Family Research Council does not condone state-sanctioned violence against gay people, "nor any other penalty which would have the effect of inhibiting compassionate pastoral, psychological and medical care and treatment for those who experience same-sex attractions or who engage in

homosexual conduct"; J. P. Duffy, quoted in David Weigel, "Family Research Council Explains: It Lobbied for Changes to Uganda Legislation," *Washington Post*, June 4, 2010, http://voices.washingtonpost.com/right-now/2010/06/family _research_council_explai.html. Notably, the Family Research Council does not differentiate between those who would seek such "medical care and treatment" under their own volition and those who are content pursuing their same-sex attraction. Jerry Falwell also spoke out against violence against gay people after a joint conference involving members of his Thomas Road Baptist Church and Soulforce; see Falwell, *Frontline* interview. Westboro Baptist Church stresses its own nonviolence toward gay people as well as toward counterprotesters; indeed, members have been disfellowshipped for their inability to maintain their calm in the face of violence on the picket line.

74. "Southern Baptists May Not Say 'God Hates Fags' as Fred Phelps Does but the Effect Is the Same."

CHAPTER 5. CIVILITY, CIVIL LIBERTIES, AND RELIGIOUS NATIONALISM

1. James A. Aho, *The Politics of Righteousness: Idaho Christian Patriotism* (Seattle: University of Washington Press, 1990), 3–4.

2. Nancy T. Ammerman, "Accounting for Christian Fundamentalisms: Social Dynamics and Rhetorical Strategies," in *Accounting for Fundamentalisms: The Dynamic Character of Movements*, The Fundamentalism Project, vol. 4, edited by Martin E. Marty and R. Scott Appleby (Chicago: University of Chicago Press, 1991), 149–150.

3. Glenn T. Miller, *Religious Liberty in America: History and Prospects* (Philadelphia, PA: Westminster Press, 1976), 79.

4. Gabriel A. Almond, Emmanual Sivan, and R. Scott Appleby, "Explaining Fundamentalisms," in *Fundamentalisms Comprehended*, The Fundamentalism Project, vol. 5, edited by Martin E. Marty and R. Scott Appleby (Chicago: University of Chicago Press, 1991), 428.

5. For example, Candi Cushman, who serves as an education analyst for Focus on the Family's political action group, Focus on the Family Action, has spoken extensively in opposition to school policies that would target bullying based on a victim's real or perceived sexuality. Candi Cushman, "Parents Beware: 'Anti-Bullying' Initiatives Are Gay Activists' Latest Tools of Choice for Sneaking Homosexuality Lessons into Classrooms," *Citizen Link*, June/July 2010, http://www.truetolerance .org/p9_June_Jul_Citizen_10_antibullying.pdf. Likewise, students working to start gay-straight alliances (GSAs) in public schools often face opposition rooted

in religious principles or supported by conservative religious groups. For an archive of public writing opposing GSAs, see American Civil Liberties Union (ACLU), "Should Public Schools Allow Gay Straight Alliances?" ProCon, July 28, 2011, http://aclu.procon.org/view.answers.php?questionID=000710.

6. Ruth Murray Brown, For a "Christian America": A History of the Religious Right (Amherst, NY: Prometheus Books, 2003), 81.

7. Fred Phelps, interview in Fall from Grace, DVD, directed by K. Ryan Jones (New York: Docurama, 2008).

8. Timothy J. Dailey, "The Other Side of Tolerance: How Homosexual Activism Threatens Liberty" (Washington, DC: Family Research Council, 2006), 17.

9. Bryan Fischer, "Gay Lobby Brings Slavery Back to the South," The Stand, August 18, 2015, http://www.afa.net/the-stand/government/gay-lobby-brings -slavery-back-to-the-south.

10. "Manhattan Declaration: A Call to Christian Conscience," November 20, 2009, http://manhattandeclaration.org/man_dec_resources/Manhattan _Declaration_full_text.pdf 38. The L.A. Times calls these "strong words, but also irresponsible and dangerous ones," for "this is a nation of laws, not of men—even holy men." The logic displayed in the Manhattan Declaration's call to civil disobedience calls into question Religious Right leaders' roles in making law. They "insist on their right to shape the nation's laws [while] reserving the right to violate them in situations far removed from [Martin Luther] King's witness"; "Christian Leaders' Stance on Civil Disobedience Is Dangerous" L.A. Times, November 28, 2009, http://articles.latimes.com/2009/nov/28/opinion/la -ed-disobedience28-2009nov28.

11. Associated Press, "Bullying Legislation Prompts Opposition from Conservative Groups," Christian Science Monitor, May 21, 2102, http://www.csmonitor .com/The-Culture/Family/2012/0521/Bullying-legislation-prompts-opposition -from-conservative-groups.

12. Maggie Gallagher, "Banned in Boston: The Coming Conflict between Same-Sex Marriage and Religious Liberty," Weekly Standard, May 15, 2006, http:// www.weeklystandard.com/content/public/articles/000/000/012/191kgwgh.asp ?page=4.

13. Dailey, "The Other Side of Tolerance."

14. Tony Perkins, fund-raising letter for the Family Research Council, May 2010.

15. Such is the picture painted by the Family Research Council's Peter Sprigg in his report "Homosexual Assault within the Military," Insight, May 1010, http:// downloads.frc.org/EF/EF10E118.pdf. Here, Sprigg uses questionable statistical

228

analysis to argue that gay male soldiers are more likely than their straight counterparts to assault their peers. Since the repeal of DADT, the Family Research Council and other organizations have pointed to the increased number of sexual assaults reported in the military, including male-male assaults; see, for example, Ret. Lt. Gen. Jerry Boykin's remarks on Frank Gaffney's *Secure Freedom Radio*, "The New Islamic Republic of America?," May 20, 2013, https://www.centerfor securitypolicy.org/tag/jerry-boykin/page/2. Boykin was undersecretary of defense for intelligence from 2002 to 2007, among other high-profile government positions. Since 2012 he has served as the executive vice president of the Family Research Council.

16. Bryan Fischer, "Gay Sex = Domestic Terrorism," *Rightly Concerned*, blog associated with the American Family Association, June 10, 2010, http://action.afa .net/Blogs/BlogPost.aspx?id=2147495382.

17. Perkins, fund-raising letter for the Family Research Council.

18. Cliff Kincaid, "Saving Soldiers from Gay Death," *America's Survival*, May 27, 2010, http://www.worldviewweekend.com/news/article/saving-soldiers-gay -death.

19. Earl Taylor, Jr., "The Destructive Sin of Homosexuality," National Center for Constitutional Studies, August 1999, archived at Restoring Social Virtue & Purity to America, http://rsvpamerica.org/wp-content/uploads/2014/03/Letter-about -homosexuality_Earl-Taylor-Jr_-Aug-1999_National-center-for-Constitutions -Studies.pdf.

20. Associated Press, "Oklahoma Rep. Sally Kern on YouTube Clip: Homosexuality Bigger Threat Than Terrorism," Fox News, March 16, 2008, http://www .foxnews.com/story/0,2933,338271,00.html.

21. Cynthia Burack, "Compassion Campaigns and Antigay Politics: What Would Arendt Do?" *Politics and Religion* 2 (April 2009): 49.

22. Ammerman, "Accounting for Christian Fundamentalisms," 151 (italics in original).

23. Fred Phelps, sermon, February 7, 2010, http://www.godhatesfags.com /sermons/outlines/Sermon_20100207.pdf.

24. Fred Phelps, interview in *Fall from Grace*.

25. "Falwell Apologizes to Gays, Feminists, Lesbians," CNN.com/US, September 14, 2001, http://www.cnn.com/2001/US/09/14/Falwell.apology.

26. Fred Phelps, sermon, April 18, 2010, http://www.godhatesfags.com /sermons/outlines/Sermon_20100418.pdf. Here, Phelps referred to 2 Peter 2:4– 10, which says in the King James translation, "For if God spared not the angels that sinned, but cast them down to hell, and delivered them into chains of dark-

ness, to be reserved unto judgment; And spared not the old world, but saved Noah the eighth person, a preacher of righteousness, bringing in the flood upon the world of the ungodly; And turning the cities of Sodom and Gomorrah into ashes condemned them with an overthrow, making them an ensample unto those that after should live ungodly; And delivered just Lot, vexed with the filthy conversation of the wicked: (For that righteous man dwelling among them, in seeing and hearing, vexed his righteous soul from day to day with their unlawful deeds:) The Lord knoweth how to deliver the godly out of temptation, and to reserve the unjust unto the day of judgment to be punished: But chiefly them that walk after the flesh in the lust of uncleanness, and despise government. Presumptuous are they, self-willed, they are not afraid to speak evil of dignities."

27. Tim Phelps, interview in *Fall from Grace.*

28. Ibid.

29. "Man, 26, Convicted for Role in Phelps Pipe-Bomb Incident," http://www.godhatesfags.com/bombing/19960227_man-convicted.html, quoting from a February 27, 1996, article by Steve Fry in *Topeka Capital-Journal.* The defendant received twenty-four months of supervised probation, according to Shawnee County court records (https://public.shawneecourt.org/PublicAccess/public Access/publicAccess/?goto=caseLookup). On October 29, 2007, a similar bomb threat was made against the church, though no bomb was found; Phil Anderson, "Church Target of Bomb Threat," *Topeka Capital-Journal,* October 30, 2007, archived at *Religion News Blog,* http://www.religionnewsblog.com/19789/hate -group-3. In August 2008, an arsonist set a fire at the church; no one was injured. Phil Anderson, "Westboro Baptist Fire Ruled Arson," *Topeka Capital-Journal,* August 27, 2008, http://cjonline.com/stories/082708/loc_323443016.shtml#.Vnih ELYrJaQ.

30. Sara Phelps, interview in *Fall from Grace.*

31. Fred Phelps, interview in *Fall from Grace.*

32. Transcript of oral arguments in *Snyder v. Phelps,* October 6, 2010, Supreme Court, http://www.supremecourt.gov/oral_arguments/argument_transcripts/09 -751.pdf.

33. Coincidentally, Military Missions Network, a fundamentalist outreach to servicemen and women, encourages strategic evangelization at moments of vulnerability (details about the network and how it connects service members to evangelical churches can be found at http://www.militarymissionsnetwork.com). In contrast to the many people who believe that evangelizing at a funeral is inappropriate, relatively few people raised a protest against this exploitation of military-related stress to produce religious conversion.

34. Marine Captain Bret Miner wrote the report of the accident that killed Matthew Snyder and injured three others. In it, he recommended holding superior officers responsible for seat-belt use, providing further training on driving in the desert, reviewing protocol regarding convoy formation, and retiring the Humvee involved in the accident. His superiors rejected all of his suggestions. See Michele Canty, "Military Report Details Crash," York (PA) Daily Times, May 27, 2008, http://www.ydr.com/ci_7555437?IADID=Search-www.ydr.com-www.ydr.com.

35. Maryland Code, Criminal Law §10-205.

36. Both sides agreed to the facts of the case as presented here (oral arguments of Snyder v. Phelps are available at Supreme Court, http://www.supremecourt.gov/oral_arguments/argument_transcripts/09-751.pdf.

37. Citizen Media Project, "Defamation," Glossary, http://www.citmedialaw.org/glossary/8/ letterp#term290.

38. American Law Institute, "Intrusion upon Seclusion," Restatement of the Law, Second, Torts, 1977, Harvard University, https://cyber.law.harvard.edu/privacy/Privacy_R2d_Torts_Sections.htm.

39. Citizen Media Project, "Publication of Private Facts," Glossary, http://www.citmedialaw.org/glossary/8/ letterp#term290.

40. Shirley Phelps-Roper, interview with the author, July 30, 2008.

41. The decision is available at Fourth Court of Appeals, http://pacer.ca4.uscourts.gov/opinion.pdf/081026.P.pdf.

42. "The Phelpses are not asserting exaggerated opinions or hyperbolic overstatements for rhetorical purposes. The Phelpses cannot and do not claim that their messages are parody or satire; they mean every word they say. . . . Yet the Fourth Circuit immunized the Phelpses from liability in part because their statements were so outrageous and vile. That result turns traditional tort law on its head: the messages were much more likely to inflict serious emotional harm on their target precisely because they were so unconscionable. In fact, the Fourth Circuit created a perverse incentive for emotional terrorists to be outrageous and extreme, because First Amendment immunity will apply if reasonable people would not actually believe the statements." "Brief for the State of Kansas and 47 Other States, and the District of Columbia as Amici Curiae in Support of Petitioner," American Bar Association, June 2010, http://www.abanet.org/publiced/preview/briefs/pdfs/09-10/09-751_PetitionerAmCu48StatesandDC.pdf.

43. The compensatory damages are payment for the actual harm suffered by Snyder, while the punitive damages are a kind of punishment for Westboro Baptist Church.

44. Justices King and Duncan wrote the majority opinion. Justice Shedd wrote

a concurring opinion that argued that the original decision should be reversed because of Snyder's failure to prove his tort rather than on First Amendment grounds. *Snyder v. Phelps*, 2009, http://www.citmedialaw.org/sites/citmedialaw.org/files/2009-09-24-Snyder%20v.%20Phelps%20Appellate%20Decision.pdf.

45. Westboro Baptist Church, "You May Not Agree with the Westboro Baptist Church, but There Are Fundamental Rights That Were Established in This Country in Her Infancy! You Don't Get to Outlaw Words You Hate/Disagree with—You Get to Say MORE WORDS! Most People Don't Get It, but Sometimes There Are Little Friendlies Sprinkled around That Understand That Simple Concept," *Workmen* blog, November 8, 2010, http://blogs.sparenot.com/workmen/2010/11/08/you-may-not-agree-with-the-westboro-baptist-church-but-there-are-fundamental-rights-that-were-established-in-this-country-in-her-infancy-you-dont-get-to-outlaw-words-you-hatedisagree-with.

46. All amicus briefs are available online under "Snyder v. Phelps" at American Bar Association, http://www.abanet.org/publiced/preview/briefs/oct2010.shtml #snyder. They were filed by groups as diverse as the Thomas Jefferson Center for the Protection of Free Speech, the Marion B. Brechner First Amendment Project, the National Coalition against Censorship, and the Pennsylvania Center for the First Amendment; Scholars of First Amendment Law; Reporters Committee for Freedom of the Press, which was joined by twenty-one news media groups; Liberty Counsel; the ACLU and the ACLU of Maryland; and the Foundation for Individual Rights in Education, which was joined by law professors Ash Bhagwat, David Post, Martin Redish, Nadine Strossen, and Eugene Volokh.

47. The American Legion's brief is available at American Bar Association, http://www.abanet.org/publiced/preview/briefs/pdfs/09-10/09-751_Petitioner AmCuAmericanLegion.pdf. See page 2.

48. The Veterans of Foreign Wars brief is available at American Bar Association, http://www.abanet.org/publiced/preview/briefs/pdfs/09-10/09-751_Petitioner AmCuVFW.pdf. See page 4.

49. The state of Kansas brief is available at American Bar Association, http://www.abanet.org/publiced/preview/briefs/pdfs/09-10/09-751_PetitionerAm Cu48StatesandDC.pdf. See page 10.

50. Westboro Baptist Church tactics at military funerals are not "unprecedented." To begin with, the church itself has been picketing at funerals for nearly twenty years. Further, as illustrated in the amicus brief filed by the Reporters Committee for Freedom of the Press, which was joined by twenty-one other news organizations, other groups have used funerals as opportunities to picket for their own reasons. For example, Teamsters have picketed at nonunionized funeral homes,

and prolife protesters have picketed at the funerals of judges who defended the legality of abortion as well as the funerals of slain abortion providers. The brief is available at American Bar Association, http://www.americanbar.org/content /dam/aba/publishing/preview/publiced_preview_briefs_pdfs_09_10_09_751 _RespondentAmCuReportersCommitteeforFreedomofthePressetal.authcheck dam.pdf. See especially pages 24–25.

51. *Snyder v. Phelps* (2011). The opinion is available at http://www.supreme court.gov/opinions/10pdf/09-751.pdf.

52. Julie Francis, "Matthew Snyder's Mom: The Right to Freedom of Speech Is Absolute," *Baltimore Sun*, March 14, 2011, http://articles.baltimoresun.com/2011 -03-14/news/bs-ed-snyder-westboro-letter-20110314_1_free-speech-wbc-west boro-baptist-church.

53. Joshua Lawrence, *A Patriotic Discourse*, July 4, 1830, quoted in James R. Mathis, *The Making of the Primitive Baptists: A Cultural and Intellectual History of the Antimission Movement, 1800–1840* (New York: Routledge, 2004), 92.

54. *Snyder v. Phelps*.

55. According to reporting by the *Advocate*, while the assailant, Billy Spade, admitted to spitting on Phelps-Roper's sign, and both the victim and the attending officer testified that he actually had spit tobacco juice on Phelps-Roper herself, "the jury, ruling in less than an hour, said Spade committed no crime, considering the highly charged events of the day." Editors, "Jury: Feel Free to Spit on Shirley Phelps," *Advocate*, April 10, 2011, http://www.advocate.com/news /daily-news/2011/04/10/jury-feel-free-spit-shirley-phelps.

56. According to church members, God protected them in the attack; Matthew Hansen, "Marine Veteran Haunted by Memories," *Omaha World-Herald*, August 31, 2010, 1A.

57. Manny Gamallo, "Tires on Westboro Baptist Church Van Slashed in Oklahoma," November 15, 2010, http://www2.ljworld.com/news/2010/nov/15 /tires-westboro-baptist-church-van-slashed-oklahoma.

58. Nexstar Broadcasting, "Soldier's Supporters Turn Back Funeral Protestors," *Ozarks First*, November 24, 2010, http://www.ozarksfirst.com/news /regional-news/soldiers-supporters-turn-back-funeral-protestors.

59. Lucia Blackwell, "Beau Biden Funeral: How the Day Unfolded," *Delaware News Journal*, June 22, 2015, http://www.delawareonline.com/story/news /2015/06/06/beau-biden-funeral-saturday-wilmington-delaware/28594017.

60. Indeed, Westboro Baptist Church often partners with progressive civil liberties defense groups in fighting its legal battles. For example, Shirley Phelps-Roper was represented by the ACLU when she was charged with the crime of flag

desecration in Nebraska. Said Amy Miller, the legal director of ACLU Nebraska, "Clearly, the ACLU disagrees with the Westboro Baptist Church's message that gay people are an abomination. . . . The ACLU spends a significant amount of time working for equality on the basis of sexual orientation and I myself am gay. But disagreeing with the message doesn't mean that we can allow the government to try to silence protected free speech. Punishing this use of the flag is contrary to the very spirit of freedom the flag stands for"; "ACLU Nebraska Challenges Flag Desecration Law," ACLU, June 8, 2007, http://www.aclu.org/free-speech /aclu-nebraska-challenges-flag-desecration-law.

61. Westboro Baptist Church, "You May Not Agree with the Westboro Baptist Church."

62. Anonymous, interview with the author, September 11, 2010.

63. Anonymous, interview with the author, September 11, 2010.

64. Footage of Banderas's interview with Shirley Phelps-Rope is available on YouTube, http://www.youtube.com/watch?v=b3PyoUPcobA.

65. Kathleen C. Boone, *The Bible Tells Them So: The Discourse of Protestant Fundamentalism* (Albany: State University of New York Press, 1989), 6.

66. Jonathan Phelps, interview in *Fall from Grace*.

67. Fred Phelps, sermon, February 7, 2010, http://www.godhatesfags.com /sermons/outlines/Sermon_20100207.pdf.

68. Order of Judge Richard G. Kopf to Margy [Megan] M. Phelps-Roper and Jon Bruning, Nebraska attorney general; Col. Bryan Tuma, superintendent of Nebraska State Patrol; Kenneth Polikov, Sarpy County attorney; Leonard Houloose, chief of Papillion Police Department; Donald Kleine, Douglas County attorney; Alex Hays, chief of Omaha Police Department; and John Stacey, chief of Bellevue Police Department, July 15, 2010.

69. Indeed, prior to her arrest for flag desecration and contributing to the delinquency of a minor (because she encouraged her minor child to stand on the flag), Shirley Phelps-Roper politely reminded the officer who arrested her that she was within her legal right to tread on the flag because the Supreme Court said in *Johnson v. Texas* that flag desecration was legal in an otherwise lawful protest. The officer replied, "You're not in Texas." Phelps-Roper attempted to correct the officer by stressing that the Supreme Court has jurisdiction nationwide. Nonetheless, he arrested her, sparking a three-year legal battle. Westboro Baptist Church, "Why Nebraska Is Now Funding WBC Picket Trips," Sign Movies, http://www .signmovies.com/videos/news/index.html.

70. Nate Phelps, interview in *Fall from Grace*.

71. Tim Hrenchir and Kevin Elliott, "City: Westboro Graffiti May Stay,"

*Topeka Capital-Journal*, May 8, 2010, http://cjonline.com/news/local/2010-05-07 /city_westboro_graffiti_may_stay.

72. Fred Phelps, sermon, February 7, 2010, http://www.godhatesfags.com /sermons/outlines/Sermon_20100207.pdf.

73. Joe Taschler and Steve Fry, "Phelps Is No Stranger to Court System," *Topeka Capital-Journal*, August 3, 1994, http://cjonline.com/indepth/phelps/stories /080394_phelps22.shtml.

74. Martin E. Marty and R. Scott Appleby, "Conclusion: Remaking the State: The Limits of the Fundamentalist Imagination," in *Fundamentalisms and the State: Remaking Polities, Economies, and Militance*, edited by Martin E. Marty and R. Scott Appleby (Chicago: University of Chicago Press, 1991), 640.

75. Benedict Anderson, *Imagined Communities: Reflections on the Origins and Spread of Nationalism* (New York: Verso, 1991), 7.

76. Ibid., 6.

77. For examples, see the essays in Stefan Dudnik, Karen Hagemann, and John Tosh, eds., *Masculinities in Politics and War: Gendering Modern History* (New York: Manchester University Press, 2004), especially Joan B. Landes, "Republican Citizenship and Heterosocial Desire: Concepts of Masculinity in Revolutionary France" (96–115).

78. For more on the use of military rhetoric in contemporary conservative Christianity, see David S. Gutterman, *Prophetic Politics: Christian Social Movements and American Democracy* (Ithaca, NY: Cornell University Press, 2005).

79. "Apoka Gun Maker Etches Scripture on Assault Rifle," Fox32, September 2, 2015, http://www.fox32chicago.com/home/15780932-story.

80. Joseph Rhee, Tahman Bradley, and Brian Ross, "U.S. Military Weapons Inscribed with Secret 'Jesus' Code," ABC News, January 18, 2010, http://abcnews.go .com/Blotter/us-military-weapons-inscribed-secret-jesus-bible-codes/story?id =9575794.

81. See, for example, Allen J. Frantzen's study of Christian masculinity among World War I servicemen in *Bloody Good: Chivalry, Sacrifice, and the Great War* (Chicago: University of Chicago Press, 2004).

82. Military Ministry, "About Us," http://www.militaryministry.org/about.

83. Ibid.

84. Jeff Sharlet, "Jesus Killed Mohammed: The Crusade for a Christian Military," *Harper's*, May 2009, http://www.harpers.org/archive/2009/05/0082488.

85. Lance Corporal Josepha Cuesta, *A Christian Marine's Journey*, http://a christianmarine.blogspot.com.

86. *Christian Military Wives*, http://christianmilitarywivescentral.blogspot.com.

87. One example that sparked public criticism was Trijicon Inc.'s practice of inscribing Bible verses on rifle scopes. After the practice became publicly known in early 2010, the military agreed to review its relationship with the military contractor. Dan Lamothe, "Bible Verses on Rifle Scopes Cause Concern," Army Times, January 21, 2010, http://www.armytimes.com/news/2010/01/military_biblical _optics_011910w. In another example, the September 2010 "Rock the Fort" evangelistic Christian music concert at Fort Bragg, North Carolina, sponsored by the Billy Graham Evangelistic Association and paid for in part with government funds, drew attention to fundamentalist Christianity's efforts to gain converts on military bases. Kevin Dolack, "Ft. Bragg Evangelical Event Draws Fire," ABC News, September 25, 2010, http://abcnews.go.com/US/ft-bragg-evangelical-event-draws -fire/story?id=11727193. Similarly, the US Air Force Academy, located in Colorado Springs, Colorado, home to many conservative Christians and Religious Right groups (including, most notably, Focus on the Family), has faced charges that evangelical Christian staff and cadets have created a climate hostile to nonbelievers and non-Christians. The Cadet and Permanent Party Climate Assessment Survey, which was released on October 29, 2010, revealed that 50 percent of non-Christians perceived low tolerance for nonreligious people, an increase of 20 percent since 2007. Indeed, 41 percent of non-Christians reported being exposed to unwanted proselytizing. Whitney Jones, "Air Force Academy Cites Progress in Tackling Religious Intolerance," Christian Century, November 2, 2010, http://www.christiancentury.org /article/2010-11/air-force-academy-cites-progress-tackling-religious-intolerance. The Air Force Academy has struggled in the past with cadet and staff intolerance of and insensitivity to non-Christians. CNN reported that fifty-five complaints of religious intolerance were filed with the school from 2001 to 2005. Mike Mount, "Air Force Probes Religious Bias Charges at Academy," CNN, May 5, 2005, http:// www.cnn.com/2005/US/05/03/airforce.religion. A civil suit against the academy included accusations that staff members inappropriately attached Bible verses to their e-mail signatures, that government e-mail systems were used to promote participation in religious events, that nonreligious events included prayer, and that the football coach hung a poster encouraging players to be part of "Team Jesus." Christine Lagorio, "Air Force Sued over Religion," CBS News, October 6, 2005, http://www.cbsnews.com/stories/2005/10/06/national/main919947.shtml. Further, in February 2010, a large wooden cross was placed in an outdoor area designed for worship by Wiccans in the community. DeeDee Correll, "Cross Found at Air Force Academy's Wicca Center," L.A. Times, February 3, 2010, http://articles .latimes.com/2010/feb/03/nation/la-na-wicca3-2010feb03.

88. Perkins, fund-raising letter for the Family Research Council.

89. See, for example, Bryan Fischer, "Freedom of Religion Does Not Mean Tolerance for Treason," *Renew America*, August 25, 2010, http://www.renewamerica .com/columns/fischer/100825. Writes Fischer, "No city council should allow itself to be browbeat into granting building permits to an organization—the religion of Islam—whose god commands his followers to kill the members of that city council. 'Slay the idolaters wherever you find them,' the god of the Holy Koran says. What kind of insanity is it to insist that special protections be granted to those whose sacred Scripture commands them to kill us? It is mind-numbed craziness to cooperate with that."

90. In a well-publicized example, Al Jazeera circulated a film clip showing American soldiers apparently discussing how to convert Afghan civilians. James Bays, "US Troops Urged to Share Faith in Afghanistan," Al Jazeera English, May 4, 2009, https://www.youtube.com/watch?v=hVGmbzDLq5c. Although the local-language Bibles in the video were not distributed to Afghan civilians, the images provided further evidence that at least some servicemen and -women view their time abroad as an opportunity to promote Christianity. In the video, Army Chaplain Lt. Col. Gary Hensley tells soldiers they have a Christian duty "to be witnesses for Him." He explained, "The special forces guys, they hunt men basically. . . . We do the same things as Christians, we hunt people for Jesus. We do, we hunt them down. Get the hound of heaven after them, so we get them into the kingdom. That's what we do, that's our business." Though a military spokesperson later said that the chaplain's words were meant to encourage evangelism within the military—itself a problematic issue—they reveal a missionary impulse that is seen as a threat by the Muslim world. David Waters, "Christian Soldiers or Crusaders?" *Under God*, blog, *Washington Post*, May 25, 2009, http://onfaith.washington post.com/onfaith/undergod/2009/05/christian_soldiers_or_crusaders.html.

91. Opposition to the repeal of DADT came from religious conservatives. A Gallup poll released on May 10, 2010, just a few months before the repeal, revealed broad, steady support for the reversal of DADT but also showed that those with more regular church attendance are more likely to support the policy. Lymari Morales, "In U.S., Broad, Steady Support for Openly Gay Service Members," Gallup, May 10, 2010, http://www.gallup.com/poll/127904/broad-steady-support -openly-gay-service-members.aspx.

92. For an example of the promotion of traditional American gender and sexual values in other cultures, see President George W. Bush's international AIDS policy, which stressed abstinence and monogamy over condom use. Writing in *Sojourners* magazine, a venue for progressive Christians, Chris Rice asks, "Why the outrage over homosexuality and not over the culture of divorce, premarital sex,

and sexual abuse—all of which affect more people and, studies show, occur with the same devastating prevalence in the church as in society? Why is homosexuality treated as a worse sin than the pervasive idolatry of money that is warned about far more throughout scripture? If Christians opposed to homosexuality were equally outraged by racial and economic injustice, we'd have racism and poverty licked by now." Chris Rice, "What I Learned When I Opened My Mouth about Gay Rights," *Sojourners*, May/June 2000, https://sojo.net/magazine/may-june-2000 /what-i-learned-when-i-opened-my-mouth-about-gay-rights.

93. Miller, *Religious Liberty in America*, 80.

94. The battle for the memorialization of Pat Tillman illustrates the cultural desire to define "fallen heroes" as brave Christians. Tillman, a safety for the Arizona Cardinals football team who became a US Army Ranger in 2002, was killed while serving in Afghanistan in 2004. His family was initially informed that he had been killed in an ambush, but five weeks after his death the military admitted that Tillman and an Afghan soldier standing near him had been killed by friendly fire. Tillman was awarded a posthumous Purple Heart and promoted, and he was awarded a Silver Star for extraordinary heroism, an award some suspect was an effort by the army to boost Tillman as a hero. Christian groups clamored to depict Tillman as a citizen-soldier, though Kevin Tillman, Pat Tillman's brother and a fellow ranger, allegedly objected to the saying of prayers and the presence of a chaplain during a repatriation ceremony for his sibling, and the Tillman family made clear that Pat Tillman was not a Christian. Mike Fish, "An Un-American Tragedy," ESPN, accessed November 21, 2015, http://sports.espn.go.com/espn /eticket/story?page=tillmanpart1. "He wasn't treated as a person, really," said Mary Tillman, Pat Tillman's mother, but as a stock character in a narrative about religion and military that served the purposes of those telling the story. Associated Press, "With Movie Upcoming, Pat Tillman's Family Still Seeking Answers," *USA Today*, August 13, 2010, http://www.usatoday.com/sports/football/nfl/2010 -08-13-pat-tillman-family_N.htm.

95. Snyder's father reacted to the news of his son's noncombat death with criticism of the war and a despondent reflection, saying, "I just want it to be over. . . . And I want answers. They said he was the gunnery on top of the Humvee and the Humvee rolled. When is this senseless war going to end?" "Marine Lance Cpl. Matthew Snyder," *Military Times*, accessed November 21, 2015, http://military times.com/valor/marine-lance-cpl-matthew-a-snyder/1582584.

96. Robert A. Nye, "Western Masculinities in War and Peace," *American Historical Review* (April 2007): 421.

97. Associated Press, "How Casper, Wyo., Reconciled Rights of Protesters,

Funeral-Goers," October 23, 1998, First Amendment Center, http://www.first amendmentcenter.org/how-casper-wyo-reconciled-rights-of-protesters-funeral -goers. Throughout the legal debates regarding funeral pickets, conservative Christians have been rightly fearful that limits on funeral pickets could affect the rights of antiabortion picketers picketing near abortion clinics. Said Jay Sekulow, chief counsel for the ACLJ, regarding Casper's ordinance, "I don't think that a speech-free zone (at a funeral) is any more constitutional than a buffer zone around an abortion clinic." In contrast to the ACLJ's "no exceptions" position, Fred Phelps called Casper's ordinance "altogether constitutional when the distance is so minuscule" (ibid).

98. The brief, filed September 27, 2006, is available at http://www.american bar.org/content/dam/aba/publishing/preview/publiced_preview_briefs_pdfs _09_10_09_751_NeutralAmCuACLJ.authcheckdam.pdf.

99. When the Supreme Court agreed to hear *Snyder v. Phelps*, the ACLJ offered a carefully worded brief in support of neither party, recommending retrial because of faulty jury instructions in the original trial. This was likely because, although the reversal of the original decision was intolerable to the ACLJ's promilitary and antigay sensibilities, the original decision opened new possibilities for further limits of abortion-clinic pickets, limits that the ACLJ certainly does not want to support.

100. Anderson, *Imagined Communities*, 9.

101. Mark Redfield, "Imagi-nation: The Imagined Community and the Aesthetics of Mourning," *Diacritics* 29, no. 4 (Winter 1999): 68–69.

102. Shirley Phelps-Roper, interview with the author, September 11, 2010.

103. Video footage of the September 27, 2010, debate between McAllister and University of Missouri Enoch H. Crowder law professor Christina Wells has been archived by the Dole Institute of Politics, https://www.youtube.com/watch ?v=HUw507fUCoA.

104. Nathan Dinsdale, "Father Knows Best," *Santa Fe Reporter*, April 20, 2005, http://www.altweeklies.com/aan/father_knows_best/Story?oid=145872.

105. Aho, *The Politics of Righteousness*, 3.

106. Fred Phelps, sermon, April 21, 2010.

107. Cushing Biggs Hassell and Sylvester Hassell, *History of the Church of God, from the Creation to A.D. 1885; Including Especially the History of the Kehukee Primitive Baptist* (Middleton, NY: Gilbert Beebe's Sons, 1886), 333.

## CONCLUSION. AFTER WESTBORO

1. Tweeted by ex-member Grace Phelps-Roper (@gracethecurious), August 3, 2015.

2. Steve Drain, interview with the author, April 16, 2015.

3. Amanda van Eck Duymaer van Twist, *Perfect Children: Growing Up on the Religious Fringe* (New York: Oxford University Press, 2015).

4. Libby Phelps-Alvarez, "I'm an Ex–Westboro Baptist Church Member Who Has Renounced the Group My Grandfather Founded," *XOJane*, September 9, 2013, http://www.xojane.com/issues/libby-phelps-alvarez-westoboro-baptist-church.

5. Sam Harris, "Leaving the Church: An Interview with Megan Phelps-Roper," *Waking Up with Sam Harris*, podcast, July 2, 2015, http://www.samharris.org/blog/item/leaving-the-church.

6. Phelps-Alvarez, "I'm an Ex–Westboro Baptist Church Member."

7. Bill Chappell, "'We Hurt a Lot of People,' Westboro Pastor's Granddaughter Says," *The Two-Way*, National Public Radio, October 29, 2013, http://www.npr.org/sections/thetwo-way/2013/10/29/241643924/we-hurt-a-lot-of-people-westboro-pastors-granddaughter-says.

8. Harris, "Leaving the Church."

9. Zach Phelps-Roper, interview with the author, June 27, 2015.

10. Phelps-Alvarez, "I'm an Ex–Westboro Baptist Church Member."

11. "I Am Zach Phelps-Roper. I Am a Former Member of the Westboro Baptist Church. Ask Me Anything!" Reddit, July 27, 2014, https://www.reddit.com/r/IAmA/comments/2bvjz6.

12. Westboro Baptist Church, "An Appropriate, Timely, Imprecatory Prayer for America," http://godhatesfags.com/prayers/20040801_imprecatory-prayer.pdf.

13. Harris, "Leaving the Church."

14. Ibid.

15. Ibid.

16. Ibid.

17. Ibid.

18. Ibid.

19. Ibid.

20. Lauren Drain worked with Lisa Pulitzer, who has worked on several other sensationalistic memoirs about fringe religions, including scientology and fundamentalist Latter Day Saints, on her memoir, *Banished: Surviving My Years in the Westboro Baptist Church* (New York: Grand Central Publishing, 2013).

21. Zach Phelps-Roper, interview with the author, June 27, 2015.

22. Phelps-Alvarez, "I'm an Ex–Westboro Baptist Church Member."

23. "Liberty U Student Plotted to Set Off Explosives, Police Say," CNN, May 22, 2007, http://www.cnn.com/2007/US/05/22/va.bombarrest.

24. Mike Spies, "Exiled from Westboro: Leaving America's Most Hated

Church," *The Week*, December 11, 2014, http://theweek.com/articles/441674
/exiled-from-westboro-leaving-americas-most-hated-church.

25. Zach Phelps-Roper, interview with the author, September 16, 2015.

26. James Michael Nichols, "Planting Peace Travels with Grace Phelps to
Document Jamaican LGBT Homeless Youth," *Huffington Post*, December 2, 2014,
http://www.huffingtonpost.com/2014/12/02/planting-peace-lgbt-homeless_n
_6255526.html.

27. Spies, "Exiled from Westboro."

28. Ann Marie Bush, "One Year Later: A Look inside Westboro Baptist Church,"
*Topeka Capital-Journal*, March 18, 2015, http://m.cjonline.com/news/2015-03-18
/one-year-later-look-inside-westboro-baptist-church.

29. Harris, "Leaving the Church."

30. Megan Phelps-Roper, "Head Full of Doubt/Road Full of Promise," *Medium*,
February 6, 2013, https://medium.com/@meganphelps/head-full-of-doubt-road
-full-of-promise-83d2ef8ba4f5.

31. Harris, "Leaving the Church."

32. Sam Phelps-Roper, interview with the author, June 8, 2014.

33. Harris, "Leaving the Church."

34. Nate Phelps, "Lessons from My Father," Recovering from Religion, March
24, 2014, http://recoveringfromreligion.org/584-2.

35. Zach Phelps-Roper, posted to Equality House's Facebook page, May 22,
2014, archived at https://www.facebook.com/permalink.php?story_fbid=644133
125676725&id=427599210663452.

36. Steve Drain, interview with the author, September 15, 2015.

37. Ibid.

38. Sam Phelps-Roper, interview with the author, June 8, 2014.

39. "Inside the Westboro Baptist Church," *Anderson Cooper Live*, May 7, 2013,
https://www.youtube.com/watch?v=IjWzC6mVdKM.

40. Nichols, "Planting Peace Travels with Grace Phelps."

41. Tim Phelps, interview in *Fall from Grace*, DVD, directed by K. Ryan Jones
(New York: Docurama, 2008).

42. James L. Peacock and Ruel W. Tyson, Jr., *Pilgrims of Paradox: Calvinism and
Experience among the Primitive Baptists of the Blue Ridge* (Washington, DC: Smithsonian Institution Press, 1989), 87.

43. Nate Phelps, Public Presentation at the Topeka Performing Arts Center,
April 24, 2010.

# BIBLIOGRAPHY

Ahlstrom, Sydney E. "Introduction." In *Theology in America: The Major Protestant Voices from Puritanism to Neo-Orthodoxy*, edited by Sydney E. Ahlstrom, 23–92. Indianapolis, IN: Bobbs-Merrill Company: 1967.

Aho, James A. *The Politics of Righteousness: Idaho Christian Patriotism.* Seattle: University of Washington Press, 1990.

Almond, Gabriel A., Emmanual Sivan, and R. Scott Appleby. "Explaining Fundamentalisms." In *Fundamentalisms Comprehended*, The Fundamentalism Project, vol. 5, edited by Martin E. Marty and R. Scott Appleby, 425–444. Chicago: University of Chicago Press, 1991.

———. "Fundamentalisms: Genus and Species." In *Fundamentalisms Comprehended*, The Fundamentalism Project, vol. 5, edited by Martin E. Marty and R. Scott Appleby, 399–424. Chicago: University of Chicago Press, 1991.

Ammerman, Nancy T. "Accounting for Christian Fundamentalisms: Social Dynamics and Rhetorical Strategies." In *Accounting for Fundamentalisms: The Dynamic Character of Movements*, The Fundamentalism Project, vol. 4, edited by Martin E. Marty and R. Scott Appleby, 149–172. Chicago: University of Chicago Press, 1991.

Anderson, Benedict. *Imagined Communities: Reflections on the Origins and Spread of Nationalism.* New York: Verso, 1991.

Anthony, Dick, and Thomas Robbins. "Religious Totalism, Violence, and Exemplary Dualism: Beyond the Extrinsic Model." In *Millennialism and Violence*, edited by Michael Barkun, 10–50. Portland, OR: Frank Cass, 1996.

Barton, Bernadette C. *Pray the Gay Away: The Extraordinary Lives of Bible Belt Christians.* New York: New York University Press, 2012.

Baxter, Richard. "Directions for Hating Sin." *The Practical Works of Richard Baxter*, vol. 1, 89–91. London: George Virtue, 1838.

Beem, Christopher. "Can Legislation Solve Our Moral Problems?" *The Responsive Community* 11, no. 4 (Fall 2001), http://www.gwu.edu/ffiiccps/rcq/legislating _morality.html.

Binning, Hugh. "Of Predestination (I)." *The Works of the Pious, Reverend and Learn'd Mr. Hugh Binning*, 134–140. Edinburgh: R. Fleming and Company, 1735. Eighteenth Century Collections Online.

———. "Of Predestination (II)." *The Works of the Pious, Reverend and Learn'd Mr. Hugh Binning*, 141–145. Edinburgh: R. Fleming and Company, 1735. Eighteenth Century Collections Online.

———. *The Works of the Pious, Reverend and Learn'd Mr. Hugh Binning.* Edinburgh: R. Fleming and Company, 1735. Eighteenth Century Collections Online.

Blee, Kathleen M. *Inside Organized Racism: Women in the Hate Movement.* Berkeley: University of California Press, 2002.

Boone, Kathleen C. *The Bible Tells Them So: The Discourse of Protestant Fundamentalism.* Albany: State University of New York Press, 1989.

Booth, Leo. *When God Becomes a Drug: Breaking the Chains of Religious Addiction and Abuse.* Los Angeles: Jeremy P. Tarcher, 1991.

Brandmeyer, Gerard A., and R. Serge Denisoff. "Status Politics: An Appraisal of the Application of a Concept." *Pacific Sociological Review* 12, no. 1 (Spring 1969): 5–11.

Brown, Ruth Murray. *For a "Christian America": A History of the Religious Right.* Amherst, NY: Prometheus Books, 2003.

Burack, Cynthia. "Compassion Campaigns and Antigay Politics: What Would Arendt Do?" *Politics and Religion* 2 (April 2009): 31–53.

———. "Contesting Compassion: Love Wins Out in the Ex-Gay Movement." Paper presented at the Western Political Science Association, Albuquerque, NM, March 16–18, 2006, http://www.allacademic.com//meta/p_mla_apa_research _citation/0/9/7/6/0/pages97608/p97608-1.php.

———. "From Doom Town to Sin City: Chick Tracts and Antigay Politics." *New Political Science* 28, no. 2 (June 2006): 163–179.

———. "Getting What 'We' Deserve: Terrorism, Sexuality, and the Christian Right." *New Political Science* 25, no. 3 (2005): 329–349.

———. *Sin, Sex, and Democracy: Antigay Rhetoric and the Christian Right.* Albany: State University of New York Press, 2008.

Burack, Cynthia, and Jyl J. Josephson. "Origin Stories." In Cynthia Burack, *Sin, Sex, and Democracy: Antigay Rhetoric and the Christian Right*, 67–100. Albany, NY: State University of New York Press, 2008.

Burke, Kelsy. *Christians under Covers: Evangelicals and Sexual Pleasure on the Internet.* Berkeley: University of California Press, 2016.

Calvin, John. "The Institutes of the Christian Religion." In *The Protestant Reformation*, edited by Hans J. Hillerbrand, 213–254. New York: Harper Torchbooks, 1968.

Castelli, Elizabeth A., and Rosamond C. Rodman. *Women, Gender, and Religion: A Reader.* New York: Palgrave, 2001.

Clark, Elmer T. *The Small Sects in America*, rev. ed. New York: Abingdon, 1937.

Cobb, Michael. *God Hates Fags: The Rhetoric of Religious Violence.* New York: New York University Press, 2006.

Cotton, John. *An Exposition of First John.* Master's Commentary Series. Jay P. Green, Sr., 2001.

Countrymen, L. William. "The Bible, Heterosexism, and the American Public Discussion of Sexual Orientation." In *God Forbid: Religion and Sex in American Public Life*, edited by Kathleen M. Sands, 167–185. New York: Oxford University Press, 2003.

Crowley, John G. *Primitive Baptists of the Wiregrass South: 1815 to the Present*. Gainesville: University Press of Florida, 1998.

———. "The Primitive or Old School Baptists." In *The Baptist River: Essays on the Many Tributaries of a Diverse Tradition*, edited by W. Glenn Jonas, Jr., 158–181. Macon, GA: Mercer University Press, 2006.

Daily, Timothy J. "The Other Side of Tolerance: How Homosexual Activism Threatens Liberty." Washington, DC: Family Research Council: 2006.

Dobson, James. *Marriage Under Fire: Why We Must Win this Battle*. Sisters, OR: Multnomah, 2004.

Dorgan, Howard. *In the Hands of a Happy God*. Knoxville: University of Tennessee Press, 1997.

Douglas, Ann. *The Feminization of American Culture*. New York: Anchor Press/Doubleday, 1988.

Drain, Lauren, with Lisa Pulitzer. *Banished: Surviving My Years in the Westboro Baptist Church*. New York: Grand Central Publishing, 2013.

Driscoll, Mark, and Grace Driscoll. *Real Marriage: The Truth about Sex, Friendship, and Life Together*. Nashville, TN: Thomas Nelson, 2012.

Edwards, Jonathan. "God Glorified in Man's Dependence." In *Selected Writings of Jonathan Edwards*, edited by Harold P. Simonson, 45–64. New York: Frederick Ungar Publishing, 1970.

———. *Selected Writings of Jonathan Edwards*, edited by Harold P. Simonson. New York: Frederick Ungar Publishing, 1970.

———. "Sinners in the Hands of an Angry God." In *Selected Writings of Jonathan Edwards*, edited by Harold P. Simonson, 96–113. New York: Frederick Ungar Publishing, 1970.

Ellison, Christopher G., and Darren E. Sherkat. "Obedience and Authority: Religion and Parental Values Reconsidered," *Journal for the Scientific Study of Religion* 32, no. 4 (December 1993): 313–329.

Eskridge, William N., Jr. "Body Politics: *Lawrence v. Texas* and the Constitution of the Disgust and Contagion." *Florida Law Review* 57, no. 5 (2005): 1011–1064.

*Fall from Grace*. DVD. Directed by K. Ryan Jones. New York: Docurama, 2008.

Farrel, Pam, and Doreen Hanna. *Raising a Modern-Day Princess: Inspiring Purpose, Value, and Strength in Your Daughter*. Carol Stream, IL: Tyndale, 2009.

*For the Bible Tells Me So*. DVD. Directed by Daniel Karslake. New York: First Run Features, 2008.

Foxcroft, Thomas. "The Earthquake, a Divine Visitation: A Sermon Preached to the Old Church in Boston, January 8, 1756." Boston: S. Kneeland, 1756.

Frantzen, Allen J. *Bloody Good: Chivalry, Sacrifice, and the Great War.* Chicago: University of Chicago Press, 2004.

Freeman, Jo. *The Politics of Women's Liberation.* New York: McKay, 1975.

Friedland, Roger. "Money, Sex, and God: The Erotic Logic of Religious Nationalism." *Sociological Theory* 20, no. 3 (November 2002): 381–425.

Froese, Paul, and Christopher D. Bader. *America's Four Gods: What We Say about God—and What That Says about Us.* New York: Oxford University Press, 2010.

———. "God in America: Why Theology Is Not Simply the Concern of Philosophers." *Journal for the Scientific Study of Religion* 46, no. 4 (2007): 465–481.

Froese, Paul, Christopher Bader, and Buster Smith. "Political Tolerance and God's Wrath in the United States." *Sociology of Religion* 69, no. 1 (2008): 29–44.

Garrett, James Leo, Jr. *Baptist Theology: A Four Century Study.* Macon, GA: Mercer University Press, 2009.

Gill, John. *Body of Divinity.* London, 1769. Eighteenth Century Collections Online.

Ginsburg, Faye. "Preface." *Contested Lives: The Abortion Debate in an American Community,* xxxiii–xxxv. Berkeley: University of California Press, 1998 [1987].

Glass, Jennifer, and Philip Levchak. "Red States, Blue States, and Divorce: Understanding the Impact of Conservative Protestantism on Regional Variation in Divorce Rates." *American Journal of Sociology* 119, no. 4 (2014): 1–44.

Gutterman, David S. *Prophetic Politics: Christian Social Movements and American Democracy.* Ithaca, NY: Cornell University Press, 2005.

Hagee, John. *What Every Man Wants in a Woman.* Lake Mary, FL: Charisma House, 2005.

Haines, Herbert H. *Black Radicals and the Civil Rights Mainstream, 1954–1970.* Knoxville: University of Tennessee Press, 1988.

Hardesty, Jean. *Mobilizing Resentment: Conservative Resurgence from the John Birch Society to the Promise Keepers.* Boston: Beacon, 1999.

Hassell, Cushing Biggs, and Sylvester Hassell. *History of the Church of God, from the Creation to A.D. 1885; Including Especially the History of the Kehukee Primitive Baptist.* Middleton, NY: Gilbert Beebe's Sons, 1886. Google Books.

Herman, Didi. *The Antigay Agenda: Orthodox Vision and the Christian Right.* Chicago: University of Chicago Press, 1997.

Hostetler, John A. *Amish Roots: A Treasury of History, Wisdom, and Lore.* Baltimore, MD: Johns Hopkins University Press, 1992.

Hussey, Joseph. *God's Operations of Grace but No Offers of His Grace.* London: D. Bridge, 1707. Eighteenth Century Collections Online.

Hutchison, William R. *Religious Pluralism in America: The Contentious History of a Founding Ideal.* New Haven, CT: Yale University Press, 2003.

Jefferson, Thomas. *Jefferson's Extracts from the Gospels: "The Philosophy of Jesus" and "The Life and Morals of Jesus,"* edited by Dickinson W. Adams and Ruth W. Lester. Princeton, NJ: Princeton University Press, 1983.

Jones-Correa, Michael A., and David L. Leal. "Political Participation: Does Religion Matter?" *Political Research Quarterly* 54, no 4 (December 2001): 751–770.

Kaufman, Moisés. *The Laramie Project.* New York: Dramatists Play Service, 2001.

Kaufman, Peter Iver. *Prayer, Despair, and Drama: Elizabethan Introspection.* Urbana: University of Illinois Press, 1996.

Khan, Surina. "Calculated Compassion: How The Ex-Gay Movement Serves the Right's Attack on Democracy." *Public Eye: The Website of Political Research Associates,* 1998, http://www.publiceye.org/equality/x-gay/X-Gay.html.

LaHaye, Tim and Beverly. *The Act of Marriage: The Beauty of Sexual Love.* Grand Rapids, MI: Zondervan, 1998.

Landes, Joan B. "Republican Citizenship and Heterosocial Desire: Concepts of Masculinity in Revolutionary France." In *Masculinities in Politics and War: Gendering Modern History,* edited by Stefan Dudnick, Karen Hagemann, and John Tosh, 95–115. New York: Manchester University Press, 2004.

Lawrence, Joshua. "Address to the Particular Baptist Churches of the 'Old School' in the United States (1832)." In *Antirevivalism in Antebellum America: A Collection of Religious Voices,* edited by James D. Bratt, 69–77. New Brunswick, NJ: Rutgers University Press, 2006.

Lehman, Kevin. *Sheet Music: Uncovering the Secrets of Sexual Intimacy in Marriage.* Carol Stream, IL: Tyndale 2003.

Levie, David, Zachary Navit, and Kara Tappan. "Special Report: Constitutionality of State Funeral-Picketing Laws since *Snyder v. Phelps.*" The First Amendment Center, February 11, 2014, http://www.firstamendmentcenter.org/special -report-constitutionality-of-state-funeral-picketing-laws-since-snyder-v -phelps.

Lewis, Clara S. *Tough on Hate? The Cultural Politics of Hate Crimes.* New Brunswick, NJ: Rutgers University Press, 2013.

Lewis, Robert. *Raising a Modern-Day Knight: A Father's Role in Guiding His Son to Authentic Manhood.* Carol Stream, IL: Tyndale, 1999.

Marsden, George. *Jonathan Edwards: A Life.* New Haven, CT: Yale University Press, 2004.

Marty, Martin E., and R. Scott Appleby. "Conclusion: Remaking the State: The Limits of the Fundamentalist Imagination." In *Fundamentalisms and the State:*

*Remaking Polities, Economies, and Militance*, The Fundamentalism Project, vol. 3, edited by Martin E. Marty and R. Scott Appleby, 620–643. Chicago: University of Chicago Press, 1991.

———. "Introduction." In *Fundamentalisms and the State: Remaking Polities, Economies, and Militance*, edited by Martin E. Marty and R. Scott Appleby, 1–9. Chicago: University of Chicago Press, 1991.

———, eds. *Accounting for Fundamentalisms: The Dynamic Character of Movements*, The Fundamentalism Project, vol. 4. Chicago: University of Chicago Press, 1991.

———, eds. *Fundamentalisms and the State: Remaking Polities, Economies, and Militance*, The Fundamentalism Project, vol. 5. Chicago: University of Chicago Press, 1991.

———, eds. *Fundamentalisms Comprehended*, The Fundamentalism Project, vol. 5. Chicago: University of Chicago Press, 1991.

Mather, Cotton. "Free Grace Maintained and Improved." Boston: B. Green, 1706. Eighteenth Century Collections Online.

Mathis, James R. *The Making of the Primitive Baptists: A Cultural and Intellectual History of the Antimission Movement, 1800–1840*. New York: Routledge, 2004.

Miller, Glenn T. *Piety and Intellect: The Aims and Purposes of Ante-Bellum Theological Education*. Atlanta, GA: Scholars Press, 1990.

———. *Religious Liberty in America: History and Prospects*. Philadelphia, PA: Westminster Press, 1976.

Minor, Robert N. *When Religion Is an Addiction*. St. Louis, MO: HumanityWorks!, 2007.

Monto, Martin A., and Jessica Supinski. "Discomfort with Homosexuality: A New Measure Captures Differences in Attitudes toward Gay Men and Lesbians." *Journal of Homosexuality* 61, no. 6 (2014): 899–916.

*The Most Hated Family in America*. Television documentary. Written by Louis Theroux and directed by Geoffrey O'Conner. London: BBC, 2007.

Nye, Robert A. "Western Masculinities in War and Peace." *American Historical Review* (April 2007): 417–438.

Peacock, James L., and Tim Pettyjohn. "Fundamentalisms Narrated: Muslim, Christian, and Mystical." In *Fundamentalisms Comprehended*, The Fundamentalism Project, vol. 5, edited by Martin E. Marty and R. Scott Appleby, 115–134. Chicago: University of Chicago Press.

Peacock, James L., and Ruel W. Tyson, Jr. *Pilgrims of Paradox: Calvinism and Experience among the Primitive Baptists of the Blue Ridge*. Washington, DC: Smithsonian Institution Press, 1989.

Pestana, Carla Gardina. *Quakers and Baptists in Colonial Massachusetts*. New York: Cambridge University Press, 1991.

Peters, Peter J. "Intolerance of, Discrimination against, and the Death Penalty for Homosexuals Is Prescribed in the Bible." Laport, CO: Scriptures for America, 1992.

Rainey, Dennis. *Stepping Up: A Call to Courageous Manhood*. Little Rock, AR: Family Life, 2011.

Redfield, Mark. "Imagi-nation: The Imagined Community and the Aesthetics of Mourning," *Diacritics* 29, no. 4 (Winter 1999): 58–83.

Robinson, Carin, and Clyde Wilcox. "The Faith of George W. Bush: The Personal, Practical, and Political." In *Religion and the American Presidency*, The Evolving American Presidency, edited by Mark J. Rozell and Gleaves Whitney, 215–238. New York: Palgrave MacMillan, 2007.

Sands, Kathleen M., ed. *God Forbid: Religion and Sex in American Public Life*. New York: Oxford University Press, 2000.

Scott, Thomas, ed. and trans. *The Articles of the Synod of Dort and Its Rejection of Errors: With the Events Which Made Way for That Synod*. Utica, NY: William Williams, 1831. Google Books.

Scott, William A. *Historical Protestantism: An Historical Introduction to Protestant Theology*. Englewood Cliffs, NJ: Prentice-Hall, 1971.

Sears, Alan, and Craig Osten. *The Homosexual Agenda: Exposing the Principal Threat to Religion Today*. Nashville, TN: Broadman and Holman, 2003.

Sears, Brad. "Kansas—Sexual Orientation and Gender Identity Law and Documentation of Discrimination." Documenting Discrimination on the Basis of Sexual Orientation and Gender Identity in State Employment, the Williams Institute, University of California–Los Angeles School of Law, September 2009, http://escholarship.org/uc/item/05g290fb;jsessionid=4FE0B56ABECE5A1A 04A813933208008D#page-1.

Sivan, Emmanual. "The Enclave Culture." In *Fundamentalisms Comprehended*, The Fundamentalism Project, vol. 5, edited by Martin E. Marty and R. Scott Appleby, 11–70. Chicago: University of Chicago Press, 1991.

Spivey, Susan E., and Christine M. Robinson. "Genocidal Intentions: Social Death and the Ex-Gay Movement." *Genocide Studies and Prevention* 5, no. 1 (April 2010): 68–88.

Stanley, Ralph, with Eddie Dean. *Man of Constant Sorrow: My Life and Times*. New York: Gotham, 2009.

Sullivan, Susan Crawford. *Living Faith: Everyday Religion and Mothers in Poverty*. Chicago: University of Chicago Press, 2011.

Thuesen, Peter J. *Predestination: The American Career of a Contentious Doctrine*. New York: Oxford University Press, 2009.

Toon, Peter. *The New Dictionary of Theology*. Leicester, England: IVP, 1988.

Van Delinder, Jean. "Brown *v.* Board of Education of Topeka: A Landmark Case Unresolved Fifty Years Later, Part 2." *Prologue: The Journal of the National Archives* 36, no. 1 (Spring 2004), http://www.archives.gov/publications/prologue/2004/spring/brown-v-board-2.html.

Van Eck Duymaer van Twist, Amanda. *Perfect Children: Growing Up on the Religious Fringe*. New York: Oxford University Press, 2015.

Warren, Rick. *The Purpose Driven Life*. Grand Rapids, MI: Zondervan, 2002.

Wax, Rosalie H. *Doing Fieldwork: Warnings and Advice*. Chicago: University of Chicago Press, 1971.

Weber, Max. *The Protestant Ethic and the Spirit of Capitalism*, translated by Talcott Parsons. Mineola, NY: Dover, 2003 [1936].

Weber, Stu. *The Tender Warrior: Every Man's Purpose, Every Woman's Dream, Every Child's Hope*. Sisters, OR: Multnomah, 2006.

Weber, Timothy P. "The Two-Edged Sword: The Fundamentalist Use of the Bible." In *The Bible in America: Essays in Cultural History*, edited by Nathan O. Hatch and Mark A. Noll, 101–120. New York: Oxford University Press, 1982.

Wheat, Ed, and Gaye Wheat. *Intended for Pleasure: Sex Technique and Sexual Fulfillment in Christian Marriage*. Grand Rapids, MI: Fleming H. Revel, 1997.

Wilcox, Clyde, and Leopoldo Gomez. "Religion, Group Identification, and Politics among American Blacks." *Sociological Analyses* 51, no. 3 (Autumn 1990): 271–285.

Willard, Samuel. "What Is Effectual Calling?" Sermon CXV, Question XXXI, from *Compleat Body of Divinity*. Boston: B. Green and S. Kneeland, 1726. Eighteenth Century Collections Online.

———. "What Is the Duty That God Requires of Man?" Sermon CXLVII, Question XXXIX, from *Compleat Body of Divinity*. Boston: B. Green and S. Kneeland, 1726. Eighteenth Century Collections Online.

Winthrop, John. "A Model of Christian Charity." In *Life and Letters of John Winthrop*, vol. 2, 2nd ed., edited by Robert C. Winthrop. Boston: Little, Brown, 1866, 18–20. Google Books.

Wuthnow, Robert, and Matthew P. Lawson. "Sources of Christian Fundamentalism in the United States." In *Accounting for Fundamentalisms: The Dynamic Character of Movements*, The Fundamentalism Project, vol. 4, edited by Martin E. Marty and R. Scott Appleby, 18–56. Chicago: University of Chicago Press, 1994.

Wyatt-Brown, Bertram. *The Shaping of Southern Culture: Honor, Grace, and War, 1760s–1880s*. Chapel Hill: University of North Carolina Press, 2011.

# INDEX